Principles of Micro Economics

Principles of Micro Economics

Dr. Seema Mahlawat

PRASHANT PUBLISHING HOUSE
DELHI-110094

Published by :
Prashant Publishing House
C-34, 28 Foota Road, Gali-3,
West Karwal Nagar, Delhi-110094
Phone : 011-22963970, Mob. : 9810396373
e-mail.: prashantpublishinghouse@gmail.com

Principles of Micro Economics

First Published 2019

ISBN 978-93-80565-99-6

PRINTED IN INDIA
Published by Mr. R.K. Jha M/s Prashant Publishing House and Published at H.S. Offset House Press, Delhi.

Contents

Preface

Microeconomics stresses the relevance and application of microeconomic theory to decision making in both managerial and public policy.

Micro economics examines how entities, forming a market structure, interact within a market to create a market system. These entities include private and public players with various classifications, typically operating under scarcity of tradeable units and government regulation. The item traded may be a tangible product such as apples or a service such as repair services, legal counsel, or entertainment.

Demand is often represented by a table or a graph showing price and quantity demanded. Demand theory describes individual consumers as rationally choosing the most preferred quantity of each good, given income, prices, tastes, etc. A term for this is "constrained utility maximization" (with income and wealth as the constraints on demand). Here, utility refers to the hypothesized relation of each individual consumer for ranking different commodity bundles as more or less preferred.

The production function thus contains the limitations that technology places on the firm. The mathematical forms of the production function and the utility function are identical. In one case, inputs of goods and services combine to produce utility; in the other, inputs of resources combine to produce goods or services.

Economic analysis has recognised the role of key variables in determining demand and consumption. In practice, the distinction between demand and consumption as an equilibrium quantity at a given price, is frequently ignored. The development of "gap" type models emphasise the common approach of projecting 'demand' as a fixed quantity independent of price. Demand, as the relationship between price and quantity, is subject to change over time due to changes in the underlying factors held constant by the static notion of demand. Changes in demand "shifters" are often included in economic estimation of demand representing anticipated dynamics in these determinants.

Price discrimination requires market segmentation and some means to discourage discount customers from becoming resellers and, by extension, competitors. This usually entails using one or more means of preventing any resale, keeping the different price groups separate, making price comparisons difficult, or restricting pricing information. The boundary set up by the marketer to keep segments separate are referred to as a rate fence.

Price discrimination is thus very common in services, where resale is not possible; an example is student discounts at museums. Price discrimination in intellectual property is also enforced by law and by technology. In the market for DVDs, DVD players are designed - by law - with chips to prevent use of an inexpensive copy of the DVD from being used in a higher price market. The Digital Millenium Copyright Act has provisions to outlaw circumventing of such devices to protect the enhanced monopoly profits that copyright holders can obtain from price discrimination against higher price market segments.

This is a reference book. All the matter is just compiled and edited in nature, taken from the various sources which are in public domain.

A new approach has been used to make the learning of economics easy. It is a student-friendly and teacher-friendly book.

—*Editor*

1

An Introduction

MARKETS

Micro economics examines how entities, forming a market structure, interact within a market to create a market system. These entities include private and public players with various classifications, typically operating under scarcity of tradeable units and government regulation. The item traded may be a tangible product such as apples or a service such as repair services, legal counsel, or entertainment.

In theory, in a free market the aggregates (sum of) of *quantity demanded* by buyers and *quantity supplied* by sellers will be equal and reach economic equilibrium over time in reaction to price changes; in practice, various issues may prevent equilibrium, and any equilibrium reached may not necessarily morally equitable. For example, if the supply of health care services is limited by external factors, the equilibrium price may be unaffordable for many who desire it but cannot pay for it.

Various market structures exist. In perfectly competitive markets, no participants are large enough to have the market power to set the price of a homogeneous product. In other words, every participant is a "price taker" as no participant influences the price of a product. In the real world, markets often experience imperfect competition.

Forms include monopoly (in which there is only one seller of a good), duopoly (in which there are only two sellers of a good), oligopoly (in which there are few sellers of a good), monopolistic competition (in which there are many sellers producing highly differentiated goods), monopsony (in which there is only one buyer of a good), and oligopsony (in which there are few buyers of a good). Unlike perfect competition, imperfect competition invariably means market power is unequally distributed. Firms under imperfect competition have the potential to be "price makers", which means that, by holding a disproportionately high share of market power, they can influence the prices of their products.

Micro economics studies individual markets by simplifying the economic system by assuming that activity in the market being analysed does not affect other markets. This method of analysis is known as partial-equilibrium analysis (supply and demand). This method aggregates (the sum of all activity) in only one market. General-equilibrium theory studies various markets and their behaviour. It aggregates (the sum of all activity) across *all* markets. This method studies both changes in markets and their interactions leading towards equilibrium.

MICROECONOMICS IN ACTION

In order to best understand how microeconomics applies to the real world, we'll go over the case of a car maker, General Motors (OTCBB:GMGMQ). Once, General Motors was among America's most profitable companies and a colossus of the automobile industry.

Microeconomic Breakdown

By 2008, GM had fallen on hard times, the victim of a slumping U.S., and global economy and a series of microeconomic decisions that turned out to be wrong. Trouble at the microeconomic level began for General Motors several years before its problems worsened in late 2008. As Japanese automaker Toyota (NYSE:TM) began steadily eating into GM's market share, GM did not meet its competition head-on.

Toyota made a cheaper car with better gas mileage that was of better overall quality, and was engineered for greater durability than its chief competitor, GM. Consumers naturally gravitated away from GM to Toyota and demand for the once-popular GM automobiles declined slowly and continually as Toyota and other Japanese cars won an ever-increasing share of the automobile market.

Dreadful Decision-Making

Although the general economy may also be responsible to some degree for GM's fall, which eventually led to its bankruptcy in 2009, several GM management decisions at the microeconomic level contributed to the problem.

First, prior to its bankruptcy, GM was selling eight different brands of cars – Buick, Cadillac, Chevrolet, GMC, Hummer, Pontiac, Saab and Saturn. The number of units manufactured for each of these brands represented too much output, a situation in which the marginal revenue is less than the marginal costs.

Second, as gasoline prices rose, spurred by rising oil prices, GM continued to build gas-guzzling SUVs and pick-up trucks, and failed to produce cars that kept pace with the high mileage-per-gallon vehicles produced by Toyota and other Japanese manufacturers. Despite the obvious decline in demand for automobiles that were not fuel-efficient, GM persisted in marketing them, reflecting a microeconomic decision of management that seemed to disregard data on consumer preferences.

Finally, in response to high consumer demand for fuel-efficient or alternative-energy vehicles, GM began developing hybrid vehicles, but only long after its competitors had brought them to the market.

GM's problems staggering debt and the costs of honouring contracts to provide pensions to its retirees and handsome health benefits and other costly benefits to its union-represented employees only contributed to its decline. Too many microeconomic decisions at GM have apparently proved unsuccessful. The result was abankruptcy filing for a firm that once made huge profits and reigned supreme over its industry.

Microeconomic Achievement

On the success side of the microeconomic ledger are many companies whose top management made the right decisions as start-ups, or in their restructuring efforts in the face of changing market conditions.

One typical success story is FedEx (NYSE:FDX). Founded in 1971, the service firm is now the world's largest express transportation company. Initially, FedEx had a simple but powerfully effective business strategy that was summed up in its early advertising slogan: "When it absolutely, positively has to be there overnight."

Frederick W. Smith, who founded FedEx, was aware of the growing consumer demand for prompt, dependable overnight delivery of packages and documents. Smith's microeconomic research in advance of starting his firm provided the data necessary to confirm an idea he first developed when he was studying economics at Yale.

Understanding Demand and Adaptation

In the early 1970s, the U.S. Postal Service was not as reliable as it would later become, and postal rates were increasing. Smith's unknown start-up firm would provide the service that the post office could not, at a reasonable price, and demand for Fed Ex service grew exponentially through the years. As the firm matured, several new and critical price and technological challenges arose, which threatened FedEx's market share. These included the entry into the express carrier business of the U.S. Postal Service, Emory Airborne Freight and United Parcel Service of America (UPS), among others.

On the technological side, fax transmissions and e-mails could now deliver almost instantaneously what previously could only be delivered overnight. In response to this challenge, FedEx concentrated on items that could not be dispatched via phone lines or electronically and expanded into foreign markets.

With its own fleet of aircraft, FedEx was an effective competitor against most of the other carriers, which used commercial flights for delivery.

These moves reflect simple microeconomic decisions - when demand declined for overnight deliveries of materials which could be sent via e-mail or fax, the firm focused on other services, vigourously advertising what the market demanded at a competitive price. In the slumping economy of late 2008, with consumer budgets and disposable income shrinking through job loss, the declining value of their investments, and a lack of consumer confidence, consumer decision-making took a new direction.

Customer Spending During a Downturn

Consumer spending during the period of economic downturn that began in 2008 still expressed the microeconomic concepts of opportunity costs, cardinal utility and ordinal utility, which are used in decision-making in good economic times. Opportunity costs, as discussed in a previous chapter, are the tradeoff concept. With a limited budget, a consumer may be able to afford two items he or she desires, but cannot buy both. Buying one rather than the other is the opportunity cost.

Suppose a consumer wants an expensive chocolate cake, a loaf of bread and a pound of sliced ham to make sandwiches for her school children. In a down economy the consumer on an abbreviated budget would likely chose the more practical purchases, the bread and ham. The cost for this decision - the opportunity cost - is the chocolate cake. (To learn more see, Economics Basics.)

The cardinal utility - in microeconomics, the numerical value of satisfaction to the consumer - may not be measurable. But the ordinal value, which only denotes consumer preference, without assigning actual numbers, is obvious. In hard times, consumers prefer the necessities. This consumer preference for necessities and competitive pricing during a recessionary period was also demonstrated in a reported increase in brand switching and the use of discount coupons at supermarkets and other retailers. A consumer may prefer one brand of toothpaste at a certain price, but if a coupon for a different brand of toothpaste is offered at a significant discount, consumers may decide to buy the cheaper brand.

Micro Meets Macro

At this point, the principles of macroeconomics - the big-picture economy - came into play in the 2007-2009 recession. The Federal Reserve lowered the key interest rate to encourage borrowing. The federal government embarked on a costly but necessary rescue plan for the financial industry, and a plan to help home owners either facing default, or in default of their mortgages.

The government also rescued certain mortgage firms and investment banks with infusions of cash, principally Fannie Mae and Freddie Mac, and JPMorgan Chase to purchase failing investment firm Bear Sterns.

Additionally, through a legislative act called The Troubled Assets Relief Programme (commonly called "the bailout"), the federal government appropriated some $750 billion to buy toxic debt (non-performing or questionable debt) and to lend money to banks and other institutions to get the economy moving again.

PRODUCTION, COST, AND EFFICIENCY

In micro economics, production is the conversion of inputs into outputs. It is an economic process that uses inputs to create a commodity for exchange or direct use. Production is a flow and thus a rate of output per period of time. Distinctions include such production alternatives as for consumption (food, haircuts, etc.) vs. investment goods (new tractors, buildings, roads, etc.), public goods (national defence, small-pox vaccinations, etc.) or private goods (new computers, bananas, etc.), and “guns” vs. “butter”.

Opportunity cost refers to the economic cost of production: the value of the next best opportunity foregone. Choices must be made between desirable yet mutually exclusive actions. It has been described as expressing "the basic relationship between scarcity and choice.". The opportunity cost of an activity is an element in ensuring that scarce resources are used efficiently, such that the cost is weighed against the value of that activity in deciding on more or less of it. Opportunity costs are not restricted to monetary or financial costs but could be measured by the real cost of output forgone, leisure, or anything else that provides the alternative benefit (utility).

Inputs used in the production process include such primary factors of production as labour services, capital (durable produced goods used in production, such as an existing factory), and land (including natural resources). Other inputs may include intermediate goods used in production of final goods, such as the steel in a new car.

Economic efficiency describes how well a system generates desired output with a given set of inputs and available technology. Efficiency is improved if more output is generated without changing inputs, or in other words, the amount of "waste" is reduced. A widely accepted general standard is Pareto efficiency, which is reached when no further change can make someone better off without making someone else worse off.

The production–possibility frontier (PPF) is an expository figure for representing scarcity, cost, and efficiency. In the simplest case an economy can produce just two goods (say "guns" and "butter").

Scarcity is represented in the figure by people being willing but unable in the aggregate to consume *beyond the PPF* (such as at *X*) and by the negative slope of the curve. If production of one good *increases* along the curve, production of the other good *decreases*, an inverse relationship. This is because increasing output of one good requires transferring inputs to it from production of the other good, decreasing the latter.

The slope of the curve at a point on it gives the trade-off between the two goods. It measures what an additional unit of one good costs in units forgone of the other good, an example of a *real opportunity cost*. Thus, if one more Gun costs 100 units of butter, the opportunity cost of one Gun is 100 Butter. *Along the PPF*, scarcity implies that choosing *more* of one good in the aggregate entails doing with *less* of the other good. Still, in a market economy, movement along the curve may indicate that the choice of the increased output is anticipated to be worth the cost to the agents.

By construction, each point on the curve shows *productive efficiency* in maximizing output for given total inputs. A point *inside* the curve (as at *A*), is feasible but represents *production inefficiency* (wasteful use of inputs), in that output of *one or both goods* could increase by moving in a northeast direction to a point on the curve. Examples cited of such inefficiency include high unemployment during a business-cycle recession or economic organization of a country that discourages full use of resources. Being on the curve might still not fully satisfy allocative efficiency (also called Pareto efficiency) if it does not produce a mix of goods that consumers prefer over other points.

Much applied economics in public policy is concerned with determining how the efficiency of an economy can be improved. Recognizing the reality of scarcity and then figuring out how to organize society for the most efficient use of resources has been described as the "essence of economics", where the subject "makes its unique contribution."

Specialization

Specialization is considered key to economic efficiency based on theoretical and empirical considerations. Different individuals or nations may have different real opportunity costs of production, say from differences in stocks of human capital per worker or capital/labour ratios. According to theory, this may give a comparative advantage in production of goods that make more intensive use of the relatively more abundant, thus *relatively* cheaper, input.

Even if one region has an absolute advantage as to the ratio of its outputs to inputs in every type of output, it may still specialize in the output in which it has a comparative advantage and thereby gain from trading with a region that lacks any absolute advantage but has a comparative advantage in producing something else.

It has been observed that a high volume of trade occurs among regions even with access to a similar technology and mix of factor inputs, including high-income countries. This has led to investigation of economies of scale and agglomeration to explain specialization in similar but differentiated product lines, to the overall benefit of respective trading parties or regions.

The general theory of specialization applies to trade among individuals, farms, manufacturers, service providers, and economies. Among each of these production systems, there may be a corresponding *division of labour* with different work groups specializing, or correspondingly different types of capital equipment and differentiated land uses.

An example that combines features above is a country that specializes in the production of high-tech knowledge products, as developed countries do, and trades with developing nations for goods produced in factories where labour is relatively cheap and plentiful, resulting in different in opportunity costs of production. More total output and utility thereby results from specializing in production and trading than if each country produced its own high-tech and low-tech products.

Theory and observation set out the conditions such that market prices of outputs and productive inputs select an allocation of factor inputs by comparative advantage, so that (relatively) low-cost inputs go to producing low-cost outputs. In the process, aggregate output may increase as a by-product or by design. Such specialization of production creates opportunities for *gains from trade* whereby resource owners benefit from trade in the sale of one type of output for other, more highly valued goods. A measure of gains from trade is the *increased income levels* that trade may facilitate.

SUPPLY AND DEMAND

Prices and quantities have been described as the most directly observable attributes of goods produced and exchanged in a market economy. The theory of supply and demand is an organizing principle for explaining how prices coordinate the amounts produced and consumed. In micro economics, it applies to price and output determination for a market with perfect competition, which includes the condition of no buyers or sellers large enough to have price-setting power. For a given market of a commodity, *demand* is the relation of the quantity that all buyers would be prepared to purchase at each unit price of the good.

Demand is often represented by a table or a graph showing price and quantity demanded. Demand theory describes individual consumers as rationally choosing the most preferred quantity of each good, given income, prices, tastes, etc.

A term for this is "constrained utility maximization" (with income and wealth as the constraints on demand). Here, utility refers to the hypothesized relation of each individual consumer for ranking different commodity bundles as more or less preferred.

The law of demand states that, in general, price and quantity demanded in a given market are inversely related. That is, the higher the price of a product, the less of it people would be prepared to buy of it (other things unchanged). As the price of a commodity falls, consumers move towards it from relatively more expensive goods (the substitution effect). In addition, purchasing power from the price decline increases ability to buy (the income effect). Other factors can change demand; for example an increase in income will shift the demand curve for a normal good outward relative to the origin. All determinants are predominantly taken as constant factors of demand and supply.

Supply is the relation between the price of a good and the quantity available for sale at that price. It may be represented as a table or graph relating price and quantity supplied. Producers, for example business firms, are hypothesized to be *profit-maximizers*, meaning that they attempt to produce and supply the amount of goods that will bring them the highest profit. Supply is typically represented as a directly proportional relation between price and quantity supplied (other things unchanged).

That is, the higher the price at which the good can be sold, the more of it producers will supply. The higher price makes it profitable to increase production. Just as on the demand side, the position of the supply can shift, say from a change in the price of a productive input or a technical improvement. The "Law of Supply" states that, in general, a rise in price leads to an expansion in supply and a fall in price leads to a contraction in supply. Here as well, the determinants of supply, such as price of substitutes, cost of production, technology applied and various factors inputs of production are all taken to be constant for a specific time period of evaluation of supply.

Market equilibrium occurs where quantity supplied equals quantity demanded, the intersection of the supply and demand curves. At a price below equilibrium, there is a shortage of quantity supplied compared to quantity demanded. This is posited to bid the price up. At a price above equilibrium, there is a surplus of quantity supplied compared to quantity demanded. This pushes the price down. The model of supply and demand predicts that for given supply and demand curves, price and quantity will stabilize at the price that makes quantity supplied equal to quantity demanded. Similarly, demand-and-supply theory predicts a new price-quantity combination from a shift in demand, or in supply.

For a given quantity of a consumer good, the point on the demand curve indicates the value, or marginal utility, to consumers for that unit. It measures what the consumer would be prepared to pay for that unit. The corresponding point on the supply curve measures marginal cost, the increase in total cost to the supplier for the corresponding unit of the good. The price in equilibrium is determined by supply and demand. In a perfectly competitive market, supply and demand equate marginal cost and marginal utility at equilibrium.

On the supply side of the market, some factors of production are described as (relatively) *variable* in the short run, which affects the cost of changing output levels. Their usage rates can be changed easily, such as electrical power, raw-material inputs, and over-time and temp work. Other inputs are relatively *fixed*, such as plant and equipment and key personnel. In the long run, all inputs may be adjusted by management. These distinctions translate to differences in the elasticity (responsiveness) of the supply curve in the short and long runs and corresponding differences in the price-quantity change from a shift on the supply or demand side of the market.

Marginalist theory describes the consumers as attempting to reach most-preferred positions, subject to income and wealth constraints while producers attempt to maximize profits subject to their own constraints, including demand for goods produced, technology, and the price of inputs. For the consumer, that point comes where marginal utility of a good, net of price, reaches zero, leaving no net gain from further consumption increases.

Analogously, the producer compares marginal revenue (identical to price for the perfect competitor) against the marginal cost of a good, with *marginal profit* the difference. At the point where marginal profit reaches zero, further increases in production of the good stop. For movement to market equilibrium and for changes in equilibrium, price and quantity also change "at the margin": more-or-less of something, rather than necessarily all-or-nothing.

Other applications of demand and supply include the distribution of income among the factors of production, including labour and capital, through factor markets. In a competitive labour market for example the quantity of labour employed and the price of labour (the wage rate) depends on the demand for labour (from employers for production) and supply of labour (from potential workers). Labour economics examines the interaction of workers and employers through such markets to explain patterns and changes of wages and other labour income, labour mobility, and (un)employment, productivity through human capital, and related public-policy issues.

Demand-and-supply analysis is used to explain the behaviour of perfectly competitive markets, but as a standard of comparison it can be extended to any type of market. It can also be generalized to explain variables across the economy, for example, total output (estimated as real GDP) and the general price level, as studied in macroeconomics. Tracing the qualitative and quantitative effects of variables that change supply and demand, whether in the short or long run, is a standard exercise in applied economics. Economic theory may also specify conditions such that supply and demand through the market is an efficient mechanism for allocating resources.

Firms

People frequently do not trade directly on markets. Instead, on the supply side, they may work in and produce through *firms*. The most obvious kinds of firms are corporations, partnerships and trusts. According to Ronald Coase people begin to organise their production in firms when the costs of doing business becomes lower than doing it on the market. Firms combine labour and capital, and can achieve far greater economies of scale than individual market trading.

In perfectly competitive markets studied in the theory of supply and demand, there are many producers, none of which significantly influence price. Industrial organization generalizes from that special case to study the strategic behaviour of firms that do have significant control of price. It considers the structure of such markets and their interactions. Common market structures studied besides perfect competition include monopolistic competition, various forms of oligopoly, and monopoly.

Managerial economics applies micro economic analysis to specific decisions in business firms or other management units. It draws heavily from quantitative methods such as operations research and programming and from statistical methods such as regression analysis in the absence of certainty and perfect knowledge. A unifying theme is the attempt to optimize business decisions, including unit-cost minimization and profit maximization, given the firm's objectives and constraints imposed by technology and market conditions.

UNCERTAINTY AND GAME THEORY

Uncertainty in economics is an unknown prospect of gain or loss, whether quantifiable as risk or not. Without it, household behaviour would be unaffected by uncertain employment and income prospects, financial and capital markets would reduce to exchange of a single instrument in each market period, and there would be no communications industry. Given its different forms, there are various ways of representing uncertainty and modelling economic agents' responses to it.

Game theory is a branch of applied mathematics that considers strategic interactions between agents, one kind of uncertainty. It provides a mathematical foundation of industrial organization to model different types of firm behaviour, for example in an oligopolistic industry (few sellers), but equally applicable to wage negotiations, bargaining, contract design, and any situation where individual agents are few enough to have perceptible effects on each other. As a method heavily used in behavioural economics, it postulates that agents choose strategies to maximize their payoffs, given the strategies of other agents with at least partially conflicting interests.

In this, it generalizes maximization approaches developed to analyze market actors such as in the supply and demand model and allows for incomplete information of actors. The field dates from the 1944 classic *Theory of Games and Economic Behaviour* by John von Neumann and Oskar Morgenstern. It has significant applications seemingly outside of economics in such diverse subjects as formulation of nuclear strategies, ethics, political science, and evolutionary biology.

Risk aversion may stimulate activity that in well-functioning markets smooths out risk and communicates information about risk, as in markets for insurance, commodity futures contracts, and financial instruments. Financial economics or simply finance describes the allocation of financial resources. It also analyzes the pricing of financial instruments, the financial structure of companies, the efficiency and fragility of financial markets, financial crises, and related government policy or regulation.

Some market organizations may give rise to inefficiencies associated with uncertainty. Based on George Akerlof's "Market for Lemons" article, the paradigm example is of a dodgy second-hand car market. Customers without knowledge of whether a car is a "lemon" depress its price below what a quality second-hand car would be. Information asymmetry arises here, if the seller has more relevant information than the buyer but no incentive to disclose it. Related problems in insurance are adverse selection, such that those at most risk are most likely to insure (say reckless drivers), and moral hazard, such that insurance results in riskier behaviour (say more reckless driving).

Both problems may raise insurance costs and reduce efficiency in driving otherwise willing transactors from the market ("incomplete markets"). Moreover, attempting to reduce one problem, say adverse selection by mandating insurance, may add to another, say moral hazard. Information economics, which studies such problems, has relevance in subjects such as insurance, contract law, mechanism design, monetary economics, and health care. Applied subjects include market and legal remedies to spread or reduce risk, such as warranties, government-mandated partial insurance, restructuring or bankruptcy law, inspection, and regulation for quality and information disclosure.

Market failure

The term "market failure" encompasses several problems which may undermine standard economic assumptions. Although economists categorise market failures differently, the following categories emerge in the main texts.

Information asymmetries and incomplete markets may result in economic inefficiency but also a possibility of improving efficiency through market, legal, and regulatory remedies.

Natural monopoly, or the overlapping concepts of "practical" and "technical" monopoly, is an extreme case of *failure of competition* as a restraint on producers. The problem is described as one where the more of a product is made, the lower the unit costs are. This means it only makes economic sense to have one producer.

Public goods are goods which are undersupplied in a typical market. The defining features are that people can consume public goods without having to pay for them and that more than one person can consume the good at the same time.

Externalities occur where there are significant social costs or benefits from production or consumption that are not reflected in market prices. For example, air pollution may generate a negative externality, and education may generate a positive externality (less crime, etc.). Governments often tax and otherwise restrict the sale of goods that have negative externalities and subsidize or otherwise promote the purchase of goods that have positive externalities in an effort to correct the price distortions caused by these externalities. Elementary demand-and-supply theory predicts equilibrium but not the speed of adjustment for changes of equilibrium due to a shift in demand or supply.

In many areas, some form of price stickiness is postulated to account for quantities, rather than prices, adjusting in the short run to changes on the demand side or the supply side. This includes standard analysis of the business cycle in macroeconomics. Analysis often revolves around causes of such price stickiness and their implications for reaching a hypothesized long-run equilibrium. Examples of such price stickiness in particular markets include wage rates in labour markets and posted prices in markets deviating from perfect competition.

Macroeconomic instability, addressed below, is a prime source of market failure, whereby a general loss of business confidence or external shock can grind production and distribution to a halt, undermining ordinary markets that are otherwise sound.

Some specialised fields of economics deal in market failure more than others. The economics of the public sector is one example, since where markets fail, some kind of regulatory or government programme is the remedy. Much environmental economics concerns externalities or "public bads".

Policy options include regulations that reflect cost-benefit analysis or market solutions that change incentives, such as emission fees or redefinition of property rights.

Public sector

Public finance is the field of economics that deals with budgeting the revenues and expenditures of a public sector entity, usually government. The subject addresses such matters as tax incidence (who really pays a particular tax), cost-benefit analysis of government programmes, effects on economic efficiency and income distribution of different kinds of spending and taxes, and fiscal politics. The latter, an aspect of public choice theory, models public-sector behaviour analogously to micro economics, involving interactions of self-interested voters, politicians, and bureaucrats.

Much of economics is positive, seeking to describe and predict economic phenomena. Normative economics seeks to identify what economies *ought* to be like.

Welfare economics is a normative branch of economics that uses micro economic techniques to simultaneously determine the allocative efficiency within an economy and the income distribution associated with it. It attempts to measure social welfare by examining the economic activities of the individuals that comprise society.

ECONOMIC IDEOLOGY

An economic ideology distinguishes itself from economic theory in being normative rather than just explanatory in its approach. It expresses a perspective on the way an economy should run and to what end, whereas the aim of economic theories is to create accurate explanatory models. However the two are closely interrelated.

A good way of discerning whether an ideology can be classified an economic ideology is to query if it inherently takes a specific and detailed economic standpoint. For instance, Anarchism cannot be said to be an economic ideology as such, because it has amongst others Anarcho-capitalism on the one hand and Anarcho-communism on the other as subcategories thereof, which are in themselves opposing ideological standpoints.

Furthermore, economic ideology is distinct from an economic system that it supports, such as a capitalist ideology, to the extent that explaining an economic system (positive economics) is distinct from advocating it (normative economics). The theory of economic ideology explains its occurrence, evolution, and relation to an economy.

Examples

Capitalism

Capitalism is a broad economic system where competition in a free market determines the price, production and consumption of goods through the invisible hand of supply and demand reaching efficient market equilibrium. Capital, property and enterprise are privately owned and managed for a profit.

New enterprises may freely gain market entry without State restriction. Employment and wages are determined by a labour market that will result in some unemployment. Government and Judicial intervention are employed at times to change the economic incentives for people for various reasons. The capitalist economy will likely follow a business cycle of economic growth along with a steady cycle of small booms and busts.

There are several implementations of capitalism that are loosely based around how much government involvement exists. The main ones that exist today are mixed economies, where the state intervenes in market activity and provides some services; Laissez faire, where the state only supplies a court, a military, and a police; and anarcho-capitalism, where the state does not exist and thus cannot interfere in economic activity.

Socialism

Socialism refers to the various theories of economic organization which advocate either public or direct labour ownership and administration of the means of production and allocation of resources. In certain socialist models, government or state institutions approve of the prices and products grown or otherwise produced in the economy, subjecting the market system to direct external regulations. Alternatively, the state may oversee the production of goods but then sell them in competitive markets.

A socialist state will primarily concern itself with the welfare of its citizens. Socialist doctrines essentially promote the collectivist idea that an economy's resources should be used in the interest all participants, and not simply for private gain.

This notion historically alienated the market economy, and tended to favour central planning. Unfortunately, countries that favoured excessive central controls experienced economic decline and collapse in the long run, as was the case with the Soviet Union.

Communism

As Friedrich Engels described it (in *Anti-Dühring*), communism is the evolution of socialism so that the central role of the State has 'withered away' and is no longer necessary for the functioning of a planned economy. All property and capital are collectively owned and managed in a communal, classless and egalitarian society. Currency is no longer needed, and all economic activity, enterprise, labour, production and consumption is freely exchanged "from each according to his ability, to each according to his needs".

Communism is also a political system as much an economic one—with various models in how it is implemented—the well known being the Marxist Leninist model, which argues for the use of a vanguard party to bring about a workers state to be used as a transitional tool to bring about stateless communism, the economic arrangement. Other models to bring about communism include democratic socialism, which argues for slow social transformation and evolution, or anarcho-communism, which argues similarly to Marxist schools for a revolutionary transformation to the above economic arrangement, but does not use a transitional period or vanguard party.

ECONOMIC POLICY

Economic policy refers to the actions that governments take in the economic field. It covers the systems for setting interest rates and government budget as well as the labour market, national ownership, and many other areas of government interventions into the economy.

Such policies are often influenced by international institutions like the International Monetary Fund or World Bank as well as political beliefs and the consequent policies of parties.

Types of economic policy

Almost every aspect of government has an economic aspect involving a near superfluous quantity of terms. A few examples of the kinds of economic policies that exist include:

- Macroeconomic stabilization policy, which attempts to keep the money supply growing at a rate that doesn't result in excessive inflation.
- Trade policy, which refers to tariffs, trade agreements and the international institutions that govern them.
- Policies designed to create economic growth
  - Policies related to development economics
- Policies dealing with the redistribution of income, property and/or wealth
- As well as: regulatory policy, anti-trust policy, industrial policy and technology-based economic development policy

Macroeconomic stabilization policy== Stabilization policy attempts to stimulate an economy out of recession or constrain the money supply to prevent excessive inflation.

- Fiscal policy, often tied to Keynesian economics, uses government spending and taxes to guide the economy.
  - Fiscal stance: The size of the deficit or surplus
  - Tax policy: The taxes used to collect government income.
  - Government spending on just about any area of government
- Monetary policy controls the value of currency by lowering the supply of money to control inflation and raising it to stimulate economic growth. It is concerned with the amount of money in circulation and, consequently, interest rates and inflation.
  - Interest rates, if set by the Government
  - Incomes policies and price controls that aim at imposing non-monetary controls on inflation
  - Reserve requirements which affect the money multiplier there are many types of economic policies

Tools and goals

Policy is generally directed to achieve particular objectives, like targets for inflation, unemployment, or economic growth. Sometimes other objectives, like military spending or nationalization are important.

These are referred to as the policy goals: the outcomes which the economic policy aims to achieve.

To achieve these goals, governments use policy tools which are under the control of the government. These generally include the interest rate and money supply, tax and government spending, tariffs, exchange rates, labour market regulations, and many other aspects of government.

Selecting Tools and Goals

Government and central banks are limited in the number of goals they can achieve in the short term. For instance, there may be pressure on the government to reduce inflation, reduce unemployment, and reduce interest rates while maintaining currency stability. If all of these are selected as goals for the short term, then policy is likely to be incoherent, because a normal consequence of reducing inflation and maintaining currency stability is increasing unemployment and increasing interest rates.

Demand-side vs. Supply-side Tools

This dilemma can in part be resolved by using micro economics, supply-side policy to help adjust markets. For instance, unemployment could potentially be reduced by altering laws relating to trade unions or unemployment insurance, as well as by macroeconomic (demand-side) factors like interest rates.

Discretionary policy vs policy rules

For much of the 20th century, governments adopted discretionary policies like demand management designed to correct the business cycle. These typically used fiscal and monetary policy to adjust inflation, output and unemployment.

However, following the stagflation of the 1970s, policymakers began to be attracted to policy rules.

A discretionary policy is supported because it allows policymakers to respond quickly to events. However, discretionary policy can be subject to dynamic inconsistency: a government may say it intends to raise interest rates indefinitely to bring inflation under control, but then relax its stance later. This makes policy non-credible and ultimately ineffective.

A rule-based policy can be more credible, because it is more transparent and easier to anticipate. Examples of rule-based policies are fixed exchange rates, interest rate rules, the stability and growth pact and the Golden Rule. Some policy rules can be imposed by external bodies, for instance the Exchange Rate Mechanism for currency.

A compromise between strict discretionary and strict rule-based policy is to grant discretionary power to an independent body. For instance, the Federal Reserve Bank, European Central Bank, Bank of England and Reserve Bank of Australia all set interest rates without government interference, but do not adopt rules.

Another type of non-discretionary policy is a set of policies which are imposed by an international body. This can occur (for example) as a result of intervention by the International Monetary Fund.

Economic policy through history

The first economic problem was how to gain the resources it needed to be able to perform the functions of an early government: the military, roads and other projects like building the Pyramids. Early governments generally relied on tax in kind and forced labour for their economic resources. However, with the development of money came the first policy choice. A government could raise money through taxing its citizens. However, it could now also debase the coinage and so increase the money supply.

Early civilizations also made decisions about whether to permit and how to tax trade. Some early civilizations, such as Ptolemaic Egypt adopted a closed currency policy whereby foreign merchants had to exchange their coin for local money. This effectively levied a very high tariff on foreign trade.

By the early modern age, more policy choices had been developed. There was considerable debate about mercantilism and other restrictive trade practices like the Navigation Acts, as trade policy became associated with both national wealth and with foreign and colonial policy.

Throughout the 19th Century, monetary standards became an important issue. Gold and silver were in supply in different proportions. Which metal was adopted influenced the wealth of different groups in society.

The First Fiscal Policy

With the accumulation of private capital in the Renaissance, states developed methods of financing deficits without debasing their coin. The development of capital markets meant that a government could borrow money to finance war or expansion while causing less economic hardship.

This was the beginning of modern fiscal policy.

The same markets made it easy for private entities to raise bonds or sell shares to fund private initiatives.

Business Cycles

The business cycle became a predominant issue in the 19th century, as it became clear that industrial output, employment, and profit behaved in a cyclical manner. One of the first proposed policy solutions to the problem came with the work of Keynes, who proposed that fiscal policy could be used actively to ward off depressions, recessions and slumps. The Austrian school argues that central banks create the business cycle.

2

Supply: Benefits and Costs

What determines the amount of a good or service that people are willing and ready to sell during some period of time? A discussion of exchange suggested that people sell things because it is a way, indirect but effective, of obtaining other things that they prefer.

Sellers intend to make a profit from their sales, and economists assume that they want their profits to be as large as possible. Because profit is the difference between benefits in the form of revenues and costs, anything that influences revenues or costs can influence the amounts sellers want to sell. Revenue, the benefit that sellers get from producing and selling, is found by multiplying the price of the product by the amount sold.

A change in price changes revenues and hence profits, so it is a major determinant of the amount sellers will want to sell. Because a higher price leads to higher profit, and a higher profit leads to a larger amount that sellers will want to sell, one expects that a greater quantity should be supplied when the price is higher. Thus, the relationship between quantity that sellers will sell and price should be direct or positive. Though the positive relationship is almost always the case, there are a few exceptions. An example is labour; as wages go up, people may decide to enjoy their higher wages and work less. As a result, there is no law of supply that matches the law of demand. The cost of something is what must be given up in order to get it.

When costs are only monetary, they are easy to see. If the price of an input increases, the cost of the output will increase, and, other things held constant, profits will decrease. The seller will then have to decide if shifting part of his resources and effort to other products will improve his well-being. Production costs are determined not only by the prices of inputs, but also by technology.

Technology represents the knowledge of how inputs can be combined to produce the product. If this knowledge increases so that people find cheaper ways to make the same output, then, other things held constant, profit increases and we expect sellers to respond by producing more. Costs may be non-monetary as well as monetary. For example, a farmer takes the expected price of soybeans into account in deciding how much corn to plant.

If soybeans are expected to sell for a high price, then the farmer may find that shifting some of his land from corn production to soybean production will increase profit. The decision to plant corn means that the farmer gives up the opportunity to plant soybeans. Because we have defined cost as what must be given up to get something, the prices of other goods that sellers could otherwise produce and sell must be part of the calculation of the cost of production.

There are other factors that can influence the amount of a product that sellers will sell, such as the number of sellers, expectations about the future, and whether or not there are by-products in production that are valuable. But as in the discussion of demand, the emphasis in the discussion of supply is on the relationship between quantity and price. To focus on this relationship, all other factors must be assumed to be constant.

THE SUPPLY CURVE

The relationship between the quantity sellers want to sell during some time period and price is what economists call the supply curve.Though usually the relationship is positive, so that when price increases so does quantity supplied, there are exceptions.

Hence there is no law of supply that parallels the law of demand. The supply curve can be expressed mathematically in functional form as Qs = f. It can also be emphasised in the form of a table or a graph.

A Supply Curve

Price of Widgets Sellers Want to Sell	Number of Widgets
$1.00	10
$2.00	40
$3.00	70
$4.00	140

The graph shown has a positive slope, which is the slope one normally expects from a supply curve.

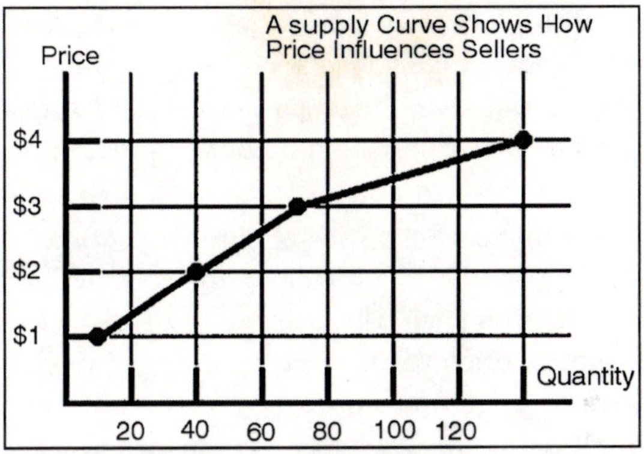

If one of the factors that is held constant changes, the relationship between price and quantity, will change. If the price of an input falls, for example, the supply relationship may change, as in the following table.

A Supply Curve can Shift

Price of Widgets Want to Sell	Number of Widgets Sellers
$1.00	[10] becomes 20
$2.00	[40] becomes 60
$3.00	[70] becomes 100
$4.00	[140] becomes 180

The same changes can be shown with a graph that shows the supply curve shifting to the right. Notice each price has a larger quantity associated with it.

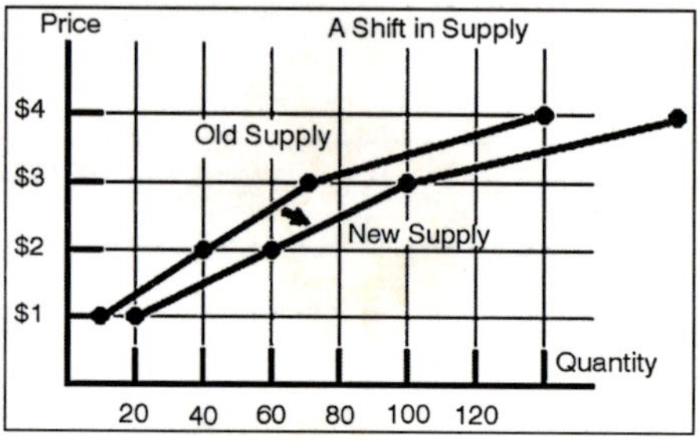

Supply Terminology

As with demand, economists separate changes in the amount that sellers will sell into two categories. A change in supply refers to a change in behaviour of sellers caused because a factor held constant has changed. As a result of a change in supply, there is a new relationship between price and quantity.

At each price there will be a new quantity and at each quantity there will be a new price. A change in quantity supplied refers to a change in behaviour of sellers caused because price has changed. In this case, the relationship between price and quantity remains unchanged, but a new pair in the list of all possible pairs of price and quantity has been realised. Supply curves as well as demand curves appear much more concrete on an economist's graph than they appear in real markets.

A supply curve is mostly potential—what will happen if certain prices are charged, most of which will never be charged. From the buyer's perspective, the supply curve has more meaning as a boundary than as a relationship. The supply curve says that only certain price-quantity pairs will be available to buyers—those lying to the left of the supply curve.

SPECIAL CASES OF A SUPPLY CURVE

As described above, the general form of a supply curve is upward sloping. There are cases, however, when supply curves do not slope upwards. A well known example is for the supply curve for Labour: backward bending supply curve of labour. As a person's wage increases, they are willing to supply a greater number of hours working, but when the wage reaches an extremely high amount (say a wage of $4,000 per hour), the amount of Labour supplied actually decreases. Another example of a nontraditional supply curve is generally the supply curve for utility production companies. Because a large portion of their total costs are in the form of fixed costs, the marginal cost (supply curve) for these firms is often depicted as a constant.

Supply Curve Shifts

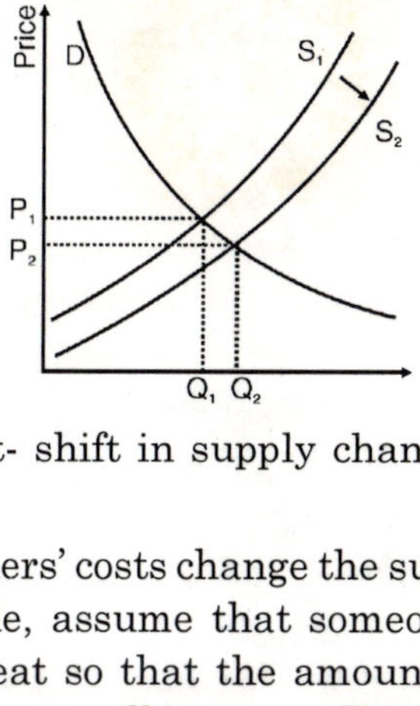

An out- or right- shift in supply changes the equilibrium price and quantity

When the suppliers' costs change the supply curve will shift (or fly). For example, assume that someone invents a better way of growing wheat so that the amount of wheat that can be grown for a given cost will increase. Producers will be willing to supply more wheat at every price and this shifts the supply curve S0 to the right, to S1—an *increase in supply*. This causes the equilibrium price to decrease from P0 to P1. The equilibrium quantity increases from Q0 to Q1 as the quantity demanded increases at the new lower prices. Notice that in the case of a supply curve shift, the price and the quantity move in opposite directions.

Conversely, if the quantity supplied *decreases*, the opposite happens. If the supply curve starts at S1 and then shifts to S0, the equilibrium price will increase and the quantity will decrease. Notice that this is purely an effect of supply changing.

The quantity demanded at each price is the same as before the supply shift (at both Q0 and Q1). The reason that the equilibrium quantity and price are different is the *supply* is different.

There are only 4 possible movements to a demand/supply curve diagram. The demand curve can move to the left and right, and the supply curve can also move only to the left or right. If they do not move at all then they will stay in the middle where they already are.

Market Clearance

The market "clears" at the point where all the supply and demand at a given price are balanced. That is, the amount of a commodity available at a given price equals the amount that buyers are willing to purchase at that price. It is assumed that there is a process that will result in the market reaching this point, but exactly what the process is in a real situation is an ongoing subject of research. Markets which do not clear will react in some way, either by a change in price, or in the amount produced, or in the amount demanded.

Graphically the situation can be represented by two curves: one showing the price-quantity combinations buyers will pay for, or the demand curve; and one showing the combinations sellers will sell for, or the supply curve. The market clears where the two are in equilibrium, that is, where the curves intersect. In a general equilibrium model, all markets in all goods clear simultaneously and the "price" can be described entirely in terms of tradeoffs with other goods. For a century most economists believed in Say's Law, which states that markets, as a whole, would always clear and thus be in balance.

For traditional economics, the market clearing price contains no maximization basis. As a result, any disequilibrium (excess demand or excess supply) is just a matter of graphical exercises. Some economists regarded that a demand curve could be represented by a diminishing marginal use value curve (the schedule of a consumer's maximum willing to pay with different quantity endowments). By this framework, people will buy when the market price is low enough, and they will sell when the price is high enough. In market clearing condition, the market price implies that the marginal use value of all participants are equalized. In other words, mutual gain of exchange is exhausted. Here come the basis of maximization for the concept of market equilibrium.

Vertical Supply Curve

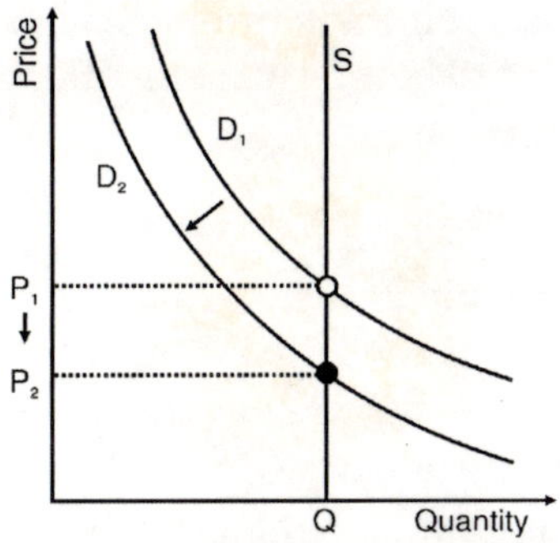

When demand D_1 is in effect, the price will be P_1. When D_2 is occurring, the price will be P_2. Notice that at both values the quantity is Q. Since the supply is fixed, any shifts in demand will only affect price.

It is sometimes the case that the supply curve is vertical: that is the quantity supplied is fixed, no matter what the market price. For example, the amount of land in the world can be considered fixed. In this case, no matter how much someone would be willing to pay for a piece of land, the extra cannot be created. Also, even if no one wanted all the land, it still would exist. If land is considered in this way, then it warrants a vertical supply curve, giving it zero elasticity (i.e., no matter how large the change in price, the quantity supplied will not change). On the other hand, the supply of useful land can be increased in response to demand — by irrigation. And land that otherwise would be below sea level can be kept dry by a system of dikes, which might also be regarded as a response to demand. So even in this case, the vertical line is a bit of a simplification.

In the short run near vertical supply curves are more common. For example, if the Super Bowl is next week, increasing the number of seats in the stadium is almost impossible. The supply of tickets for the game can be considered vertical in this case. If the organizers of this event underestimated demand, then it may very well be the case that the price that they set is below the equilibrium price. In this case there will likely be people who paid the lower price who only value the ticket at that price, and people who could not get tickets, even though they would be willing to pay more. If some of the people who value the tickets less sell them to people who are willing to pay more (i.e., scalp the tickets), then the effective price will rise to the equilibrium price.

Other Market Forms

In a situation in which there are many buyers but a single monopoly supplier that can adjust the supply or price of a good at will, the monopolist will adjust the price so that his profit is maximized given the amount that is demanded at that price.

This price will be higher than in a competitive market. A similar analysis using supply and demand can be applied when a good has a single buyer, a monopsony, but many sellers.

Where there are both few buyers or few sellers, the theory of supply and demand cannot be applied because both decisions of the buyers and sellers are interdependent—changes in supply can affect demand and vice versa. Game theory can be used to analyze this kind of situation.

The supply curve does not have to be linear. However, if the supply is from a profit-maximizing firm, it can be proven that supply curves are not downward sloping (i.e., if the price increases, the quantity supplied will not decrease). Supply curves from profit-maximizing firms can be vertical, horizontal or upward sloping. While it is possible for industry supply curves to be downward sloping, supply curves for individual firms are never downward sloping.

Standard microeconomic assumptions cannot be used to prove that the demand curve is downward sloping. However, despite years of searching, no generally agreed upon example of a good that has an upward-sloping demand curve has been found (also known as a giffen good). Non-economists sometimes think that certain goods would have such a curve.

For example, some people will buy a luxury car because it is expensive. In this case the good demanded is actually prestige, and not a car, so when the price of the luxury car decreases, it is actually changing the amount of prestige so the demand is not decreasing since it is a different good. Even with downward-sloping demand curves, it is possible that an increase in income may lead to a decrease in demand for a particular good, probably due to the existence of more attractive alternatives which become affordable: a good with this property is known as an inferior good.

An example: Supply and demand in a 6-person economy

Supply and demand can be thought of in terms of individual people interacting at a market. Suppose the following six people participate in this simplified economy:

- Alice is willing to pay $10 for a sack of potatoes.
- Bob is willing to pay $20 for a sack of potatoes.
- Cathy is willing to pay $30 for a sack of potatoes.
- Dan is willing to sell a sack of potatoes for $5.
- Emily is willing to sell a sack of potatoes for $15.
- Fred is willing to sell a sack of potatoes for $25.

There are many possible trades that would be mutually agreeable to both people, but not all of them will happen. For example, Cathy and Fred would be interested in trading with each other for any price between $25 and $30. If the price is above $30, Cathy is not interested, since the price is too high. If the price is below $25, Fred is not interested, since the price is too low. However, at the market Cathy will discover that there are other sellers willing to sell at well below $25, so she will not trade with Fred at all. In an efficient market, each seller will get as high a price as possible, and each buyer will get as low a price as possible.

Imagine that Cathy and Fred are bartering over the price. Fred offers $25 for a sack of potatoes. Before Cathy can agree,

Emily offers a sack of potatoes for $24. Fred is not willing to sell at $24, so he drops out. At this point, Dan offers to sell for $12. Emily won't sell for that amount so it looks like the deal might go through. At this point Bob steps in and offers $14. Now we have two people willing to pay $14 for a sack of potatoes, but only one person willing to sell for $14. Cathy notices this and doesn't want to lose a good deal, so she offers Dan $16 for his potatoes.

Now Emily also offers to sell for $16, so there are two buyers and two sellers at that price (note that they could have settled on any price between $15 and $20), and the bartering can stop. But what about Fred and Alice? Well, Fred and Alice are not willing to trade with each other, since Alice is only willing to pay $10 and Fred will not sell for any amount under $25. Alice can't outbid Cathy or Bob to purchase from Dan, so Alice will not be able to get a trade with them. Fred can't underbid Dan or Emily, so he will not be able to get a trade with Cathy. In other words, a stable equilibrium has been reached.

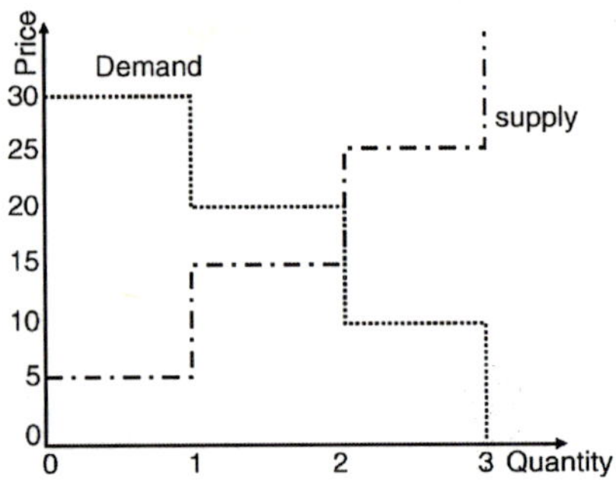

Fig. Discrete Supply and Demand Curves

A supply and demand graph could also be drawn from this. The demand would be:

- 1 person is willing to pay $30 (Cathy).
- 2 people are willing to pay $20 (Cathy and Bob).
- 3 people are willing to pay $10 (Cathy, Bob, and Alice).

The supply would be:

- 1 person is willing to sell for $5 (Dan).

- 2 people are willing to sell for $15 (Dan and Emily).
- 3 people are willing to sell for $25 (Dan, Emily, and Fred).

Supply and demand match when the quantity traded is two sacks and the price is between $15 and $20. Whether Dan sells to Cathy, and Emily to Bob, or the other way round, and what precisely is the price agreed cannot be determined.

This is the only limitation of this simple model. When considering the full assumptions of perfect competition the price would be fully determined, since there would be enough participants to determine the price.

For example, if the "last trade" was between someone willing to sell at $15.50 and someone willing to pay $15.51, then the price could be determined to the penny. As more participants enter, the more likely there will be a close bracketing of the equilibrium price.

It is important to note that this example violates the assumption of perfect competition in that there are a limited number of market participants. However, this simplification shows how the equilibrium price and quantity can be determined in an easily understood situation. The results are similar when unlimited market participants and the other assumptions of perfect competition are considered.

History of Supply and Demand

Attempts to determine how supply and demand interact began with Adam Smith's *The Wealth of Nations*, first published in 1776. In this book, he mostly assumed that the supply price was fixed but that the demand would increase or decrease as the price decreased or increased. David Ricardo in 1817 published the book *Principles of Political Economy and Taxation*, in which the first idea of an economic model was proposed. In this, he more rigorously laid down the idea of the assumptions that were used to build his ideas of supply and demand.

During the late 19th century the marginalist school of thought emerged. This field mainly was started by Stanley

Jevons, Carl Menger, and Léon Walras. The key idea was that the price was set by the most expensive price, that is, the price at the margin. This was a substantial change from Adam Smith's thoughts on determining the supply price.

Finally, most of the basics of the modern school theory of supply and demand were finalized by Alfred Marshall and Léon Walras, when they combined the ideas about supply and the ideas about demand and began looking at the equilibrium point where the two curves crossed.

They also began looking at the effect of markets on each other. Since the late 19th century, the theory of supply and demand has mainly been unchanged. Most of the work has been in examining the exceptions to the model (like oligarchy, transaction costs, non-rationality).

Criticism of Marshall's Theory of Supply and Demand

Marshall's theory of supply and demand runs counter to the ideas of economists from Adam Smith and David Ricardo through the creation of the marginalist school of thought. Although Marshall's theories are dominant in universities today, other economists have disagreed with it. One theory counter to Marshall is that price is already known in a commodity before it reaches the market, negating his idea that some abstract market is conveying price information. The only thing the market communicates is whether or not an object is exchangeable or not (in which case it would change from an object to a commodity).

This would mean that the producer creates the goods without already having customers — blindly producing, hoping that someone will buy them ("buy" meaning exchange money for the commodities). Modern producers often have market studies prepared well in advance of production decisions; however, misallocation of factors of production can still occur.

Keynesian economics also runs counter to the theory of supply and demand. In Keynesian theory, prices can become "sticky" or resistant to change, especially in the case of price decreases. This leads to a market failure. Modern supporters of Keynes, such as Paul Krugman, have noted this in recent history, such as when the Boston housing market dried up in the early 1990s, with neither buyers nor sellers willing to exchange at the price equilibrium.

Gregory Mankiw's work on the irrationality of actors in the markets also undermines Marshall's simplistic view of the forces involved in supply and demand.

3

Production and Supply

In investigating the foundations of supply and demand, we will look at demand and supply as separate headings. It doesn't matter much, logically, which we take first. Historically, the first stages of the economists' Reasonable Dialog were focused more on supply. In investigating the foundations of supply, we are investigating the economics of production and that was the central topic for the classical economists.

Adam Smith, we recall, had been very optimistic about the future economic development of the industrializing countries. With increased division of labour leading to higher wages and growing demand, he felt, production could continue to grow. However, Thomas Malthus criticized Smith's optimism. Malthus spoke for the pessimistic view and, of course, Malthus is best known for his claim that increasing population would lead to poverty. In supporting this idea, Malthus began to study the limits on production. It was this study that has made his work important particularly for Neoclassical economics.

Limits on production stem from limited resources with a given technology. With a given technology, limited quantities of inputs will yield only limited quantities of outputs. The relationship between the quantities of inputs and the maximum quantities of outputs produced is called the "production function."

The "production function." is a relationship between quantities of input and quantities of output that tells us, for each quantity of input, the greatest output that can be produced with those inputs. Malthus didn't work out the details, but he clearly had this idea in mind as he originated the key concept of Diminishing Returns.

Diminishing Returns

As we recall, Malthus is best known for his pessimistic idea that population growth would force incomes down to the subsistence level. What we are interested in here is not his conclusion, but the reasoning that took him there.

Malthus argued that l and is a fixed input, but the growth of population makes labour a variable input.

Malthus proposed a general law of economics, the Law of Diminishing Returns: when a fixed input is combined in production with a variable input, using a given technology, increases in the quantity of the variable input will eventually depress the productivity of the variable input. (Malthus argued that decreasing productivity of labour would depress incomes). Was Malthus right? The answer is, of course, yes and no.

There is plenty of evidence, both observational and statistical, that the Law of Diminishing Returns is valid. For example, agricultural economists have carried out experimental tests of the theory. They have selected plots of l and of identical size and fertility and used different quantities of fertilizer on the different plots of l and. In this example, l and was the fixed input and fertilizer the variable input. They found that, as the quantity of fertilizer increased, the productivity of fertilizer declines. This is only one of many bits of evidence that the Law of Diminishing Returns is true in general.

On the other h and, in the two hundred years since Malthus wrote, on the whole, population has increased but labour productivity and incomes have not declined.

On the whole, they have risen. What seems to have happened is that technology has improved. Malthus recognized that if technology improved (in agriculture, at least), that might postpone what he saw as the inevitable poverty as a consequence of rising population. Some economists and other people, believe that the Malthusian prediction will eventually come true. Perhaps: what is clear is that in two hundred years it has not. But that doesn't mean the Law of Diminishing Returns is wrong! A "law" such as this can be true in general but cannot be applied when its assumptions (such as an unchanging technology) aren't true. The "Law" isn't wrong—just inapplicable to that case.There are many valid and useful applications of the Law of Diminishing Returns in economics. In this chapter we will look at two.

- We will use Diminishing Returns and related concepts to get a better idea of the meaning of the phrase "efficient allocation of resources" and some guidelines for efficiency in that sense.
- We will explore how a business firm should direct its production in order to get maximum profits and that will give us a basis for a better underst anding of the economics of supply.

First, though, we will need to look at production and diminishing returns in general in a little more detail.

Production Function

Production is the transformation of inputs into outputs. Inputs are the factors of production—l and, labour and capital—plus raw materials and business services. The transformation of inputs into outputs is determined by the technology in use. Limited quantities of inputs will yield only limited quantities of outputs. The relationship between the quantities of inputs and the maximum quantities of outputs produced is called the "production function. "But how do these outputs change when the input quantities vary? Let's take a look at an example of a production function.In general, we would allow for varying amounts of l and, labour and capital. However, in this example, labour will be the only input, for the sake of simplicity.

A Production Function Example

The production function thus contains the limitations that technology places on the firm. The mathematical forms of the production function and the utility function are identical. In one case, inputs of goods and services combine to produce utility; in the other, inputs of resources combine to produce goods or services. As one moves to the right, one reaches higher levels of production. If one can visualize this as a three-dimensional graph, one can see that the production surface rises increasingly high above the surface of the page; the isoquants indicate a hill.

Marginal Productivity

Productivity, by definition, is a ratio of output to labour input. In most statistical discussions of productivity, we refer to the average productivity of labour:

$$AP = \frac{\text{Output}}{\text{Labor Input}}$$

Average labour productivity is an important concept, especially in macroeconomics. In microeconomics, however, we will focus more on the marginal productivity.

We can think of the marginal productivity of labour as the additional output as a result of adding one unit of labour, with all other inputs held steady and ceteris paribus.

In algebraic terms, an equally correct definition is:

$$MP = \frac{\Delta\text{Output}}{\Delta\text{Labor}}$$

Let's have a numerical example to illustrate the application of the theory. Suppose that:

- When 300 labour-days per week are employed the firm produces 2505 units of output per week.
- When 400 labour-days per week are employed the firm produces 3120 units of output per week.
- It follows that the change in labour input, ýÿLabor, is 100.
- It also follows that the change in output, ýÿOutput, is 615.
- Applying the formula above, we approximate the marginal productivity of labour by the quotient 615/100 = 6.15.

- We can interpret this result as follows: over the range of 300 to 400 man-days of labour per week, each additional worker adds approximately 6.15 units to output.

Of course, if we had more information, we could get a closer approximation. For example, if we had the outputs for 310, 320,... 390 man-days of labour, we could see how MP varies within the range 300-400. But we can be sure that the values will be in the neighborhood of 6.15.

Now let's think a little further about the Law of Diminishing Returns.

The Law of Diminishing Marginal Productivity

In his discussions of the Law of Diminishing Returns, Malthus did not distinguish between average and marginal productivity. However, in modern economics, we think of diminishing returns primarily in terms of marginal, not average, productivity.

Law of Diminishing Returns (Modern Statement): When the technology of production and some of the inputs are held constant and the quantity of a variable input increases continually, the marginal productivity of the variable input will eventually decline. The inputs that are held steady are called the "fixed inputs." In these pages we are treating l and and capital as fixed inputs. The inputs that are allowed to vary are called the "variable inputs." In these pages we are treating labour as the variable input. Another way to express the law of diminishing returns, is that, as the variable input increases, the output also increases, but at a decreasing rate. The marginal productivity of labour is the rate of increase in output as the labour input increases. To say that output increases at a decreasing rate when the variable input increases is another way to say that the marginal productivity declines.

Marginal Productivity

Let's extend the numerical example in the page before last and see how marginal productivity varies over a wide range of labour inputs. Here is a hypothetical example of production with the inputs of l and and labour held steady and varying quantities of labour and the output and average and marginal productivities.

Table

Labour	Output	Average Productivity	Marginal Productivity
0	0	0	0
100	945	9.45	9.45
200	1780	8.90	8.35
300	2505	8.35	7.25
400	3120	7.80	6.15
500	3625	7.25	5.05
600	4020	6.70	3.95
700	4305	6.15	2.85
800	4480	5.60	1.75
900	4545	5.05	0.65
1000	4500	4.50	-0.45

Output Diagram

Here is a picture of the relationship between the variable input and the output in the numerical example in the previous table. Notice how the slope gets flatter: as the variable input increases, output increases at a decreasing rate. This is a visualization of the Law of Diminishing Marginal Productivity.

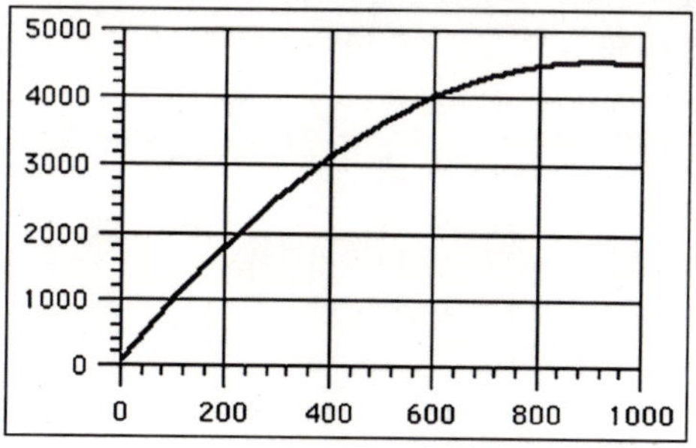

Fig: Production with Diminishing Returns

Average and Marginal Productivity Diagram

We have put some stress on the difference between average

and marginal productivity. Both are important, but for a model of short-run profit-maximizing supply, marginal productivity is the more important. and the two are quite different.

Here are the average and marginal productivities for the same numerical example in the page before last. Notice how both average and marginal productivity decrease as the labour input increases. But the marginal productivity declines faster than the average productivity, pulling the average productivity down after it. The downward slope of the marginal productivity line expresses the Law of Diminishing Returns and the downward slope of the average productivity is also a result of the law.

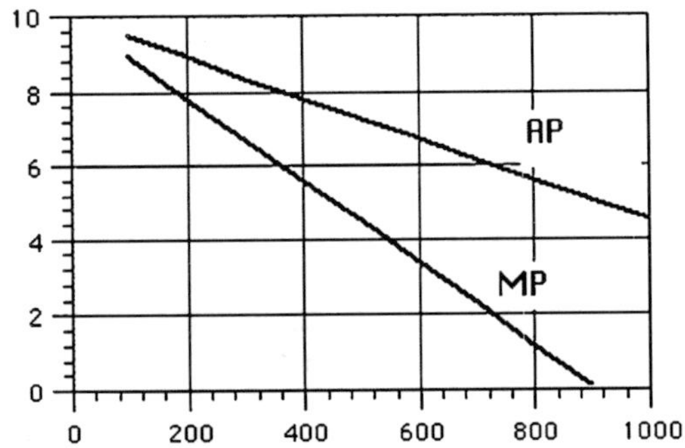

Fig: Average and Marginal Productivity

The relationship between average and marginal productivity in the diagram is important in itself and we will see similar relationships in future chapters. So let's look at it a little more closely. Average and marginal productivity will not always have the same slope. In general,

- Whenever average productivity is greater than marginal productivity, average productivity will slope downward.
- Whenever average productivity is less than marginal productivity, average productivity will slope upward.

The diagram does not show any values where average productivity is less, but a more complicated example might and then we would see the second part of the relationship visualized. To underst and the relationship, think of it this way: as we add labour input, one unit after another, we add a bit more to output at each step. When the addition is greater than the average, it pulls the average up toward it. When the addition is less than the average, it pulls the average down toward it.

AGENTS OF PRODUCTION

Land, labour, capital and entrepreneurship are the four generally recognized factors of production in classical economics. Example: Last year Farmer Brown's crop yielded $100 worth of produce. To generate that selling price, Brown incurred $25 to rent the land, $25 to pay for labour, and $25 for the use of equipment. The remaining $25 compensates him for his effort as an entrepreneur.

FACTORS OF PRODUCTION

Naturally, in a literal sense anything contributing to the productive process is a factor of production. However, economists seek to classify all inputs into a few broad categories, so standard usage refers to the categories themselves as factors. Earlier only three factors making up the "*classical triad*" were recognized: *land, labour*, and *capital*. Entrepreneurship is a fairly recent addition.

The concept of these factors is used to construct models illustrating general features of the economic process without getting caught up in inessential details. These include models purporting to explain growth, value, choice of production method, income distribution, and social classes. A major conceptual application is in the theory of production functions.

One intuitive basis for the classification of the factors of production is the manner of payment for their services: rent for land, wages for labour, interest for capital, and profit for entrepreneurship.

Land

Sometimes this factor however, extends over all natural resources. It is intended to represent the contribution to production of nonhuman resources as found in their original, unimproved form. For the French physiocrats led by Francois Quesnay in the 1750s and 1760s, land was the only factor yielding a reliable gain to its owner. In their view, labourers and artisans were powerless and in excess supply, and hence they earned on average only a subsistence-level income; and in the same way what they produced outside of agriculture fetched enough to cover only their wages and input costs with no margin for profit. Only in agriculture, due to soil fertility and other "*gifts of nature*," could a labourer palpably produce more than required to cover subsistence and other costs, so only in agriculture could proprietors collect surplus. Thus the physiocrats explained land rent as coming from surplus produced by the land. They recommended taxes on land as the only sound way to raise revenue and land-grabbing as the best means to increase the government's revenue base.

In 1821, David Ricardo, in *The Principles of Political Economy and Taxation*, stated what came to be known as the classical view: that rent reflects scarcity of good land. The value of a crop depends on the labour required to produce it on the worst land under cultivation. This worst land yields no rent—as long as some of it remains unused—and rent collected on better land is simply its yield in excess of that on the worst land. Ricardo saw rent as coming from differences in land quality (including accessibility) and scarcity. The classical economists assumed only land—understood as natural resources—could be scarce in the long term.

In 1899, John Bates enlarge Marginalism in *The Distribution of Wealth*, takes a different approach. It declares that rent reflects the marginal productivity of land—not, as with Ricardo, the productivity of good versus marginal land. Marginal productivity is the extra output obtained by extending a constant amount of labour and capital over an additional unit of land of uniform quality. Marginalists held that any factor of production could be scarce. Their theory is based on the possibility of substituting among factors to design alternative production methods, whereby the optimal production method allocates all the factors to equalize their marginal productivity with their marginal costs. Long thought of as a self-sustaining input, land might depreciate just like produced assets do.

In 1989 Herman Daly and Jonathan Cobb, in *For the Common Good*, distinguished between nonrenewable resources that are consumed or depreciate irretrievably and renewable resources where the rate of natural renewal is important. One consequence of this work in environmental economics is that natural resource accounting increasingly resembles capital accounting.

Labour

In this factor the classical "*labour theory of value*" was an innovative theory in response to the physiocratic doctrine that only land could yield surplus. In 1776 Adam Smith, in *The Wealth of Nations*, observed that with expansion of production and trade, enterprises were making profits over long periods of time, although they either had nothing to do with agriculture or else as agricultural enterprises. Classical economists tried to answer the question: Where does profit come from? Their answer was that it came from labour.

In various industries, labour can yield a surplus over subsistence costs at prevailing prices. The question arises of why proprietors, but not labourers, earn profit. Ricardo arrived at one answer: Technical innovation increases labour productivity. Owners of innovative equipment, until its general adoption, get the premium from reduced costs. In 1867 Karl Marx in *Capital*, added that wages reflect the cost of subsistence, not what labourers can produce, and that profit is the difference between the two. Even without innovation proprietors would reap surpluses, Marx held, since labourers lack market power and cannot afford their own equipment.

Why wages are differ for different types of labour? Marx's answer was that higher wages cover costs, beyond personal subsistence, of training and cultivation of skills, acknowledging that one kind of "*equipment*" now known as human capital, was available at least to some labourers. Marginalist economists noticed the advance of technology, which according to classical and Marxist views made labour ever more productive, continually throws labourers out of work. This led them to attribute productivity to equipment rather than only to labour. Referring to equipment as capital, they developed production functions featuring labour and capital as substitutes for each other. In marinalist growth theory, choice among production techniques involving different combinations of labour and capital became a major theme.

Capital

This most controversial of factors is variously defined as produced equipment; as finance used to acquire produced equipment; as all finance used to begin and carry on production, including the "*wage fund*"; and as the assessed value of the whole productive enterprise, including intangibles such as "*goodwill.*" In 1960 Piero Sraffa, in *Production of Commodities by Means of Commodities*, showed that capital in the sense of produced equipment can fail to behave as expected in marginalist production functions when an entire economy is modeled.

Specifically, equipment adopted to replace labour after wages rise from a low level, relative to interest on capital, may be abandoned again in favour of labour as wages rise still higher. This counterintuitive "*reswitching*" can happen because the equipment used is itself a product of labour and equipment, and because the ratio of labour to equipment varies for different products.

Frequently capital is treated as finance, associated with the payment of interest. Yet the connection with equipment, in spite of Sraffa's demonstration, has never been severed entirely. One still studies capital depreciation, distinguishing wear-and-tear from obsolescence, and from the present value of investments in capital. Increasingly, theory has come to treat any investment as a capital investment. Furthermore, acquired skills (as opposed to "know-how," an attribute of society rather than individuals) have come to be viewed as analogous to physical equipment, capable of yielding their owners a return.

This analogy suggests their current designation as human capital. Thus capital is a concept still mired in confusion, and care must be taken in its use to be sure what it means.

Entrepreneurship

Before the twentieth century, this function was assigned to the capitalist and frequently conflated with capital. In the classical view, profit rather than interest was attributed to ownership of capital. In the marginalist view, capital earned interest, and profit was a mere residual after all the factors of production were compensated. In his *Principles of Economics*, first published in 1890, Alfred Marshall made extensive references to "*organization*" and "*management,*" referring to the coordination function of entrepreneurship but to neither risk-assuming nor innovation. But in 1912 Joseph Schumpeter, in *The Theory of Economic Development*, featured the revolutionary role of organizer and innovator and contrasted it with that of the conservative financier, thus vividly distinguishing the entrepreneur from the capitalist.

In this view, the entrepreneur's role is not merely that of manager and risk-taker, but also of visionary—someone who seeks as much to destroy the old order as to create something new. Since innovation usually requires destroying old ways of doing things, Schumpeter gave it the name "*creative destruction.*" Profit is now assigned to entrepreneurship, to innovation. With the rise of "*venture capitalists*" and other financiers willing to take on more risk and do more for innovation in the hope for supernormal returns, the distinction between capitalist and entrepreneur has again become fuzzier. Instantly, there are entrepreneurial financiers as well as entrepreneurial producers and distributors.

Although in business usage stock dividends are distributed profits, in economic analysis they figure as returns to capital, a kind of interest payment, since they are a return to finance rather than to entrepreneurship. The fact that stocks are legally equity rather than debt shares are thereby ignored. Similarly, salaries of corporate executive officers are treated as profit, a return to entrepreneurship, rather than as wages for labour services.

Costs and Supply

In the field of business it can be looked by us in two points of view: productivity, inputs, and outputs (as we have just done) or outputs and costs. In advanced microeconomics, these two points of view are called "*duals*." They are equally valid, but they point up different things. They are also opposites from a certain point of view — the higher the productivity, the lower the costs. By looking at the firm from the point of view of costs, we shift our perspective somewhat, and gain a much more direct understanding of supply. We also look more directly at the difference between the long and short run. In the short run, we have two major categories of costs:

- Fixed costs, and
- Variable costs

However, all costs are variable in the long run. Thus, we must study costs under two quite different headings. Costs will vary quite differently in the long run and in the short.

Fixed and Variable Costs

Variable costs can be defined as the costs that can be varied flexibly as conditions change. In the John Bates Clark model of the firm that we are studying, labour costs are the variable costs. Fixed costs are the costs of the investment goods used by the firm, on the idea that these reflect a long-term commitment that can be recovered only by wearing them out in the production of goods and services for sale.

Here, the view is that labour is a much more flexible resource than capital investment. People can change from one task to another flexibly (whether within the same firm or in a new job at another firm), while machinery tends to be designed for a very specific use.

If it isn't used for that purpose, it can't produce anything at all. Thus, capital investment is much more of a commitment than hiring is. In the eighteen-hundreds, when John Bates

Clark was writing, this was pretty clearly true. Over the past century,

- Education and experience have become more important for labour, and have made labour more specialized, and
- Increasing automatic control has made some machinery more flexible. So the differences between capital and labour are less than they once were, but all the same, it seems labour is still relatively more flexible than capital. It is this (relative) difference in flexibility that is expressed by the simplified distinction of long and short run. Of course, productivity and costs are inversely related, so the variable costs will change as the productivity of labour changes.

Here is a picture of the fixed costs (FC), variable costs (VC) and the total of both kinds of costs (TC) for the productivity example in the last unit:

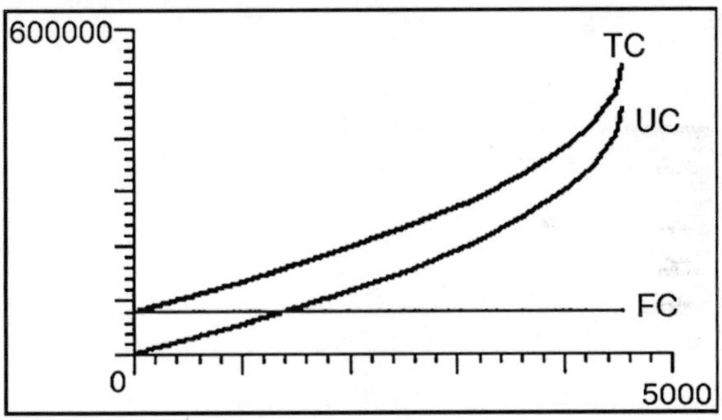

Fig. Output Produced is Measured towards the Right on the Horizontal Axis.

The cost numbers are on the vertical axis. Notice that the variable and total cost curves are parallel, since the distance between them is a constant number — the fixed cost.

Opportunity Cost, Again

What is the connection between the distinctions we have just made — fixed vs variable costs — and opportunity cost, the key concept in some earlier units? In economics, all costs are included — whether or not they correspond to money payments. If we have opportunity costs with no corresponding money payments, they are called implicit costs. The implicit costs (as well as the money costs) are included in the cost analysis we have just given. There is some correlation between implicit costs and fixed or variable costs, but this correlation will be different in such different kinds of firms as a factory owned by an absentee investor

This is the easiest case to understand. All of the labour costs to the absentee investor are money costs, including the manager's salary. If the investor has borrowed some of the money he invested in the factory, then there is some money costs of the capital invested — interest on the loan. However, we must consider the opportunity cost of invested capital as well. The investor's own money that he has used to buy the factory is money that she could have invested in some other business. The return she could have gotten on another investment is the opportunity cost of her own funds invested in the business. This is an implicit cost, and in this case the implicit cost is part of the cost of capital and probably a fixed cost.

A "Mom-and-Pop" Store

A store in which family members are self-employed and supply most of the labour is called a "*mom-and-pop*" store (family proprietorship or partnership). Typically, "*Mom*" and "*Pop"* don't pay themselves a salary — they just take money from the till when they need it, since it is their property anyway. As a result, there are no money costs for their labour. But their labour has an opportunity cost — the salary or wages they could make working similar hours in some other business — and so, in this case, the implicit costs include a large component of variable labour costs.

A Large Modern Corporation

Relatively, few implicit costs are have by the corporation but some will have generally. All labour costs will be expressed in money terms (though benefits and bonuses have to be included), since the shareholders doesn't supply labour to the corporation as "*Mom and Pop*" do in a family proprietorship. It will pay interest to bondholders and dividends to shareholders. But the dividends aren't really a cost item — they include profits distributed to the shareholders. Moreover, the typical corporation will retain some profits and invest them within the business, a "*plowback*" investment.

On the other hand, a broad part of their payout might be taken by shareholders in appreciation of the stock value — and plowback investment is one reason for the appreciation. Thus we would say that the corporation has a net equity value, that is, that the corporation "*owns*" a certain amount of capital that it invests in its own business (very much like the absentee owner in the first example). This capital has an opportunity cost and that opportunity cost is an implicit cost. The stockholders, who own the corporation, ultimately receive (as dividends or appreciation) both the opportunity cost of the equity capital and any profit left over after it is taken out.

SUPPLY FOR MONEY

In economics, the money supply or money stock, is the total amount of monetary assets available in an economy at a specific time. There are several ways to define "money," but standard measures usually include currency in circulation and demand deposits (depositors' easily accessed assets on the books of financial institutions).

Money supply data are recorded and published, usually by the government or the central bank of the country. Public and private sector analysts have long monitored changes in money supply because of its effects on the price level, inflation, the exchange rate and the business cycle.

That relation between money and prices is historically associated with the quantity theory of money. There is strong empirical evidence of a direct relation between long-term price inflation and money-supply growth, at least for rapid increases in the amount of money in the economy. That is, a country such as Zimbabwe which saw rapid increases in its money supply also saw rapid increases in prices (hyperinflation). This is one reason for the reliance on monetary policy as a means of controlling inflation.

The nature of this causal chain is the subject of contention. Some heterodox economists argue that the money supply is endogenous (determined by the workings of the economy, not by the central bank) and that the sources of inflation must be found in the distributional structure of the economy.

In addition, those economists seeing the central bank's control over the money supply as feeble say that there are two weak links between the growth of the money supply and the inflation rate. First, in the aftermath of a recession, when many resources are underutilized, an increase in the money supply can cause a sustained increase in real production instead of inflation. Second, if the velocity of money, *i.e.*, the ratio between nominal GDP and money supply, changes, an increase in the money supply could have either no effect, an exaggerated effect, or an unpredictable effect on the growth of nominal GDP.

Link with inflation

Monetary Exchange Equation

Money supply is important because it is linked to inflation by the equation of exchange in an equation proposed by Irving Fisher in 1911

$$MV = PQ$$

- M is the total dollars in the nation's money supply
- V is the number of times per year each dollar is spent (velocity of money)
- P is the average price of all the goods and services sold during the year
- Q is the quantity of assets, goods and services sold during the year

In mathematical terms, this equation is really an identity which is true by definition rather than describing economic behaviour. That is, each term is defined by the values of the other three. Unlike the other terms, the velocity of money has no independent measure and can only be estimated by dividing PQ by M. Some adherents of the quantity theory of money assume that the velocity of money is stable and predictable, being determined mostly by financial institutions. If that assumption is valid, then changes in M can be used to predict changes in PQ. If not, then the equation of exchange is useless to macroeconomics.

Most macroeconomists replace the equation of exchange with equations for the demand for money which describe more regular and predictable economic behaviour. However, predictability (or the lack thereof) of the velocity of money is equivalent to predictability (or the lack thereof) of the demand for money (since in equilibrium real money demand is simply Q/V). Either way, this unpredictability made policy-makers at the Federal Reserve rely less on the money supply in steering the U.S. economy. Instead, the policy focus has shifted to interest rates such as the fed funds rate.

In practice, macroeconomists almost always use real GDP to measure Q, omitting the role of all transactions except for those involving newly produced goods and services (*i.e.*, consumption goods, investment goods, government-purchased goods, and exports). That is, the only assets counted as part of Q are newly produced investment goods. But the original quantity theory of money did not follow this practice: PQ was the monetary value of all new transactions, whether of real goods and services or of paper assets.

The monetary value of assets, goods, and service sold during the year could be grossly estimated using nominal GDP back in the 1960s. This is not the case anymore because of the dramatic rise of the number of financial transactions relative to that of real transactions up until 2008. That is, the total value of transactions (including purchases of paper assets) rose relative to nominal GDP (which excludes those purchases).

Ignoring the effects of monetary growth on real purchases and velocity, this suggests that the growth of the money supply may cause different kinds of inflation at different times. For example, rises in the U.S. money supplies between the 1970s and the present encouraged first a rise in the inflation rate for newly produced goods and services ("inflation" as usually defined) in the seventies and then asset-price inflation in later decades: it may have encouraged a stock market boom in the '80s and '90s and then, after 2001, a rise in home prices, *i.e.*, the famous housing bubble. This story, of course, assumes that the amounts of money were the causes of these different types of inflation rather than being endogenous results of the economy's dynamics.

When home prices went down, the Federal Reserve kept its loose monetary policy and lowered interest rates; the attempt to slow price declines in one asset class, *e.g.* real estate, may well have caused prices in other asset classes to rise, *e.g.* commodities.

Rates of Growth

In terms of percentage changes (to a close approximation under small growth rates, the percentage change in a product, say XY, is equal to the sum of the percentage changes %ΔX + %ΔY). So:

$$\%\Delta P + \%\Delta Q = \%\Delta M + \%\Delta V$$

That equation rearranged gives the "basic inflation identity":

$$\%\Delta P = \%\Delta M + \%\Delta V - \%\Delta Q$$

Inflation (%ΔP) is equal to the rate of money growth (%ΔM), plus the change in velocity (%ΔV), minus the rate of output growth (%ΔQ). As before, this equation is only useful if ΔÄV follows regular behaviour. It also loses usefulness if the central bank lacks control over %ΔM.

Bank reserves at central bank

When a central bank is "easing", it triggers an increase in money supply by purchasing government securities on the open market thus increasing available funds for private banks to loan through fractional-reserve banking (the issue of new money through loans) and thus the amount of bank reserves and the monetary base rise. By purchasing government bonds (especially Treasury Bills), this bids up their prices, so that interest rates fall at the same time that the monetary base increases.

With "easy money," the central bank creates new bank reserves (in the US known as "federal funds"), which allow the banks lend more. These loans get spent, and the proceeds get deposited at other banks. Whatever is not required to be held as reserves is then lent out again, and through the "multiplying" effect of the fractional-reserve system, loans and bank deposits go up by many times the initial injection of reserves.

In contrast, when the central bank is "tightening", it slows the process of private bank issue by selling securities on the open market and pulling money (that could be loaned) out of the private banking sector. By increasing the supply of bonds, this lowers their prices and raises interest rates at the same time that the money supply is reduced.

This kind of policy reduces or increases the supply of short term government debt in the hands of banks and the non-bank public, lowering or raising interest rates. In parallel, it increases or reduces the supply of loanable funds (money) and thereby the ability of private banks to issue new money through issuing debt.

The simple connection between monetary policy and monetary aggregates such as M1 and M2 changed in the 1970s as the reserve requirements on deposits started to fall with the emergence of money funds, which require no reserves. Then in the early 1990s, reserve requirements were dropped to zero on savings deposits, CDs, and Eurodollar deposit. At present, reserve requirements apply only to "transactions deposits" – essentially checking accounts. The vast majority of funding sources used by private banks to create loans are not limited by bank reserves. Most commercial and industrial loans are financed by issuing large denomination CDs. Money market deposits are largely used to lend to corporations who issue commercial paper. Consumer loans are also made using savings deposits, which are not subject to reserve requirements. This means that instead of the amount of loans supplied responding passively to monetary policy, we often see it rising and falling with the demand for funds and the willingness of banks to lend.

Some academics argue that the money multiplier is a meaningless concept, because its relevance would require that the money supply be exogenous, *i.e.* determined by the monetary authorities via open market operations. If central banks usually target the shortest-term interest rate (as their policy instrument) then this leads to the money supply being endogenous.

Arguments

The main functions of the central bank are to maintain low inflation and a low level of unemployment, although these goals are sometimes in conflict (according to Phillips curve). A central bank may attempt to do this by artificially influencing the demand for goods by increasing or decreasing the nation's money supply (relative to trend), which lowers or raises interest rates, which stimulates or restrains spending on goods and services.

An important debate among economists in the second half of the twentieth century concerned the central bank's ability to predict how much money should be in circulation, given current employment rates and inflation rates. Economists such as Milton Friedman believed that the central bank would always get it wrong, leading to wider swings in the economy than if it were just left alone. This is why they advocated a non-interventionist approach—one of targeting a pre-specified path for the money supply independent of current economic conditions— even though in practice this might involve regular intervention with open market operations (or other monetary-policy tools) to keep the money supply on target.

The Chairman of the U.S. Federal Reserve, Ben Bernanke, has suggested that over the last 10 to 15 years, many modern central banks have become relatively adept at manipulation of the money supply, leading to a smoother business cycle, with recessions tending to be smaller and less frequent than in earlier decades, a phenomenon termed "The Great Moderation" This theory encountered criticism during the global financial crisis of 2008–2009. Furthermore, it may be that the functions of the central bank may need to encompass more than the shifting up or down of interest rates or bank reserves: these tools, although valuable, may not in fact moderate the volatility of money supply (or its velocity).

PRODUCTION TECHNOLOGY

Production is the process of transforming inputs to outputs. Typically, inputs consist of labour, capital equipment, raw materials, and intermediate goods purchased from other firms. Outputs consists of finished products or service, or intermediate goods to be sold to other firms. Often alternative methods are available for producing the same output, using different combinations of inputs. A firm produces outputs from various combinations of inputs. In order to study firm choices we need a convenient way to summarize the production possibilities of the firm, *i.e.*, which combinations of inputs and outputs are technologically feasible.

Measurement of Inputs and Outputs

It is usually most satisfactory to think of the inputs and outputs as being measured in terms of flows: a certain amount of inputs per the period are used to produce a certain amount of outputs per unit the period at some location. It is a good idea to explicitly include the time and location dimensions in a specification of inputs and outputs. The level of detail that as suggested, use in specifying inputs and outputs will depend on the problem at hand, but we should remain aware of the fact that a particular input or output good can be specified in arbitrarily fine detail. However, when discussing technological choices in the abstract, it is common to omit the time and location dimensions.

Specification of Technology

The fundamental reality firms must contend with in this process is technological feasibility. The state of technology determines and restricts what is possible in combing inputs to produce outputs, and there are several way we can represent this constraint. The most general way is to think of the firm as having a production possibility set. Suppose the firm has L possible goods to serve as inputs and/or outputs. If a firm uses y_j^0 units of a good j as an input and produces y_j^0 of the good as an output, then the net output of good j is given by,

$$y_j = y_j^o - y_j^i.$$

A production plan is simply a list of net outputs of various goods. We can represent a production plan by a vector y in R^L where y_j is negative if the jth good serves as a net input and positive if the j^{th}good serves as a net output. The set of all technologically feasible production plans is called the firm's production possibilities set and will be denoted by Y, a subset of RL. The set Y is supposed to describe all patterns of inputs and outputs that are technologically feasible. It gives us a complete description of the technological possibilities facing the firm.

When we study the behaviour of a firm in certain economic environments, we may want to distinguish between production plans that are "immediately feasible" and those that are "eventually" feasible.

As suggested, generally assume that such restrictions can be described by some vector z in R^L. The restricted or short-run production possibilities set will be denoted by $Y(z)$; this consists of all feasible net output bundles consistent with the constraint level z. The following are some examples of such restrictions.

Example: Input requirement set. Suppose a firm produces only one output. In this case we write the net output bundle as $(y,-x)$ where x is a vector of inputs that can produce y units of output. We can then define a special case of a restricted production possibilities set, the input requirement set:

$$V(y) = \left\{x \, in \, R_+^L : (y, = x) \, is \, in \, Y\right\}$$

The input requirement set is the set of all input bundles that produce at least y units of output. Note that the input requirement set, as defined here, measures inputs as positive numbers rather than negative numbers as used in the production possibilities set.

Example: Isoquant

In the case we can also define an isoquant:

$$Q(y) = \{x \text{ in } R^n_+ : x \text{ is in } V(y) \text{ and } x \text{ is not in } V(y') \text{ for } y' > y\}:$$

The isoquant gives all input bundles that produce exactly y units of output.

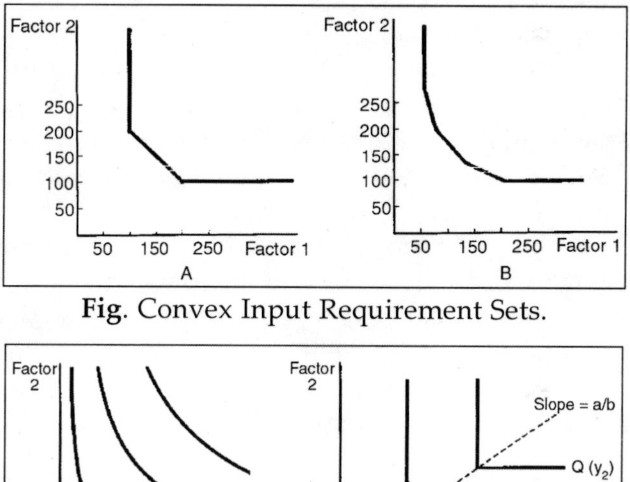

Fig. Convex Input Requirement Sets.

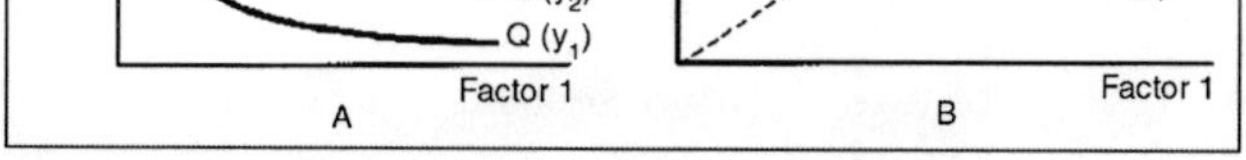

Fig: Panel A Depicts the General Shape of a Isoquant Curve, and Panel B Depicts The General Shape of a Perfect Complement (Leontief) Technology.

Example: Short-run production possibilities set.

Suppose a firm produces some output from labour and some kind of machine which as suggested, refer to as "capital."

Production plans then look like $(y,-l,-k)$ where y is the level of output, l the amount of labour input, and k the amount of capital input. We imagine that labour can be varied immediately but that capital is fixed at the level k in the short run.

Then,

$$Y(\bar{K}) = \{(y,-l,-k)\, in\, Y : k = \bar{k}\}$$

is a short-run production possibilities set.

Example: Production function

If the firm has only one output, we can define the production function: $f(x) = \{y$ in R: y is the maximum output associated with–x in $Y\}$.

Example: Transformation function

A production plan y in Y is (technologically) efficient if there is no y′ in Y such that y′ ≧ y and y′ ≠ y; that is, a production plan is efficient if there is no way to produce more output with the same inputs or to produce the same output with less inputs. We often assume that we can describe the set of technologically efficient production plans by a transformation function T: → R where $T(y) = 0$ if and only if y is efficient.

Just as a production function picks out the maximum *scalar* output as a function of the inputs, the transformation function picks out the the maximum *scalar* output as a function of the inputs, the transformation function picks out the maximal *vectors* of net outputs.

Example: Cobb-Douglas technology

Let α be a parameter such that $0 < a < 1$. Then the Cobb-Douglas technology is defined in the following manner.

$$Y = \{(y,-x_1,-x_2)\, in\, R^3 : y \leqq x_1^{\alpha} x_2^{1-\alpha}\}$$

$$V(y) = \{(x_1,x_2)\, in\, R_+^2 : y \leqq x_1^{\alpha} x_2^{1-\alpha}\}$$

$$Q(y) = \{(x_1,x_2)\, in\, R_+^2 : y = x_1^{\alpha} x_2^{1-\alpha}\}$$

$$Y(z) = \{(y,-x_1-x_2)\, in\, R^3 : \leqq x_1^{\alpha} x_2^{1-\alpha}, x_2 = z\}$$

$$T(y, x_1 x_2) = y - x_1^a x_2^{1-\alpha}$$
$$f(x_1, x_2) = x_1^a x_2^{1-\alpha}.$$

Example: Leontief technology

Let $a > 0$ and $b > 0$ be parameters. Then the Leontief technology is defined in the following manner.

$$Y = \{(y, -x_1, -x_2) \text{ in } R^3 : y \leqq \min(ax_1, bx_2)\}$$
$$V(y) = \left\{(x_1, x_2) \, in \, R_+^2 : y \leqq \min(ax_1, bx_2)\right\}$$
$$Q(y) = \left\{(x_1, x_2) \, in \, R_+^2 : y = \min(ax_1, bx_2)\right\}$$
$$T(y, x_1, x_2) = y - \min(ax_1, bx_2)$$
$$f(x_1, x_2) = \min(ax_1, bx_2).$$

Common Properties of Production Sets

Although the production possibility sets of different processes can differ widely in structure, many technologies share certain general properties.

If it can be assumed that these properties are satisfied, special theoretical results can be derived. Some important properties are:

Possibility of Inaction: $0 \in Y$. Possibility of inaction means that no action on production is a possible production plan.

Closeness: Y is closed. The possibility set Y is closed means that, whenever a sequence of production plans. y_i, $i = 1, 2, \ldots$, are in Y and $y_i \to y$, then the limit production plan y is also in Y. It guarantees that points on the boundary of Y are feasible. Note that Y is closed implies that the input requirement set $V(y)$ is a closed set for all $y \geqq 0$.

Free Disposal or Monotonicity: If $y \in Y$ implies that $y' \in Y$ for all $y' \in y$, then the set Y is said to satisfy the free disposal or monotonicity property. Free disposal implies that commodities can be thrown away. This property means that if $y \in Y$, then Y includes all vectors in the negative orthant translated to y, *i.e.*, there are only inputs, but no outputs.

A weaker requirement is that we only assume that the input requirement is monotonic: If x *is in* $V(y)$ *and* x′ ≥ x, *then* x′ *is in* $V(y)$. Monotonicity of $V(y)$ means that, if x is a feasible way to produce y units of output and x′ is an input vector with at least as much of each input, then x′ should be a feasible way to produce y.

Irreversibility: $Y \cap \{-Y\ g = \{0\}$. Irreversibility means a production plan is not reversible unless it is a non-action plan.

Convexity: Y is convex if whenever y and $y0$ are in Y, the weighted average $ty + (1-t)y$ is also in Y for any t with $0 \leqq t \leqq 1$. Convexity of Y means that, if all goods are divisible, it is often reasonable to assume that two production plans y and y' can be scaled downward and combined. However, it should be noted that the convexity of the production set is a strong hypothesis. For example, convexity of the production set rules out "start up costs" and other sorts of returns to scale.

Strict Convexity: y is strictly convex if $y \in Y$ and $y' \in Y$, then $ty + (1-t)y' \in intY$ for all $0 < t < 1$, where $intY$ denotes the interior points of Y. As as suggested, show, the strict convexity of Y can guarantee the profit maximizing production plan is unique provided it exists. A weak and more reasonable requirement is to assume that $V(y)$ is a convex set for all outputs y_o:

Convexity of Input Requirement Set: *If* x *and* x′ *are in* $V(y)$, *then* tx + $(1-t)$x′ *is in* $V(y)$ *for all* $0 \leqq t \leqq 1$. *That is,* $V(y)$ *is a convex set*. Convexity of $V(y)$ means that, if x and x' both can produce y units of output, then any weighted average $tx + (1-t)x'$ can also produce y units of output. We describe a few of the relationships between the convexity of $V(y)$, the curvature of the production function, and the convexity of Y. We first have

Proposition: *If the production set* Y *is a convex set, then the associated input requirement set,* $V(y)$, is a convex set.

Proof: If Y is a convex set then it follows that for any x and x′ such that $(y,-\text{x})$ and $(y,-\text{x}')$ are in Y for $0 \leqq t \leqq 1$, we must have $(ty + (1-t)y, t\text{x}-(1-t)\text{x}')$ in Y. This is simply requiring that $(y, (t\text{x} + (1-t)\text{x}'))$ is in Y. It follows that if x and x' are in $V(y)$, $t\text{x} + (1-t)\text{x}'$ is in $V(y)$ which shows that $V(y)$ is convex.

Proposition: *$V(y)$ is a convex set if and only if the production function $f(\mathrm{x})$ is a* quasi-concave function.

Proof: $V(y) = \{\mathrm{x}: f(\mathrm{x}) \geqq y\}$, which is just the upper contour set of $f(\mathrm{x})$. But a function is quasi-concave if and only if it has a convex upper contour set.

Returns to Scale

Suppose that we are using some vector of inputs x to produce some output y and we decide to scale all inputs up or down by some amount $t = 0$. What will happen to the level of output? The notions of returns to scale can be used to answer this question. Returns to scale refer to how output responds when all inputs are varied in the same proportion so that they consider long run production processes.

There are three possibilities: technology exhibits:

1. Constant returns to scale;
2. Decreasing returns to scale, and
3. Increasing returns to scale. Formally, we have

(Global) Returns to Scale: A production function f(x) is said to exhibits:

1. Constant returns to scale if $f(t\mathrm{x}) = tf(\mathrm{x})$ *for all* $t \geqq 0$;
2. Decreasing returns to scale if $f(t\mathrm{x}) < tf(\mathrm{x})$ *for all* $t > 1$;
3. Increasing returns to scale if $f(t\mathrm{x}) > tf(\mathrm{x})$ *for all* $t > 1$;

Constant returns to scale means that doubling inputs exactly double outputs, which is often a reasonable assumption to make about technologies. Decreasing returns to scale means that doubling inputs are less than doubling outputs. Increasing returns to scale means that doubling inputs are more than doubling outputs. Note that a technology has constant returns to scale if and only if its production function is homogeneous of degree 1. Constant returns to scale is also equivalent to: the statement y in Y implies ty is in Y for all $t \geqq 0$; or equivalent to the statement x in $V(y)$ implies tx is in $V(t\mathrm{y})$ for all $t > 1$.

It may be remarked that the various kinds of returns to scale defined are global in nature. It may well happen that a technology exhibits increasing returns to scale for some values of x and decreasing returns to scale for other values. Thus in many circumstances a local measure of returns to scale is useful. To define locally returns to scale, we first define elasticity of scale. The elasticity of scale measures the per cent increase in output due to a one per cent increase in all inputs{that is, due to an increase in the scale of operations. Let $y = f(x)$ be the production function. Let t be a positive scalar, and (consider the function $y(t) = f(tx)$. If $t = 1$, we have the current scale of operation; if $t > 1$, we are scaling all inputs up by t; and if $t < 1$, we are scaling all inputs down by t. The elasticity of scale is given by

$$e(x) = \frac{\frac{dy(t)}{y(t)}}{\frac{dt}{t}},$$

evaluated at $t = 1$. Rearranging this expression, we have,

$$e(x) = \left.\frac{dy(t)}{dt}\frac{t}{y}\right|_{t=1} = \left.\frac{df(tx)}{dt}\frac{t}{f(tx)}\right|_{t=1}$$

Note that we must evaluate the expression at $t = 1$ to calculate the elasticity of scale at the point x. Thus, we have the following the local returns to scale:

Returns to Scale: A production function $f(x)$ is said to exhibits locally increasing, constant, or decreasing returns to scale as e(x) is greater, equal, or less than 1.

The Marginal Rate of Technical Substitution

Suppose that technology is summarized by a smooth production function and that we are producing at a particular point,

$$y^* = f\left(x_1^*, x_2^*\right).$$

Suppose that we want to increase a small amount of input 1 and decrease some amount of input 2 so as to maintain a constant level of output. How can we determine this marginal rate of technical substitution (MRTS) between these two factors? The way is the same as for deriving the marginal rate of substitution of an indifference curve. Differentiating production function when output keeps constant, we have,

$$0=\frac{\partial f}{\partial x_1}dx_1+\frac{\partial f}{\partial x_2}dx_2,$$

which can be solved for,

$$\frac{dx_2}{dx_1}=-\frac{\partial f/\partial x_1}{\partial f/\partial x_2}\equiv-\frac{MP_{x_1}}{MP_{x_2}}1.$$

This gives us an explicit expression for the marginal rate technical substitution, which is the rate of marginal production of x_1 and marginal production of x_2.

Example: Given that,

$$f(x_1,x_2)=x_1^{\alpha}x_2^{1-\alpha},$$

we can take the derivatives to find,

$$\frac{\partial f(x)}{\partial x_1}=\alpha x_1^{\alpha-1}x_2^{1-\alpha}=a\left[\frac{x_2}{x_1}\right]^{1-\alpha}$$

$$\frac{\partial f(x)}{\partial x_2}=(1-a)x_1^{\alpha}x_2^{-\alpha}=(1-a)\left[\frac{x_1}{x_2}\right]^{a}.$$

It follows that,

$$\frac{\partial x_2(x_1)}{\partial x_1}=\frac{\partial f/\partial x_1}{\partial f/\partial x_2}=-\frac{a}{1-a}\frac{x_1}{x_2}.$$

The Elasticity of Substitution

The marginal rate of technical substitution measures the slope of an isoquant. The elasticity of substitution measures the curvature of an isoquant.

More specifically, the elasticity of substitution measures the percentage change in the factor ratio divided by the percentage change in the MRTS, with output being held fixed.

If we let $\Delta(x_2/x_1)$ be the change in the factor ratio and ΔMRTS be the change in the technical rate of substitution, we can express this as,

$$\sigma = \frac{\dfrac{\Delta(x_2/x_1)}{x_2/x_1}}{\dfrac{\Delta MRTS}{MRTS}}.$$

This is a relatively natural measure of curvature: it asks how the ratio of factor inputs changes as the slope of the isoquant changes.

If a small change in slope gives us a large change in the factor input ratio, the isoquant is relatively flat which means that the elasticity of substitution is large.

In practice we think of the per cent change as being very small and take the limit of this expression as Δ goes to zero. Hence, the expression for σ becomes

$$\sigma = \frac{MRTS}{(x_2/x_1)} \frac{d(x_2/x_1)}{dMRTS} = \frac{d\ln(x_2/x_1)}{d\ln|MRTS|}.$$

Example: We have seen that,

$$MRTS = -\frac{a}{1-a}\frac{x_2}{x_1}.$$

or

$$\frac{x_2}{x_1} = -\frac{1-a}{a} MRTS.$$

It follows that,

$$\ln\frac{x_2}{x_1} = \ln\frac{1-a}{a} + \ln|MRTS|.$$

This in turn implies,

$$\sigma = \frac{d\ln(x_2/x_1)}{d\ln|MRTS|} = 1.$$

Example: The constant elasticity of substitution production function has the form,

$$y = \left[a_1 x_1^{\rho} + a_2 x_2^{\rho}\right]^{\frac{1}{\rho}}.$$

It is easy to verify that the CES function exhibits constant returns to scale. It will probably not surprise you to discover that the CES production function has a constant elasticity of substitution. To verify this, note that the marginal rate of technical substitution is given by,

$$MRTS = -\left(\frac{x_1}{x_2}\right)^{\rho-1},$$

so that,

$$\frac{x_2}{x_1} = |MRTS|^{\frac{1}{1-\rho}}.$$

Taking logs, we see that,

$$\ln\frac{x_2}{x_1} = \frac{1}{1-\rho}\ln|MTRTS|.$$

Applying the definition of a using the logarithmic derivative,

$$\sigma = \frac{d\ln x_2/x_1}{d\ln|MRTS|} = \frac{1}{1-\rho}.$$

4

The Demand Curve

The relationship between price and the amount of a product people want to buy is what economists call the demand curve. This relationship is inverse or indirect because as price gets higher, people want less of a particular product. This inverse relationship is almost always found in studies of particular products, and its very widespread occurrence has given it a special name: the law of demand.

The word "law" in this case does not refer to a bill that the government has passed but to an observed regularity. There are various ways to express the relationship between price and the quantity that people will buy. Mathematically, one can say that quantity demanded is a function of price, with other factors held constant, or:

$$Qd = f$$

A more elementary way to capture the relationship is in the form of a table. The numbers in the table are what one expects in a demand curve: as price goes up, the amount people are willing to buy decreases.

A Demand Curve

Price of Widgets People Want to Buy	Number of Widgets
$1.00	100
$2.00	90
$3.00	70
$4.00	40

The same information can also be plotted on a graph, where it will look like the graph.

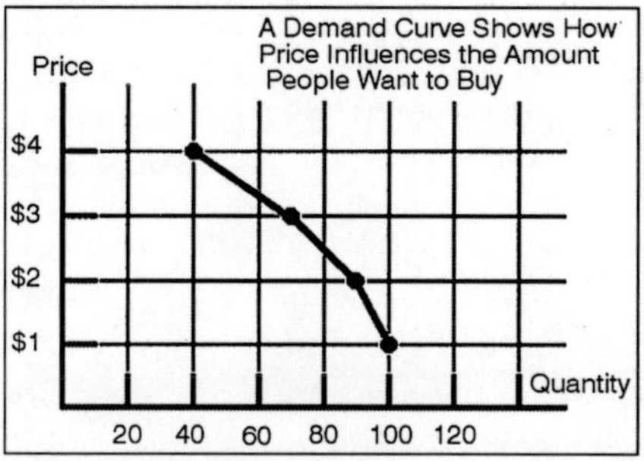

If one of the factors being held constant becomes unstuck, changes, and then is held constant again, the relationship between price and quantity will change. For example, suppose the price of getwids, a substitute for widgets, falls. Then, people who previously were buying widgets will reconsider their choices, and some may decide to switch to getwids. This would be true at all possible prices for widgets. These changes in the way people will behave at each price will change the demand curve to look like the table.

A Demand Curve can Shift

Price of Widgets People Want to Buy	Number of Widgets
$1.00	[100] becomes 80
$2.00	[90] becomes 70
$3.00	[70] becomes 50
$4.00	[40] becomes 10

Demand Terminology

If the price of widgets is originally $1.00 and people are buying 100, they may change to 90 for two reasons. One reason is that the price may rise to $2.00. The other reason is that one of the factors that is assumed to be constant may change, so that even though the price has not changed, quantity will. Economists distinguish these two cases. In the first case the demand relationship or schedule has not changed, but there has been movement within the relationship. Economists call a change of this sort a change in quantity demanded. The second sort of change is an alteration of the relationship. The original pairing of price and quantity is destroyed and replaced by a new pairing. Economists call this sort of change a change in demand.

It is important to realise that though the demand relationship looks concrete when it is emphasised with a table or graph, in everyday life demand curves are hidden. A demand curve refers to what people would do if various prices were charged, and very rarely are enough prices charged so a clear demand curve can be seen. This is not to say that the concept is of no importance to people who sell. They may not be interested in the demand curve as a relationship, but they do find it a boundary or constraint on their behaviour.

If there were an actual widget seller facing the demand curve in our demand table, he would find that he could not sell more than 90 widgets if he wanted to charge $2.00. He could of course sell fewer if he wanted to. He could sell only 70 at $2.00, but if he did this, he would earn far less than he could. If he wanted to sell more than 90, he would have to lower his price.

Thus, to an actual businessman the demand curve is important as a limitation on what he can do. A businessman may not know exactly where the demand curve is, and he may not think of it as fixed. Advertising—either informing or persuading people—can move the boundary. As we proceed further, as suggested, see that there are still other ways to view the demand curve in addition to seeing it as a mathematical relationship and as a boundary that limits sellers.

THE "LAW OF DEMAND"

Notice that, in this example, the demand curve is downward sloping. That's a common-sense point: the higher the price, the less people will want to buy. In this case, common-sense has it 100% right.

Economists call this the Law of Demand: At a higher price, the quantity dem anded will be less, ceteris paribus.(Ceteris paribus means: if nothing else changes to offset the change in price).

Ceteris Paribus: Some Economist's Jargon

Now might be a good time to explain that phrase, "ceteris paribus."

Ceteris paribus: "Ceteris paribus" is a Latin phrase often used by economists, literally meaning "other things equal." Used in the context of an economic model, it means all the the variables that might affect the equilibrium in the model, are held constant unless we explicitly say otherwise.

Only the ones we say are changing are allowed to change. In the example of the demand curve, we say that the law of demand applies "ceteris paribus," meaning that other things that might influence quantity dem anded, such as the consumers' income and the population, are treated as being constant.

If those things change, that would shift the demand curve. This is part of the economist's analytical technique, allowing us to take one thing at a time. Believe it or not, it helps to keep things simple!

The Demand Relationship: 3 More Points

The example also illustrates three important points about the demand relation:

- The price must always be adjusted for inflation. We use the "real" (adjusted) price, not the nominal price.
- The demand relationship can be represented and approximated,
  - — Numerical
  - — Graphical, or
  - — Mathematical and statistical methods
  - — Statements in a computer programming language
- Mathematically, the demand schedule and diagram we have just seen can also be expressed as

$$Q = 7617.27-54.36*P$$

Here is more detail on the mathematical approach—optional.

The Demand Relationship

Of course, the demand relationship is approximate, since many things other than the price of a good can influence the quantity dem anded of that good.

In practice, we have to use statistical methods to get an approximate estimate of the demand relationship.

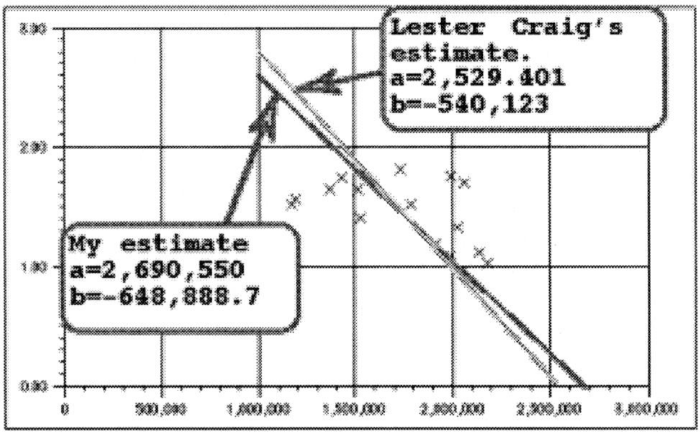

A real estimate of a demand curve, done by one of my students using a very simple statistical procedure for his class project.

My estimate used a more complex statistical procedure. Quantity is in pounds of cigarettes and price in inflation-adjusted dollars per pound.

The estimate is for 1974-1988. The actual prices and quantities dem anded for the different years are also shown, so you can see about how good an approximation it is.

Supply of Beer

Economists treat supply symmetrically as demand. That is, we treat supply (also) as a relationship between price and the quantity supplied. Usually, the relation is direct (upward sloping), rather than inverse. Here is the supply schedule corresponding to the beer demand given before.

Supply of Beer, 1960

Price, cents/gal.	Quantity supplied, millions of gals.
50	0
60	0
70	0
80	1304.4
90	2894
100	4483.6
110	6073.2
120	7662.8

As with demand, supply may be represented not only by a table of numbers, but also by a diagram or a mathematical equation. Here is a diagram of the estimated demand for beer. As before, we put the price on the vertical axis and the quantity supplied on the horizontal axis.

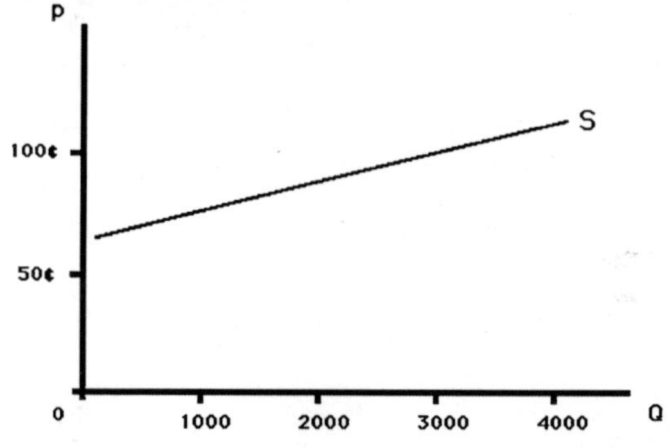

Remember, also, that when we use the term "supply" we usually mean the entire supply curve or relationship, while if we refer to the quantity people want to sell at a particular price, we say the "quantity supplied."

TYPES OF DEMAND

Some types of demand are:

- Individual demand and Market Demand.

- Demand for capital goods and demand for consumer goods.
- Autonomous demand and derived demand direct and indirect demand.
- Demand for durable and non-durable goods.
- Short term demand and long term demand.

ELASTICITY OF DEMAND

The concept of price-elasticity of demand was first of all introduced in economics by Dr. Marshall.

In simple words, price elasticity of demand is the ratio of percentage change in quantity demanded to the percentage change in price. In other words, price elasticity of demand is a measure of the relative change in quantity purchased of a good in response to a relative change in its price.

It is, thus a rate at which the demand changes to the given change in prices. So, it means the rate or the degree of response in demand to the change in price. Thus, the co-efficient of price-elasticity of demand can be expressed as under:

$$E_d = \frac{\Pr oportionate\ change\ in\ quality\ demanded}{\Pr oportionate\ change\ in\ price}$$

Definitions of Price Elasticity of Demand

The concept of price elasticity of demand has been defined by different economists as under:

- *According to Alfred Marshall:* "Elasticity of demand may be defined as the percentage change in quantity demanded to the percentage change in price."
- *According to A.K. Cairncross:* "The elasticity of demand for a commodity is the rate at which quantity bought changes as the price changes."
- *According to J.M. Keynes:* "The elasticity of demand is a measure of the relative change in quantity to a relative change in price."

- *According to Kenneth Boulding:* "Elasticity of demand measures the responsiveness of demand to changes in price."

Degrees Of Price Elasticity

Different commodities have different price elasticities. Some commodities have more elastic demand while others have relative elastic demand. Basically, the price elasticity of demand ranges from zero to infinity. It can be equal to zero, less than one, greater than one and equal to unity.

According to Dr. Marshall: "The elasticity or reponsiveness of demand in a market is great or small according as the amount demanded increases much or little for a given fall in price and diminishes much or little for a given rise in price." However, some particular values of elasticity of demand have been explained as under; Perfectly Elastic Demand. Perfectly elastic demand is said to h appen when a little change in price leads to an infinite change in quantity demanded. A small rise in price on the part of the seller reduces the demand to zero. In such a case the shape of the demand curve will be horizontal straight line as shown in figure.

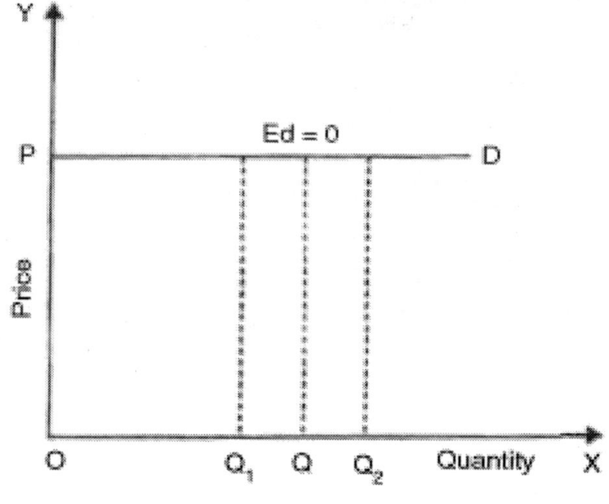

The figure shows that at the ruling price OP, the demand is infinite. A slight rise in price will contract the demand to zero. A slight fall in price will attract more consumers but the elasticiy of demand will remain infinite. But in real world, the cases of perfectly elastic demand are exceedingly rare and are not of any practical interest.

Perfectly inelastic Demand

Perfectly inelastic demand is opposite to perfectly elastic demand. Under the perfectly inelastic demand, irrespective of any rise or fall in price of a commodity, the quantity demanded remains the same. The elasticity of demand in this case will be equal to zero. In diagram 14, DD shows the perfectly inelastic demand. At price OP, the quantity demanded is OQ. Now, the price falls to OP, from OP1, demand remains the same. Similarly, if the price rises to OP2 the demand still remains the same. But just as we do not see the example of perfectly elastic demand in the real world, in the same fashion it is difficult to come across the cases of perfectly inelastic demand because even the demand for bare essentials of life does show some degree of responsiveness to change in price.

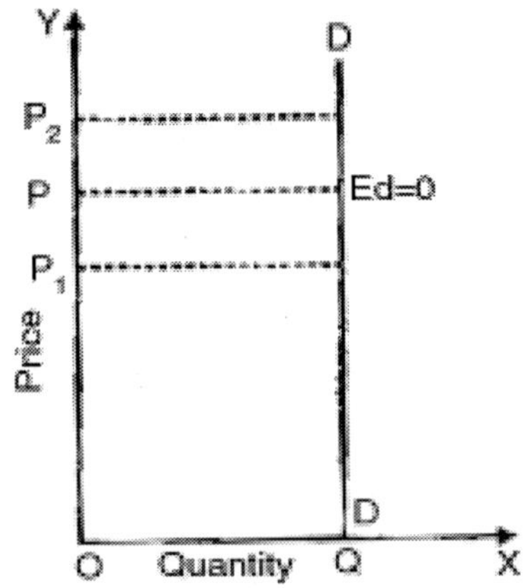

Unitary Elastic Demand

The demand is said to be unitary elastic when a given proportionate change in the price level brings about an equal proportionate change in quantity demanded, The numerical value of unitary elastic demand is exactly one *i.e.*, ed = 1. Marshall calls it unit elastic. In figure, DD demand curve represents unitary elastic demand. This demand curve is called rectangular hyperbola. When price is OP, the quantity demanded is OQ1. Now price falls to OP1, the quantity demanded increases to OQ1. The shaded area in the fig. equal in terms of price and quantity demanded denotes that in all cases price elasticity of demand is equal to one.

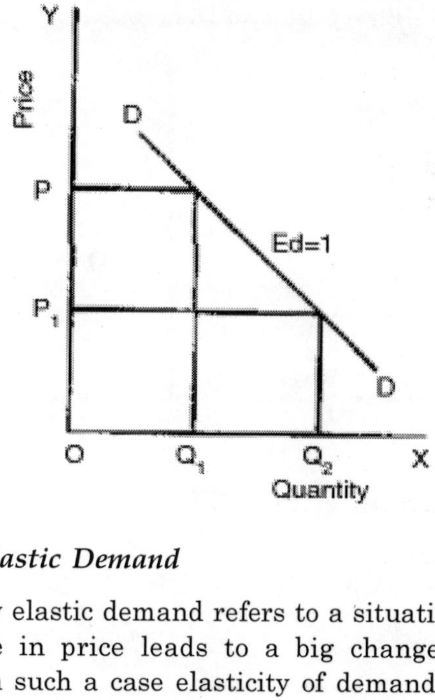

Relatively Elastic Demand

Relatively elastic demand refers to a situation in which a small change in price leads to a big change in quantity demanded. In such a case elasticity of demand is said to be more than one. This has been shown in figure. In fig., DD is the demand curve which indicates that when price is OP the quantity demanded is OQ1, Now the price falls from OP to OP1, the quantity demanded increases from OQ1 to OQ2 *i.e.* quantity demanded changes more than the change in price.

Relatively Inelastic Demand

Under the relatively inelastic demand a given percentage change in price produces a relatively less percentage change in quantity demanded. In such a case elasticity of demand is said to be less than one as shown in figure. All the five degrees of elasticity of demand have been shown in figure. On OX axis, quantity demanded and on OY axis price is given. It shows:

- AB — Perfectly Inelastic Demand
- CD — Perfectly Elastic Demand
- EQ — Less Than Unitary Elastic Demand
- EF — Greater Than Unitary Elastic Demand
- MN — Unitary Elastic Demand

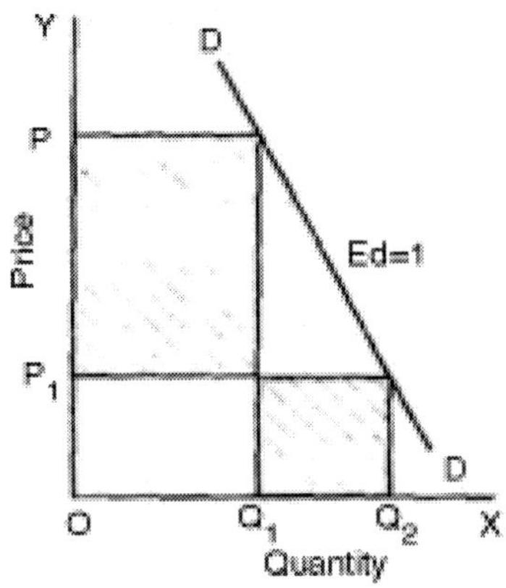

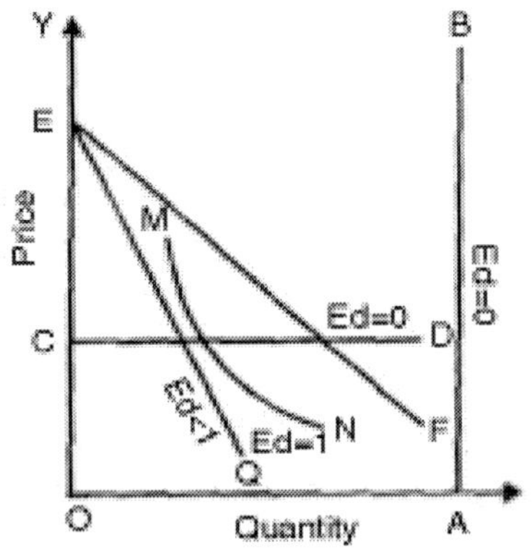

Factors Determining Price Elasticity Of Demand

The factors that determine elasticity of demand are numberless. But the most important among them are the nature, uses and prices of related goods and the level of income. They are stated below:

Nature of the Commodity

Generally, all commodities can be dividend into three categories *i.e.*

- Necessaries of Life. For necessaries of life the demand is inelastic because people buy the required amount of goods whatever their price. For example, necessaries such as rice, salt, cloth are purchased whether they are dear or cheap.

- Conventional Necessaries. The demand for conventional necessaries is less elastic or inelastic. People are accustomed to the use of goods like intoxicants which they purchase at any price. For example, drunkards consider opium and wine almost as a necessity as food and water. Therefore, they buy the same amount even when their prices are higher and highest.
- Luxury Commodities. The demand for luxury is usually elastic as people buy more of them at a lower price and less at a higher price. For example, the demand of luxuries like silk, perfumes and ornaments increases at a lower price and diminishes at a higher price. Here, we must keep in mind that luxury is a relative term, which varies from person to person, place to place and from time to time. For example, what is a luxury to a poor man is a necessity to the rich. The luxury of the past may become a necessity of today. Similarly a commodity which is a necessity to one class may be a luxury to another. Hence, the elasticity of demand in such cases should have to be carefully expressed.

Substitutes

Demand is elastic for those goods which have substitutes and inelastic for those goods which have no substitutes. The availability of substitutes, thus, determines the elasticity of demand. For instance, tea and coffee are substitutes. The change in the price of tea affects the demand for coffee. Hence, the demand for coffee and tea is elastic.

Number of Uses

Elasticity of demand for any commodity depends on its number of uses. Demand is elastic; if a commodity has more uses and inelastic if it has only one use. As coal has multiple uses, if its price falls it will be demanded more for cooking, heating, industrial purposes etc. But if its price rises, minimum will be demanded for every purpose.

Postponement

Demand is more elastic for goods the use of which can be postponed. For example, if the price of silk rises, its consumption can be postponed. The demand for silk is, therefore, elastic. Demand is inelastic for those goods the use of which is urgent and, therefore, cannot be postponed. The use of medicines cannot be put off. Hence, the demand for medicines is inelastic.

Raw Materials and Finished Goods

The demand for raw materials is inelastic but the demand for finished goods is elastic. For instance, raw cotton has inelastic demand but cloth has elastic demand. In the same way, petrol has inelastic demand but car itself has only elastic demand.

Price Level

The demand is elastic for moderate prices but inelastic for lower and higher prices. The rich and the poor do not bother about the prices of the goods that they buy. For example, rich buy Benaras silk and diamonds etc. at any price. But the poor buy coarse rice, cloth etc. whatever their prices are.

Income Level

The demand is inelastic for higher and lower income groups and elastic for middle income groups. The rich people with their higher income do not bother about the price. They may continue to buy the same amount whatever the price. The poor people with lower incomes buy always only the minimum requirements and, therefore, they are induced neither to buy more at a lower price nor less at a higher price. The middle income group is sensitive to the change in price. Thus, they buy more at a lower price and less at higher price.

Habits

If consumers are habituated of some commodities, the demand for such commodities will be usually inelastic. It is because that the consumer will use them even their prices go up. For example, a smoker does not smoke less when the price of cigarette goes up.

Nature of Expenditure

The elasticity of demand for a commodity also depends as to how much part of the income is spent on that particular commodity. The demand for such commodities where a small part of income is spent is generally highly inelastic *i.e.* newspaper, boot-polish etc. On the other hand, the demand of such commodities where a significant part of income is spent, elasticity of demand is very elastic.

Distribution of Income

If the income is uniformly distributed in the society, a small change in price will affect the demand of the whole society and the demand will be elastic. In case of unequal distribution of income and wealth, a change in price will hardly influence the poor section of the society and the demand will be relatively inelastic.

Influence of Diminishing Marginal Utility

We know that utility falls when we consume more and more units but not in a uniform way. In case utility falls rapidly, it means that the consumer has no other near substitutes. As a result, demand is inelastic. Conversely, if the utility falls slowly, demand for such commodity would be elastic and raises much for a fall in price.

DETERMINANTS OF DEMAND ANALYSIS

Economic analysis has recognised the role of key variables in determining demand and consumption. In practice, the distinction between demand and consumption as an equilibrium quantity at a given price, is frequently ignored. The development of "gap" type models emphasise the common approach of projecting 'demand' as a fixed quantity independent of price.

Demand, as the relationship between price and quantity, is subject to change over time due to changes in the underlying factors held constant by the static notion of demand. Changes in demand "shifters" are often included in economic estimation of demand representing anticipated dynamics in these determinants.

Levels of Income

A key determinant of demand is the level of income evident in the appropriate country or region under analysis. As a generality, the higher the level of aggregate and/or personal income the higher the demand for a typical commodity, including forest products. More of a good or service will be chosen at a given price where income is higher. Thus determinants of demand normally utilise some form of income measure, including Gross Domestic Product.

Population

Population is of course a key determinant of demand. Although all forest products do not necessarily enter final consumer markets, the actual markets are largely presumed to be functionally related to population. Growing populations are positively correlated to timber demands in the aggregate, as well as specifically to individual forest products. Frequently, population and income estimators are combined, as in the case of the use of Gross Domestic Product per capita.

End Market Indicators

The use of end market indicators as determinants of demand is frequently incorporated into demand analysis. For example, much of the final use of forest products is linked to construction. Indicators and trends related to construction activities, or which are determinants of construction, provide indirect estimates of the influence of these activities as the source of derived demand for wood. Housing starts, public investments, interest rates, etc., can be highly correlated to timber demand.

Availability and Price of Substitute Goods

Consumption choices related to timber are also influenced by the alternative options facing users in the relevant marketplace. The availability of potential substitute products, and their prices, weigh heavily in determining the elasticity of demand, both in the short run sense and over time. Fuelwood, as a dominant use of timber in the Asia Pacific Region, reflects conditions of very limited options for energy sources at 'reasonable' prices. Rural low income or subsistence populations simply do not have 'options' regarding energy - they use wood or go without. Demand, at this basic level, in almost perfectly inelastic. The cost does not materially affect consumption quantity. Suitability of alternative goods and services is, in part, a question of knowledge as well as availability. Market information regarding alternative products, quality, convenience, and dependability all influence choices. Under conditions of increased scarcity and rising prices for tropical hardwood panels, for example, users have a positive incentive to search for and investigate the suitability of alternatives that were previously overlooked or ignored.

Tastes and Preferences

All markets are shaped by collective and individual tastes and preferences. These patterns are partly shaped by culture and partly implanted by information and knowledge of products and services. Different societies use forest products differently because of these differences in taste and preferences. For example, markets for wood products in Japan are commonly recognised as requiring very high product quality standards, the importance of visual attributes of wood, and other preferences not commonly found in many other markets.

THE MODEL OF SUPPLY AND DEMAND

To this point, we have developed two behavioural statements, or assertions, about how people will act. The first says that the amount buyers are willing and ready to buy depends on price and other factors that are assumed constant. The second says that the amount sellers are willing and ready to sell depends on price and other factors that are assumed constant.

In mathematical terms our model is Qd = f, Qs = f. This is not a complete model. Mathematically, the problem is that we have three variables and only two equations, and this system will not have a solution.

To complete the system, we add a simple equation containing the equilibrium condition: Qd = Qs. In words, equilibrium exists if the amount sellers are willing to sell is equal to the amount buyers are willing to buy.

It should be obvious that the price of $3.00 is the equilibrium price and the quantity of 70 is the equilibrium quantity. At any other price, sellers would want to sell a different amount than buyers want to buy.

Supply and Demand Together at Last

Price of Widgets Widgets Sellers Sell	Number of Widgets People Want to Buy	Number of Want to
$1.00	100	10
$2.00	90	40
$3.00	70	70
$4.00	40	140

The same information can be shown with a graph. On the graph, the equilibrium price and quantity are indicated by the intersection of the supply and demand curves.

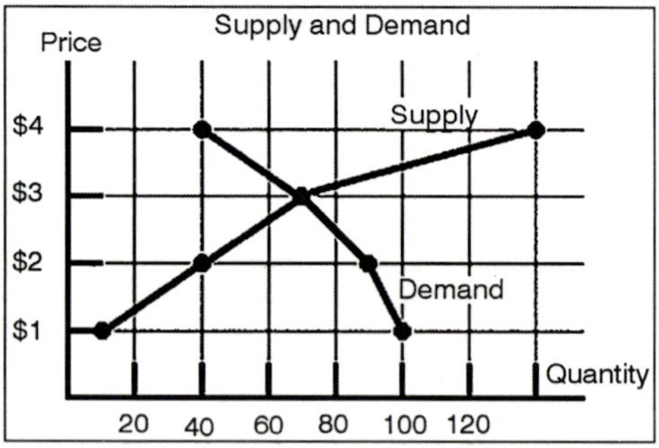

If one of the many factors that is being held constant changes, then equilibrium price and quantity will change. Further, if we know which factor changes, we can often predict the direction of changes, though rarely the exact magnitude. For example, the market for wheat fits the requirements of the supply and demand model quite well. Suppose there is a drought in the main wheat-producing areas of the United States.

How will we show this on a supply and demand graph? Should we move the demand curve, the supply curve, or both? What will happen to equilibrium price and quantity? A dangerous way to answer these questions is to first try to decide what will happen to price and quantity and then decide what will happen to the supply and demand curves. This is a route to disaster. Rather, one must first decide how the curves will shift, and then from the shifts in the curves decide how price and quantity would change. What should happen as the result of the drought? One begins by asking whether buyers would change the amount they purchased if price did not change and whether sellers would change the amount sold if price did not change. On reflection, one realises that this event will change seller behaviour at the given price, but is highly unlikely to change buyer behaviour.

Further, at any price, the drought will reduce the amount sellers will sell. Thus, the supply curve will shift to the left and the demand curve will not change. There will be a change in supply and a change in quantity demanded. The new equilibrium will have a higher price and a lower quantity.

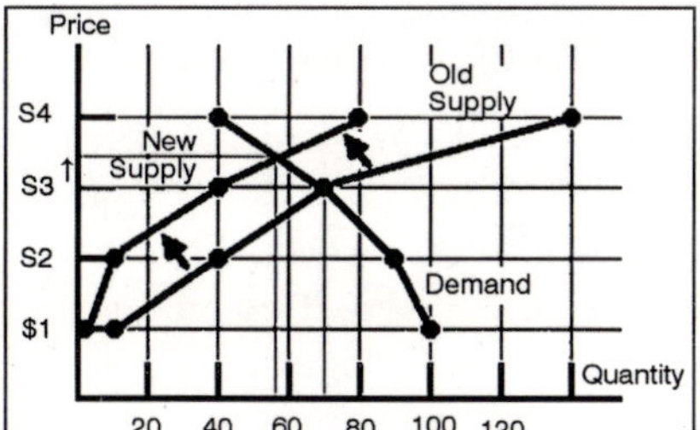

Shifting the Supply Curve Moves Us along the Demand Curve

What should one predict if a new diet calling for the consumption of two loaves of whole wheat bread sweeps through the U.S.? Again one must ask whether the behaviour of buyers or sellers will change if price does not change. Reflection should tell you that it will be the behaviour of buyers that will change.

Buyers would want more wheat at each possible price. The demand curve shifts to the right, which results in higher equilibrium price and quantity. Sellers would also change their behaviour, but only because price changed. Sellers would move along the supply curve.

Assumptions

The supply and demand model does not describe all markets—there is too much diversity in the ways buyers and sellers interact for one simple model to explain everything. When we use the supply and demand model to explain a market, we are implicitly making a number of assumptions about that market. Supply and demand analysis assumes competitive markets.

For a supply curve to exist, there must be a large number of sellers in the market; and for a demand curve to exist, there must be many buyers. In both cases there must be enough so that no one believes that what he does will influence price. In terms that were first introduced into economics in the 1950s and that have become quite popular, everyone must be a price taker and no one can be a price searcher. If there is only one seller, that seller can search along the demand curve to find the most profitable price.[1] A price taker cannot influence the price, but must take or leave it. The ordinary consumer knows the role of price taker well. When he goes to the store, he can buy one or twenty gallons of milk with no effect on price. The assumption that both buyers and sellers are price takers is a crucial assumption, and often it is not true with regard to sellers. If it is not true with regard to sellers, a supply curve will not exist because the amount a seller will want to sell will depend not on price but on marginal revenue.

The model of supply and demand also requires that buyers and sellers be clearly defined groups. Notice that in the list of factors that affected buyers and sellers, the only common factor was price. Few people who buy hamburger know or care about the price of cattle feed or the cattle breeding. Cattle raisers do not care what the income of the buyers is or what the prices of related goods are unless they affect the price of cattle. Thus, when one factor changes, it affects only one curve, not both. When buyers and sellers cannot be clearly distinguished, as on the New York Stock Exchange, where the people who are buyers one minute may be sellers the next, one cannot talk about distinct and separate supply and demand curves.

The model of supply and demand also assumes that both buyers and sellers have good information about the product's qualities and availability. If information is not good, the same product may sell for a variety of prices. Often, however, what seems to be the same product at different prices can be considered a variety of products. A pound of hamburger for which one has to wait 15 minutes in a check-out line can be considered a different product from identical meat that one can buy without waiting.

Finally, for some uses the supply and demand model needs well-defined private-property rights. Elsewhere, we discussed how private-property rights and markets provide one way of coordinating decisions. When property rights are not clearly defined, the seller may be able to ignore some of the costs of production, which will then be imposed on others. Alternatively, buyers may not get all the benefits from purchasing a product; others may get some of the benefits without payment. Even if the assumptions underlying supply and demand are not met exactly, and they rarely are, the model often provides a fairly good approximation of a situation, good enough so that predictions based on the model are in the right direction. This ability of the model to predict even when some assumptions are not quite satisfied is one reason economists like the model so much.

Buyer and Seller Equilibrium

We have developed the model of supply and demand as an equilibrium model. We have said nothing about how adjustments from disequilibrium to equilibrium take place. To develop this idea, it is useful to take still another view of supply and demand curves, to view demand as points of buyer equilibrium and supply as points of seller equilibrium.

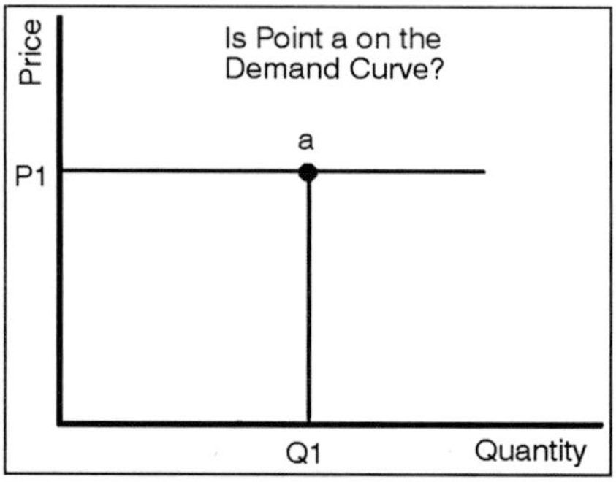

Suppose that price is at P1 in the graph. Will point a be a point on the demand curve? If people would like to buy more than Q1 at price P1, point a must lie to the left of the demand curve. In this case, some consumers are unhappy with the amount they have purchased and will try to purchase more. If there is no more to purchase, some will attempt to offer more money for the product or they will increase the time they devote to getting the product. In cease, if a position is not on the demand curve, people will change their behaviour, which indicates that only positions on the demand curve are positions of buyer equilibrium.Similar reasoning explains why the demand curve can be considered a boundary. Buyers are not in equilibrium at point a, but they can be held there and made to adjust in ways that do not change the money price. They cannot be held at point c unless there is some way to force people to buy a product when they do not want it.

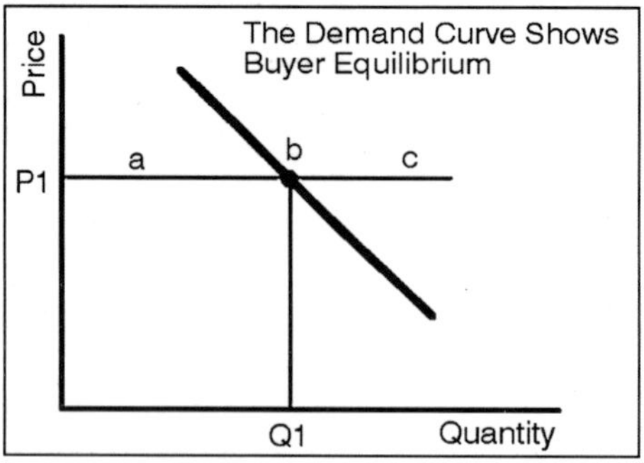

The important idea is that if point a lies to the left of the demand curve, people will be unhappy with their situation and will change their behaviour. If point a lies to the right of the demand curve, people will decide that they are buying too much of the product and will cut purchases.

Point b in the graph is a position of buyer equilibrium because, given price P1, people will be satisfied with Q1 and will do nothing to change their behaviour. Buyers would, of course, prefer a lower price than P1—they are always willing to move down the demand curve. However, this is not the issue here. Given P1, Q1 is the preferred quantity.

Just as the demand curve shows positions of buyer equilibrium, the supply curve shows positions of seller equilibrium. Suppliers find that they could increase profits by moving to the right to a larger quantity. If they could not increase profits by moving towards the right, they would stay at point a.

Because they do not, they are not in equilibrium and on the supply curve but to the left of it. If they find that they could increase profits by cutting production, they are to the right of the supply curve and out of equilibrium. There is a quantity at the price P1 that maximizes profits and towards which sellers will adjust. This point, shown as b in the picture, is on the supply curve.

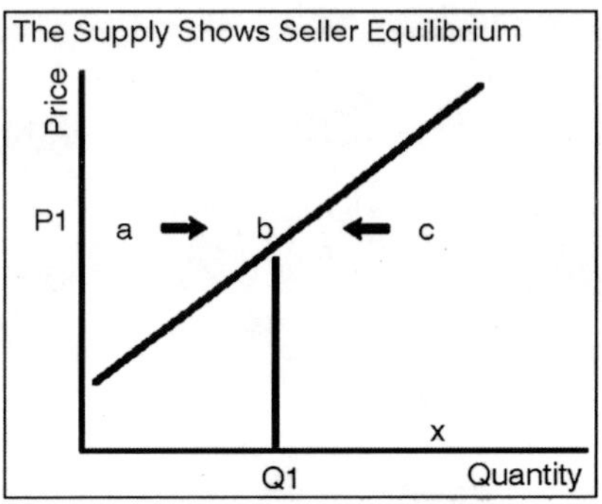

It is possible to force sellers to a position left of the supply curve. This is the case in which sellers would like to sell more at the given price, but for some reason can not. One reason might be that the buyers will not buy as much as the sellers would like to sell. It is virtually impossible—short of slavery—to force sellers to the right of the supply curve. If sellers are selling more than they want to at the given price, they can simply stop selling. Thus, the supply curve represents a boundary facing the buyers. If buyers could force sellers to the right of the supply curve, they would find it advantageous to force sellers to a position such as x in graph, which represents getting something for nothing. Sellers prefer higher prices to lower prices. Although all points on the supply curve represent points of equilibrium, not all are equally preferred by sellers. Sellers are always happy to move up along a supply curve.

Shortages and Surpluses

Viewing points on the demand curve as points of buyer equilibrium and points on the supply curve as points of seller equilibrium helps explain how an adjustment process takes place in the supply and demand model. If price is originally P1 in the graph, only Q1 will be sold even though buyers would like to buy Q2.

The difference Q2 - Q1 represents a shortage. The sellers are in equilibrium in this situation because they can sell everything they want to sell at this price, but buyers are not. Some buyers who cannot obtain the product are willing to offer more, and sellers are always willing to accept a higher price. Therefore, the actions of the buyers, as they compete with each other to obtain the amount that is available, drive the price upward in this model towards market equilibrium.

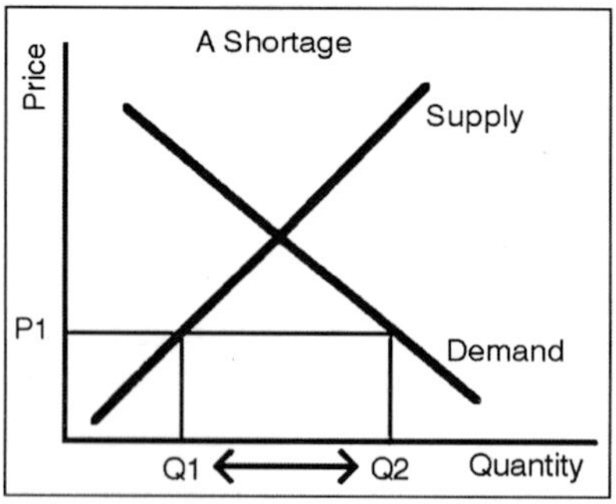

If price is originally at P1 in the picture, only Q1 will be sold because this is all that buyers will purchase, even though sellers are willing to sell more, Q2.

The difference Q2 - Q1 is called a surplus. In this situation the buyers are in equilibrium because they can buy all they want to buy at the going price. However, the sellers are not in equilibrium and will compete among themselves to get rid of the surplus.

Some sellers will be willing to offer their product at a lower price. Buyers are always willing to move down the demand curve, so there is a tendency to move downward towards market equilibrium in the picture.

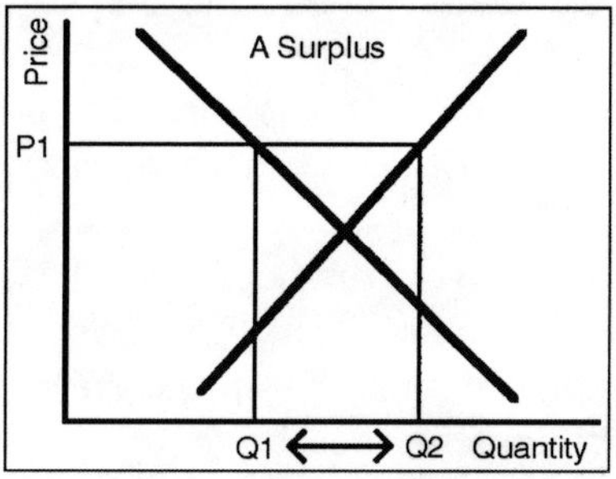

If left to itself, a supply-and-demand market tends to adjust to the point where the supply and demand curves cross. The price at this intersection is called the market-clearing price. There is, however, the possibility that the existence of lags in the adjustment process may make the adjustment more complex than the previous discussion indicates. Suppose that the price of cattle feed rises sharply. This event should affect the supply curve of cattle by shifting it to the left.

The profitability of cattle production is reduced at each possible price, and some producers will drop out of the industry while others will curtail production. Looking at the curves, we see that price should rise and quantity should drop. However, initially price might drop and quantity might rise, which is the exact opposite of the prediction from the supply and demand graph.

The higher costs of feed will encourage farmers to raise fewer cattle, but as part of that cutback, they will temporarily send more cattle to the slaughterhouses. The prediction that supply-demand analysis gives will ultimately be correct, but it will not be correct in the process of adjustment. More complicated adjustment patterns are possible. Suppose, for example, that higher beef prices shift the demand for pork to the right. Supply and demand analysis says that this should increase pork prices, and at the higher prices, farmers should produce more hogs.

However, hog production takes time, and will only happen if farmers expect the higher prices to continue for a long time. If pork producers do expect the higher prices to last, they may decrease the number of pigs sent to slaughter, further increasing price. A sow can either produce pork or baby pigs, but not both. If farmers expect high prices to last, they will keep their sows for piglet production. In six months to a year, the baby pigs will have grown enough to go to market. If enough farmers had expected the high prices to last, they may have produced so many pigs that pork prices will now plunge to a level that which is considered normal.

5

Macro-economic Policy

Macro-economic policy refers to how governments and other policy makers compensate for market failures in order to improve economic performance and well-being. Improvements in performance begin with the setting of policy objectives, which include the achievement of sustainable economic growth and development, stableprices and full employment. Some of the objectives set are potentially in conflict with each other, which means that, in attempting to achieve one objective, another one is 'sacrificed'. For example, in attempting to achieve full employment in the short-term price inflation may occur in the longer term.

Policy Targets

In order to achieve policy objectives, policy makers will set targets to aim for. Targets are often fixed, and widely known, such as the current UK inflation target of 2 per cent, but they may also be flexible and less widely known, such as exchange rate and employment targets.

Policy Instruments

Once policy objectives and targets are established, policy makers need to choose between alternative policy tools, or instruments. These instruments are the *levers of control* of the macro-economy and include monetaryinstruments such as interest rates, and fiscal instruments such as tax rates and government spending.

Policy Disagreements

Policy disagreements occur for a number of reasons. Macroeconomic policy is often shaped by long heldnormative beliefs about what is essential, and this influences the choice of model, objective, target, and instrument. For example, some economists put the eradication of poverty above the maximisation of corporate profits, and this will strongly influence their belief about how the tax system should be used. In addition, different economists may use different economic models and forecasting techniques, and this may lead them to disagree about the need for, size of, or timing of policy changes.

POST KEYNESIAN MACROECONOMICS OR "EVOLUTIONARY KEYNESIANISM"

The dominant paradigm in mainstream macroeconomics is a synthesis of New Keynesian and New Endogenous Growth economics, which has modified the New Classical and monetarist-based neo-liberal macroeconomics known as the "Washington Consensus."

The same model appears dominant in the UK, and perhaps in Euroland's European Central Bank and the EU countries as well. Evolutionary/Institutionalist and Post Keynesian economics (IPK) offers a very different approach to policy making which could be characterised as "evolutionary Keynesianism." This paper compares and contrasts the two approaches to macroeconomics.

Dominant (or hegemonic) in the mainstream means:

1. The view of most policy advisors (Federal Reserve, Council of Economic Advisors, IMF, World Bank, Bank of England, European Central Bank).
2. Appears in the most widely adopted textbooks and taught in the universities.
3. Taught and supported in the elite graduate schools.
4. Accepted by the majority of the profession.

The history of macroeconomics over last 50 years can be interpreted as a dialectical struggle between two opposing visions of the economy (as in Schumpeter's "pre-analytic visions" with which economists begin their work):

1. Stable, tending towards short run equilibrium at the natural rate of unemployment and potential output; tending towards a "steady state" long run rate of growth determined by the rate of technological change and growth in inputs. Business cycles are caused by external disturbances or supply shocks. The role of the state should be limited to providing the necessary institutional infrastructure, especially property rights, money and competitive markets. This approach originated in classical economics and reappeared in New Classical Economics (NCE); it also underlies Solovian growth theory.
2. Inherently unstable, with unemployment usually greater than optimal, and capacity utilisation lower than optimal. The actual growth rate is determined by short run cycles in production as well as the factors cited in classical, NCE and Solovian growth theory; the growth rate is usually lower than optimal. Demand is unstable and usually insufficient. Macro policy can improve performance greatly. Marx, Keynes and Institutionalist-Post Keynesian economists share this view of the economy.
3. New Keynesian economics (NKE) emerged in the 1980s; it occupies a 3rd, intermediate position.

Concept of New Keynesian Economics

NKE accepts most of the NCE microeconomic core: flexible wages, prices and interest rates lead the economy to the "natural rate" of unemployment (usually termed the NAIRU or "non-accelerating rate of inflation unemployment rate"), which can be described as a Walrasian and Hicksian general equilibrium. But the adjustment process may take a long time due to "coordination failures" caused by inflexible wages and prices. The level of GDP fluctuates around the "potential" GDP which is produced when unemployment is at the natural rate. Business cycles are temporary deviations from the long run trend growth rate, caused by supply or demand shocks. The trend growth rate and the natural rate of unemployment are both "strong attractors" dominated by the rate of technological change and the institutional and historical factors which influence labour markets.

Large demand gaps can and should be offset by demand management policies, using monetary policy. Fiscal policy is too clumsy a tool because the political and implementation time lags are too long, and the multiplier effects of fiscal policy are small. Therefore, fiscal policy is only useful for extreme crises and monetary policy should be used for normal stabilisation situations; although "fine tuning" is impossible, "rough tuning" is possible. This represents a modification of the extreme laissez-faire/non-intervention approach supported by NCE.

NKE recognises the social costs of recessions and the importance of demand factors; it defends countercyclical monetary policy and advocates demand management using "constrained rules" such as (John) Taylor's rule. In most versions, the procedure is to estimate (or forecast) potential GDP and any demand gap, then adjust (nominal and real) interest rates to move actual GDP to its potential; target interest rates rather than the money stock, since the velocity of money is unstable and the money supply is endogenous. Fiscal budgets should be balanced over the business cycle.

The principal contribution of NKE has been to provide microeconomic foundations that explain why wages and prices are sticky in modern economies (imperfect competition, management strategy, menu costs, information costs, contracts, efficiency wages are often cited) and to model the implications of this market behaviour for macroeconomics. NKE rationalises state intervention to improve short period macroeconomic performance. Reducing the natural rate of unemployment requires restructuring labour markets (increasing labour market "flexibility").

Accepts of New Endogenous Growth Theory

Most NKE economists also accept New Endogenous Growth theory (NEG), which first appeared in the late 1970s, early

1980s. NEG accepts the NCE/NKE vision of the natural rate of unemployment and the Solow growth model equilibrium steady state growth rate (the latter determined primarily by technological change) as the normal states which the economy tends towards. NEG also accepts the NCE/Solow argument that savings finances investment, so that an increase in the savings rate leads to more investment and at least temporarily a higher growth rate. But NEG rejects the NCE/Solow proposition that diminishing marginal returns to capital occurs as the capital/labour (K/L) ratio increases. Increasing returns are possible, so that the growth rate does not necessarily tend towards Solow's rate of technological change, the "steady state" growth rate for per capita real income.

Increasing or constant returns to capital are seen as possible due to phenomena such as:

1. Effects of R&D, spillover effects, externalities, learning by doing, and the interrelationships between investment in fixed and human capital.
2. Economies of scale and scope across industries, technologies and economies.

NEG implies that:

1. Higher saving and investment rates can lead to permanently higher growth rates.
2. Conditional convergence of growth rates for countries with similar savings rates may not occur.
3. Poor countries will not automatically catch up to rich countries, even if they save a lot.
4. There exists a wide range of intelligent policy choices to promote growth, including public investment in fixed capital, human capital, research and other forms of public infrastructure. Policy promoting high private investment (and saving) rates are growth promoting. Both NK and NEG support state intervention to promote the wealth of nations (full employment and higher growth rates); again, this is quite different from the "free market fundamentalism" and radical laissez-faire of New Classical Economics.

Institutionalist and Post Keynesian Economics

Institutionalist and PK economists tell similar macro stories. The macroeconomics of first and second generation evolutionary or Institutionalist economists such as Commons, Veblen, and Mitchell were similar to Keynes's in many respects. Many of the recent contributors to Institutionalist macroeconomics published in the JEI, such as John Cornwall, Paul Davidson, Hyman Minsky, Basil Moore, and Randy Wray also contributed to Post Keynesian economics.

Institutionalist and Post Keynesian economists argue that economic development is conditioned by and transforms economic institutions such as money, markets and property rights: transformational growth leads to structural and institutional change. Economies should be understood as complex systems with emerging properties that successively develop different laws of motion and pose different problems.

State intervention to create or change institutions is often necessary to promote the goals of full employment, economic growth, equity, social justice and harmony. Given the emphases on institutional change, full employment and demand management, "evolutionary Keynesianism or evolutionary macroeconomics" are appropriate terms for the IPK approach and models.

There are some similarities between IPK and NKE (the importance of aggregate demand is the chief common element) and IPK is consistent with much of NEG, there are however important distinctions between IPK and the orthodox consensus with respect to ultimate goals, assumptions, method, analysis and policy.

Differences Between IPK and NK/NEG

IPK – especially PK – emphasizes the importance of "fundamental" or "absolute uncertainty," Paul Davidson's "non-ergodicity," as a characteristic of the real world which has important implications for both theory and policy. NCE and NKE economics both assume "probabilistic risk," which is more tractable but unrealistic.

The economy is inherently unstable because of this profound uncertainty-which implies great risk for many crucial decisions-and the resultant instability of expectations regarding profits from investment and the future price of assets. Financial instability and economic instability are dialectically interactive and must be constrained with appropriate institutions. Instability is not as important a concern in NKE economics, and financial markets are discussed largely as an afterthought. Financial markets and money are central to IPK macro (following Keynes's attempt to develop a "monetary theory of production."

Economies are best understood as "complex systems" which are "self organising" and exhibit "emerging properties" as they develop - using the insights and language of complexity analysis. This proposition is a modern version of a core concept in original evolutionary economics: since institutions and economies evolve through historical time, theory must be institutionally specific if it is to be useful.

Since the behaviour of a complex system is not simply the outcome of the behaviour of its components, the complexity proposition also means that we can't adequately understand an economy (a complex system) by observing the behaviour of a component and extrapolating that behaviour to the system as a whole (as Keynes observed in his "paradox of thrift" argument). Rather than the "microeconomic foundations of macroeconomics" (as in NCE and NKE) we need to understand the "macroeconomic foundations of microeconomics."

External shocks and inflexible wages and prices explain recessions and deviations from trend for NKE; IPK argues that even if wages and prices were flexible, full employment is not guaranteed. There is no unique natural rate or NAIRU which the economy gravitates towards and which acts as a strong attractor. IPK argues that flexible wages and prices would enhance instability since falling wages and prices in a recession would probably reduce profits, investment and employment. Sticky wages, prices and interest rates are a good thing; institutions which stabilise these are useful and should be developed (national collective bargaining; incomes policy). IPK emphasizes insufficient aggregate demand as a cause for low growth as well as recessions (NKE only recessions). IPK advocates demand enhancing policy, including inequality reducing tax, transfer and expenditure systems, low interest rates, and employer of last resort programmes. Most IPK economists favour Lerner's "functional finance" theory of fiscal policy: the levels of taxation and government expenditure should be consistent with full employment and price stability.

Money is not neutral: changes in the price and availability of liquidity have powerful effects on the real economy; macroeconomics should begin with an analysis of the roles of liquidity in the economy, as in Keynes's "monetary theory of production." But IPK economists are skeptical regarding the power of monetary policy by itself and see fiscal policy as a more powerful tool for demand management. They are skeptical re "rules," in favour of "discretion" in policy.

IPK follows Keynes and Kalecki in arguing that savings do not finance or determine investment. Profit expectations, interest rates, the availability and the cost of finance are the important influences on investment - not the flow of savings - since the former variables are largely independent of saving. Savings are determined by the level of income, itself determined by aggregate demand. The NK/NEG argument that policy should encourage higher saving is generally incorrect: high saving can mean low aggregate demand, capacity utilisation and investment.

IPK puts a higher priority on full employment than on low inflation; full employment is understood as the rate of unemployment that obtains when everyone who desires employment and is willing to work at the going wage rate for workers with comparable skills is employed. Inflation is seen as the result of distributional struggles between capital and labour which can lead to "cost push" inflation. Again, institutions which socially control wages, prices and the distribution of income are necessary for full employment and price stability – some form of incomes policy. Many (but not all) IPK economists argue for government employer of last resort programmes as necessary for full employment.

IPK sees a strong reinforcing link between demand, cycles and growth: high demand leads to high employment and capacity utilisation which leads to high investment which leads to higher productivity in the next period (higher growth).

The distribution of income influences aggregate demand. More equality is demand, investment, profit and growth enhancing. IPK proposes "demand-led" growth economics; propositions 7, 8, 9 and 10 are not in NKE/NEG; IPK is richer, has more explanatory power and more usefulness in informing the design of macro policy. Most IPK economists favour some form of exchange rate regime which would reduce exchange rate instability; most NKE economists accept flexible ER systems.

IPK economists favour financial market regulation and see unregulated markets as instability enhancing; most NK economists see financial instability and crises as occasional episodes which can be handled on an *ad hoc* basis.

MACROECONOMICS: ECONOMIC PERFORMANCE AND GROWTH

Income is one of the most significant factors in measuring economic performance, and gross domestic product (GDP) is the most commonly used measure of a country's economic activity. In short, GDP reflects the value of all final goods and services legally produced in an economy in a given time period.

The distinction between final goods and intermediate goods is an important one. A tomato sold to a ketchup manufacturer would NOT be included in the GDP number, while a tomato sold in a store as produce would be included, as it represents the final use of that good. It is also worth noting that trade in illegal goods and services are also excluded from GDP figures.

There are two ways of approaching GDP – the expenditure approach and the resource cost-income approach. The expenditure approach totals the amount spent on goods and services during a year, while the resource cost-income approach adds up the payments made to suppliers of resources and other inputs that go into goods and services.

The expenditure approach is arguably more common, and it breaks GDP into four commonly watched components – personal consumption, gross profit domestic investment, government spending, and net exports to foreigners. Personal consumption has long been the largest component of GDP in the United States and is made of household spending on goods and services. Domestic investment refers to spending on fixed assets (capital expenditures) and additions made to inventories during the year.

By comparison, under the resource cost-income approach, compensation paid to employees is the largest component of GDP, with depreciation, indirect taxes, interest, corporate profits, and the income of the self-employed following. (To learn from the past, check out *A Review Of Past Recessions*.)

Going a step further, there are other types of analysis that can be applied to GDP. Real GDP is the broadest view of an economy's output, and the one most widely used by economists. Real GDP differs from nominal GDP in that it attempts to adjust for rising price levels to determine what amounts to changes in the volume of activity in an economy.

Economists observe not only the absolute level of GDP, but its growth over time. In fact, most discussions of GDP are undertaken in terms of growth. Going another step further, it is often useful to examine GDP in the context of its relationship to the number of participants in an economy.

GDP per capita often correlates to the standard of living and the extent of economic development in a country. The U.S., and China, for instance, have similar GDPs in absolute terms, but the per capita GDP in each country is much different and reflects the much higher standard of living in the United States.

There are some drawbacks and limitations to the use of GDP. GDP excludes any unpaid activity as well as illegal activity, so it cannot account for the value of all economic activity in a nation. GDP also fails to account for reductions in quality of life and losses to natural disasters or crime. The destruction wrought by an earthquake, for instance, would not be accounted for in GDP accounting, but the rebuilding efforts would be counted. Likewise, even per-capita GDP does not necessarily reflect the wealth of the typical citizen, as a majority of low-earning citizens could be offset by a small group of very high earners. (For more on GDP, read *High GDP Means Economic Prosperity, Or Does It?*)

There are other significant measures of income to consider. National income refers to the total income paid to owners of human capital (wages for labour) and physical capital, and includes both domestic and foreign income. National income can also be calculated as the sum of wages, interest, self-employment income, rent and business profits.

Personal income, in contrast, is the income received by individuals; it excludes corporate profits and social security taxes, but adds back transfer payments (like Social Security), interest and dividend. Disposable income is personal income that is actually available for spending or saving; it is personal income net of personal income taxes.

Models of Growth

While the large majority of economists basically agree with the use of metrics like GDP and GDP per capita as measures of growth, there is considerably less agreement in how to explain how economies grow over time.

Some models hold that growth is exogenous – long-term growth is determined by factors external to the economy. Other models post that growth is endogenous – long-term growth is determined by factors within the system. More specifically, there are models like the Harrod-Domar model that examine the consequences of fixed capital and labour ratios and the propensities to save. This model highlights the problems of rigidities in the capital/labour ratio and savings rate. By comparison, theSolow model holds that growth in GDP is explained by population increases, technical progress and increased investment. As with many economic models, these are not so much predictive as explanatory; seeking to identify the impact of certain variables and conditions. While economic growth is clearly an important objective for most governments, most economies do not operate at their full potential. Often there is a gap between the amount of GDP actually produced and the potential GDP that the economy could produce with full employment and full resource utilisation – this gap is called the output gap (or the GDP gap).

METHODOLOGIES FOR STUDYING MODERN ECONOMICS

Any economic theory usually consists of five aspects. Discussions on these five steps will naturally amplify into how to combine these five aspects organically. To do so, economists usually integrate various studying methods into their analysis. Two methods used in modern economics are providing various levels and aspects studying platforms and establishing reference/ benchmark systems.

Studying Platform

A studying platform in modern economics consists of some basic economic theories or principles. It provides a basis for extending the existing theories and analysing more deep economic issues.

Examples of studying platforms are:

- Consumer and producer theories provide a bedrock platform for studying individuals' independent decision choices.
- The general equilibrium theory is based on the theories of consumers and producers and is a higher level platform. It provides a basis for studying interactions of individuals within a market institution and how the market equilibrium is reached in each market.
- The mechanism design theory provides an even higher level of studying platform and can be used to study or design an economic institution. It can be used to compare

various economic institutions or mechanisms, as well as to identify which one may be an "optima".

Reference Systems/Benchmark

Modern economics provides various reference/benchmark systems for comparison and to see how far a real world is from an ideal status. A reference system is a standard economic model/theory that results in desired or ideal results, such as efficiency/the "first best".

The importance of a reference system does not rely on whether or not it describes the real world correctly or precisely, but instead gives a criterion for understanding the real world. It is a mirror that lets us see the distance between various theoretical models/realistic economic mechanisms and the one given by the reference system. For instance, the general equilibrium theory as suggested, study in the notes is such a reference system. With this reference system, we can study and compare equilibrium outcomes under various market structures with the ideal case of the perfectly competitive mechanism. The first-best results in a complete information economic environment in information economics. Other examples include the Coase Theorem in property rights theory and economic law, and the Modigliani-Miller Theorem in corporate finance theory.

Although those economic theories or economic models as reference systems may impose some unrealistic assumptions, they are still very useful, and can be used to make further analysis. They establish criterions to evaluate various theoretical models or economic mechanisms used in the real world. A reference system is not required, in most cases it is actually not needed, to predicate the real world well, but it is used to provide a benchmark to see how far a reality is from the ideal status given by a reference system.

The value of a reference system is not that it can directly explain the world, but that it provides a benchmark for developing new theories to explain the world. In fact, the establishment of a reference system is very important for any scientific subject, including modern economics. Anyone can talk about an economic issue but the main difference is that a person with systematic training in modern economics has a few reference systems in her mind while a person without training in modern economics does not so he cannot grasp essential parts of the issue and cannot provide deep analysis and insights.

Analytical Tools

Modern economics also provides various powerful analytical tools that are usually given by geometrical or mathematical models. Advantages of such tools can help us to analyse complicated economic behaviour and phenomena through a simple diagram or mathematical structure in a model.

Examples include:

- The demand-supply curve model,
- Samuelson's overlapping generation model,
- The principal-agent model, and
- The game theoretical model.

Roles, Generality, and Limitation of Economic Theory

Roles of Economic Theory

An economic theory has three possible roles:

1. It can be used to explain economic behaviour and economic phenomena in the real world.
2. It can make scientific predictions or deductions about possible outcomes and consequences of adopted economic mechanisms when economic environments and individuals' behaviour are appropriately described.
3. It can be used to refute faulty goals or projects before they are actually undertaken. If a conclusion is not possible in theory, then it is not possible in a real world setting, as long as the assumptions were approximated realistically.

Generality of Economic Theory

An economic theory is based on assumptions imposed on economic environments, individuals' behaviour, and economic institutions. The more general these assumptions are, the more powerful, useful, or meaningful the theory that comes from them is. The general equilibrium theory is considered such a theory.

Limitation of Economic Theory

When examining the generality of an economic theory, one should realise any theory or assumption has a boundary, limitation, and applicable range of economic theory. Thus, two common misunderstandings in economic theory should be avoided.

One misunderstanding is to over-evaluate the role of an economic theory. Every theory is based on some imposed assumptions. Therefore, it is important to keep in mind that every theory is not universal, cannot explain everything, but has its limitation and boundary of suitability.

When applying a theory to make an economic conclusion and discuss an economic problem, it is important to notice the boundary, limitation, and applicable range of the theory. It cannot be applied arbitrarily, or a wrong conclusion will be the result.

The other misunderstanding is to under-evaluate the role of an economic theory. Some people consider an economic theory useless because they think assumptions imposed in the theory are unrealistic. In fact, no theory, whether in economics, physics, or any other science, is perfectly correct. The validity of a theory depends on whether or not it succeeds in explaining and predicting the set of phenomena that it is intended to explain and predict. Theories, therefore, are continually tested against observations. As a result of this testing, they are often modified, refined, and even discarded.

The process of testing and refining theories is central to the development of modern economics as a science. One example is the assumption of perfect competition. In reality, no competition is perfect. Real world markets seldom achieve this ideal status. The question is then not whether any particular market is perfectly competitive, almost no one is.

The appropriate question is to what degree models of perfect competition can generate insights about real-world markets. We think this assumption is approximately correct in certain situations. Just like frictionless models in physics, such as in free falling body movement, ideal gas, and ideal fluids, frictionless models of perfect competition generate useful insights in the economic world.

It is often heard that someone is claiming they have toppled an existing theory or conclusion, or that it has been overthrown, when some condition or assumption behind it is criticized.

This is usually needless claim, because any formal rigorous theory can be criticized at anytime because no assumption can coincide fully with reality or cover everything. So, as long as there are no logic errors or inconsistency in a theory, we cannot say that the theory is wrong. We can only criticize it for being too limited or unrealistic.

What economists should do is to weaken or relax the assumptions, and obtain new theories based on old theories. We cannot say though that the new theory topples the old one, but instead that the new theory extends the old theory to cover more general situations and different economic environments.

Roles of Mathematics in Modern Economics

Mathematics has become an important tool in modern economics. Almost every field in modern economics uses mathematics and statistics.

The mathematical approach to economic analysis is used when economists make use of mathematical symbols in the statement of a problem and also draw upon known mathematical theorems to aid in reasoning.

It is not difficult to understand why the mathematical approach has become a dominant approach since finding the boundary of a theory, developing an analytical framework of a theory, establishing reference systems, and providing analytical tools all need mathematics. If we apply a theoretical result to real world without knowing the boundary of a theory, we may get a very bad consequence and hurt an economy seriously.

Some of the advantages of using mathematics are that:

- The "language" used and the descriptions of assumptions are clearer, more accurate, and more precise,
- The logical process of analysis is more rigorous and clearly sets the boundaries and limitations of a statement,
- It can give a new result that may not be easily obtained through observation alone, and
- It can reduce unnecessary debates and improve or extend existing results.

It should be remarked that, although mathematics is of critical importance in modern economics, economics is not mathematics. Economics uses mathematics as a tool in order to model and analyse various economic problems. Statistics and econometrics are used to test or measure the *accuracy* of our predication, and identify causalities among economic variables.

SEVERAL ALTERNATIVE THEORIES OR MODELS AVAILABLE EXPLAIN IN MACROECONOMICS

There are several alternative theories or models available to explain the way macro-economies function with different implications for government economic policy. There is far more disagreement in this area of macroeconomics than we ever saw in microeconomics – this is why different analysts in government and the media say completely contradictory things about what the government should do even if they agree about the current state of the economy. We will examine each of the major economic theories that has influenced economic thought and/or government policy in the US over the course of the last 100 years. In the late 1800s and early 1900s American economic theory in both microeconomics and macroeconomics was dominated by Classical theory. Classical economic theory largely came from the study of individual market behaviour in microeconomics and its macroeconomic theory was based on the contention that market based economies are just an amalgamation of individual markets and, therefore, the same behavioural patterns prevail. Classical economics viewed markets as incredibly powerful and efficient mechanisms that could not be improved upon by any intervention; as a consequence, they strongly urged laissez-faire policy by the government – that the government should leave the economy alone and let it work properly.

The Assumptions of the Classical Model

Classical economics can be traced to the pioneering work of Adam Smith (often referred to as the father of economics). The specific event launching the modern study of economics, as well as classical economics, was the publication by Adam Smith of An Enquiry into the Nature and Causes of the Wealth of Nations in 1776. In this book, Smith contended that the "wealth of a nation" was attributed to the production of goods and services (rather than stockpiles of gold in the royal vault, which was the prevailing view at the time). And this production was best achieved by unrestricted market exchanges with buyers and sellers motivated by the pursuit of self interests.

The work by Smith was refined and enhanced by scores of others over the ensuing 150 years, including Jean-Baptiste Say, John Stuart Mill, David Ricardo, Thomas Robert Malthus, and Alfred Marshall, to name just a few. Their work led to the creation of a sophisticated body of principles and analyses that offered insight into a wide range of economic phenomena—both microeconomic and macroeconomic. Many of these principles remain essential to the modern microeconomic theory. And while classical economics was largely discredited by John Maynard Keynes and advocates of Keynesian economics from the 1930s through the 1970s (due in large part to the Great Depression), it has reemerged (albeit with modifications) in recent decades.

Flexible Prices

The first assumption of classical economics is that prices are flexible. Price flexibility means that markets are able to adjust quickly and efficiently to equilibrium. While this assumption does not mean that every market in the economy is in equilibrium at all times, any imbalance (shortage or surplus) is short lived. Moreover, the adjust to equilibrium is accomplished automatically through the market forces of demand and supply without the need for government action.

The most important macroeconomic dimension of this assumption applies to resource markets, especially labour markets. The unemployment of labour, particularly involuntary unemployment, arises if a surplus exists in labour markets. With a surplus, the quantity of labour supplied exceeds the quantity of labour demanded—at the exist price of labour (wages). With flexible prices, any surplus is temporary. Wages fall to eliminate the surplus imbalance and restore equilibrium—and achieve full employment.

If, for example, aggregate demand in the economy takes a bit of a drop (perhaps due to fewer exports of goods to other countries), then production also declines (temporarily) and so too does the demand for labour, creating a surplus of labour and involuntarily unemployed workers. However, flexible prices mean that wages decline to eliminate the surplus.

Say's Law

The second assumption of classical economics is that the aggregate production of good and services in the economy generates enough income to exactly purchase all output. This notion commonly summarised by the phrase "supply creates its own demand" is attributed to the Jean-Baptiste Say, a French economist who helped to popularise the work of Adam Smith in the early 1800s. Say's law was a cornerstone of classical economics, and although it was subject to intense criticism by Keynesian economists, it remains relevant in modern times and is reflected in the circular flow model.

Say's law is occasionally misinterpreted as applying to a single good, that is, the production of a good is ensured to be purchased by waiting buyers. That law actually applies to aggregate, economy-wide supply and demand. A more accurate phrase is "aggregate supply creates its own aggregate demand." This interpretation means that the act of production adds to the overall pool of aggregate income, which is then used to buy a corresponding value of production—although most likely not the original production.

This law, first and foremost, directed attention to the production or supply-side of the economy. That is, focus on production and the rest of the economy will fall in line. Say's law further implied that extended periods of excess production and limited demand, the sort of thing that might cause an economic downturn, were unlikely. Economic downturns could occur, but not due to the lack of aggregate demand.

Saving-Investment Equality

The last assumption of classical economics is that saving by the household sector exactly matches investment expenditures on capital goods by the business sector. A potential problem with Say's law is that not all income generated by the production of goods is necessarily spent by the household sector on consumption demand—some income is saved. In other words, while the production of $100 million of output generates $100 million of income, the household sector might choose to spend only $90 million, directing the remaining $10 million to saving. If so, then supply does NOT create its own demand. Supply falls $10 million short of creating enough demand.

If this happens, then producers reduce production and lay off workers, which causes a drop in income and induces a decline in consumption, which then triggers further reductions in production, employment, income, and consumption in a contractionary downward spiral.

However, if this $10 million of saving is matched by an equal amount of investment, then no drop off in aggregate demand occurs. Such a match between saving and investment is assured in classical economics through flexible prices. However, in this case price flexibility applies to interest rates. Should saving not match investment, then interest rates adjust to restore balance. In particular, if saving exceeds investment, then interest rates fall, which stimulates investment and curtails saving until the two are once again equal.

Certain conditions or assumptions

An economic model is based on certain conditions or assumptions; it is important to examine these to understand why the theory makes the conclusions that it does. The assumptions of a model function as its foundation and flaws in the foundation undermine the structural integrity of the building. Flaws in a model's assumptions undermine the accuracy of the model itself.

The main assumptions of the Classical model are as follows:

- *Markets are highly competitive*: If markets are highly competitive, than no one can hold a market off its full employment equilibrium. Firms competing with each other will have to make the best product they can for the lowest acceptable price – any firm trying to take advantage of consumers by selling an inferior product for an inflated price will just lose its customers to other firms. Price will, therefore, always reflect the minimum efficient cost of making the good. As long as consumer benefit is high enough to justify paying for the good, they will keep buying it and we will keep making it. Consequently, if individual markets do this, all the markets together will - we will make the socially optimal level of production, *i.e.*, full employment.
- *Wages and prices are completely flexible*: Wages and prices will rapidly adjust to reflect supply and demand in the labour and goods markets. If producers are making more output than consumers want, price will simply fall until the quantity demanded and quantity supplied for goods are equal. If workers are unable to find enough jobs, wages will simply fall until the quantity demanded and quantity supplied for labour are equal. Wages and prices adjust to keep the full employment level of goods selling and the full employment level of labour working. Furthermore, this adjustment is so rapid that an

economy left alone will not experience any significant period of unemployment or falling production. This adjustment process is one of the powerful self-correcting mechanisms in the Classical model.

- *Savings will always equal investment*: The act of producing national output also generates national income and the national income is used to buy the national output. These two values must be equal since the value produced always belongs to someone (consider them GDP by the expenditures approach and GDP by the cost/income approach – with no measurement error the two would always be equal). So as long as the national income spent is equal to the national output available, there will not be unsold goods or unfulfilled demand. The Classical economists said that it always will, a belief presented as Say's Law – supply creates its own demand – the act of making national output will always generate the right amount of income to buy the output. We can, therefore, sustain the economy at full employment.

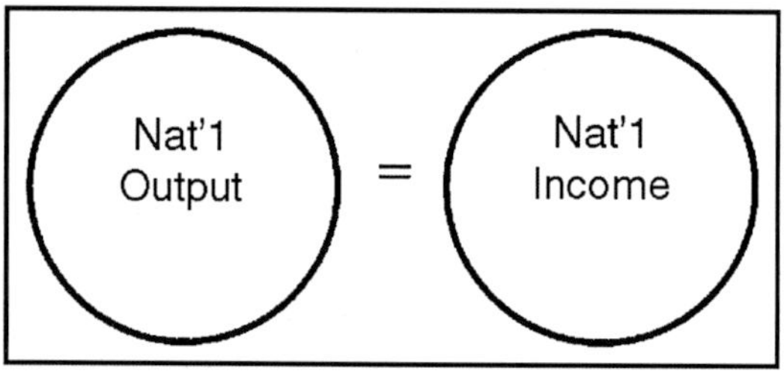

Some people pointed out a potential problem – consumers do not spend their entire income they save part of it – won't that cause the amount of national income spent to be too small to buy all the output we have made? No, the Classical economists said, because businesses don't intend to sell all their output to consumers anyway. To keep the analysis simple, imagine the economy only has consumers and businesses in it so there is only consumer spending or consumption(C) and business spending or investment (I).

When businesses invest, what they are actually doing is withholding goods and services from the household sector – they are keeping part of national output to themselves. When consumers save, they are withholding purchasing power from the business sector – they are keeping part of national income to themselves. As long as business investment is equal to consumer saving, we will still see the economy maintain equilibrium at full employment.

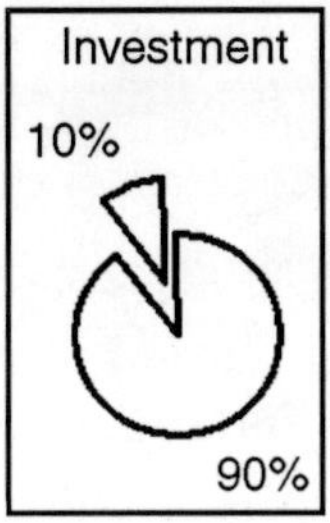

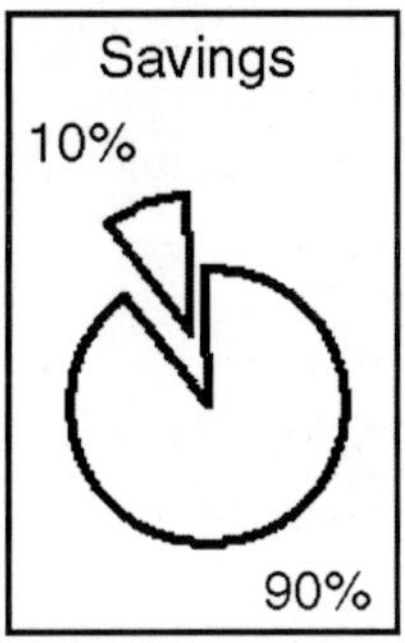

Suppose that business withhold 10 per cent of the value produced for their own uses, leaving 90 per cent available for consumers. If consumers withhold 10 per cent of value earned for savings, leaving 90 per cent available to buy goods and services, then we have a balance between quantity of national output demanded and quantity supplied. Consumers will buy all the output available to them and businesses take the remaining – both sides achieved the share of national output they were trying to acquire. There is no reason for production or employment to shift.

This sets up the situation where consumption and investment automatically correct for each other, maintaining the economy at the natural rate of output. Suppose that full employment equilibrium is at $100 billion dollars which initially is comprised of $10 billion in investment and $90 billion in consumption.

Now, what would happen if consumers for some reason reduced their spending to $80 billion dollars? When consumers spend less they must be saving more – we can examine this in a supply and demand analysis of the credit market.

In a simple economy the supply of loanable funds in the credit market is the net savings of households (amount households save minus what they borrow).

Higher levels of interest can encourage households to save more since they will earn more income on each dollar saved. The demand for loanable funds is the investment borrowing of businesses (since we have already netted out household borrowing). Higher levels of interest discourage investment since fewer projects will be profitable when the company must pay more for the loans. Consumer spending fell to $80 billion so savings must have risen to $20 billion. A rise in consumer saving shifts the supply curve to the right, depressing interest rates until firms are willing to borrow the same level of funds that households are providing. Investment borrowing will then rise to $20 billion as well. Remember, savings must equal investment.

Here we see the original level of consumption ($90B) and investment ($10B) where the economy was at full employment. After consumers drop their spending businesses MUST borrow an amount equal to savings which means that investment rises to make up for the missing consumption. The economy remains at full employment. Since all markets rapidly adjust to equilibrium, including the credit market, there is only the shortest period of time until investment has reestablished the natural rate of output. Consumption and investment corrected for each other.

Velocity of money is constant: As we saw in chapter seven, the velocity of money is the speed at which money circulates in the economy and is equal to the nominal GDP divided by money supply. This can be rearranged into the following:

Money Supply × V = Nominal GDP

Nominal GDP can be further broken down into its component parts – the price level and real GDP. Nominal GDP is the actual output made (real GDP) times the prices it sells at.

Money Supply × V = P x Y

If the velocity of money is a constant, then the only way nominal GDP can change is if the money supply changes first. This is known as the quantity theory of money – the quantity or supply of money determines nominal GDP. Attempts to use fiscal policy to change real GDP (Y) will fail since fiscal policy cannot change the value of the left-hand side of the equation. If the public sector takes a larger slice of an economic pie that is not changing in value, then the private sector must take a smaller piece. Fiscal policy is cancelled by opposite changes in private sector spending – perfect crowding out. Note that when the government increased its share of national output from $15 billion to $30, billion the private sector share fell equal to that increase.

Furthermore, monetary is also ineffective at adjusting real GDP; if the economy adjusts so rapidly that the real GDP is continually at the natural rate of output, then the only effect of a change in the money supply is a change in the price level. We can see this another way using the aggregate supply and demand model.

Implications of Assumptions

What is remarkable in cost-benefit studies of the optimal timing of mitigation is that the shape (or curvature) of the damage function matters even more than the ultimate level of damages – a fact long established by Peck and Teisberg (1995). With damage functions exhibiting smooth and regular damages (such as power functions with integer exponents or polynomial functions), GHG abatement is postponed. This is because, for several decades, the temporal rate of increase in marginal climate change damage remains low enough to conclude that investments to accelerate the rate of economic growth are more socially profitable that investing in abatement.

If all markets are competitive while wages and prices are flexible, then the economy will be rapidly pushed to full employment just as a single market is rapidly pushed to equilibrium. When there are unsold goods, output prices will fall; when there are unemployed workers, wages will fall until the natural rate of output is reached.

This means the aggregate supply curve in the economy is a vertical line (completely inelastic) set at the natural rate of output – any deviation in the economy is very temporary and is fixed quickly by our self-correcting mechanisms. Since aggregate supply is perfectly inelastic for all but the shortest time, what happens to aggregate demand is irrelevant for any real variables. No matter aggregate demand is in this graph, no matter how many times it moves, the economy makes the natural rate of output and employs the full employment level of workers (*i.e.*, unemployment will be at the natural rate of unemployment). All aggregate demand can do is establish the price level. So not only does a change in the money supply only affect the price level, but any variable that shifts aggregate demand will have no long run consequences for the economy.

Since the economy has powerful self-correcting mechanisms that work reliably and rapidly, the government has no need to intervene. In fact, government intervention will make things worse by preventing the adjustment process or slowing it down. For example, if government tried to raise income and reduce poverty by raising wages it would create unemployment and make it harder to achieve the full employment level of production.

Prices would rise reducing real wages until we eliminate the unemployment and boosted production back up to the natural level, at which time the government might raise wages again to make up for the inflation. If government tried to raise aggregate demand to increase production beyond full employment, it would only raise the price level. The more the government keeps trying to keep the temporary changes in production or income going the more the economy keeps having to work to achieve full employment. The appropriate course of action for the government would then be to do nothing – laissez-faire policy.

Historically, we know that the economy had a business cycle and sometimes spent extended periods off full employment. How is this explained in the Classical model? The Classical model explains how an economy *would* work if there were no intervention; since the economy does not work that way, intervention must have occurred. Unions which prevent the free functioning of labour markets and the adjustment of wages were a favourite factor that Classical economists used to explain persistent unemployment. Inflation was blamed on the excessive production of money shifting aggregate demand to the right and pushing the price level up.

Trade protection was viewed as a government interference that protected inefficient domestic producers at the expense of efficient foreign ones. Countries protect their firms that have difficulty competing with foreign competitors but the efficient firms lose the chance to export as other countries do the same. Since there was never any period without some level of outside intervention in the economy, the Classical economists were able to continue claiming that their model accurately predicted how the economy would work if this intervention did not exist.

It is no surprise that the Classical economists started losing influence during the Great Depression considering how severe that economic downturn was and how long it lasted. It is difficult to justify a model of rapidly adjusting self-correcting mechanisms when the economy struggles for over a decade. At first, Classical economists were able to explain the situation given the unusual nature of the stock market crash, bank failures and a growing trade war among developed countries. In 1930, soon after the October crash on Wall Street, the US government passed the Smoot-Hawley Tariff Act dramatically raising the tariffs on foreign goods. Other countries retaliated raising their tariffs on US goods and a major trade war resulted.

Since the US was a net exporter at this time, we actually lost more jobs than we protected and employment shrank.

However, we would expect the economy to bounce back if the Classical model were correct. Even if we have interfered with the reliable and rapid self-correcting mechanisms, they still should work to some degree once the economy has absorbed the initial problem. For years we do not see the kind of automatic stabilisation ever kicking in that would be predicted under the Classical model. This led to a growing number of economists and economic students questioning the accuracy and applicability of Classical theory.

The Keynesian reply

During the 1930s a British economist, John Maynard Keynes, answered the assumptions of the Classical model point by point. His position was that the Classical model was flawed from the beginning by inappropriate assumptions; if you can deny the assumptions, the model falls apart. Let's examine the Keynesian rejoinder to each of the Classical assumptions. Bear in mind that some of the arguments presented may not have been the work of John Maynard Keynes himself, but rather that of some of his students and later followers. The Keynesian model evolves over a number of years from the publication of Keynes original work.

- *Many markets are not very competitive*: Keynes argued that there are powerful oligopolies and monopolies in an industrial economy and that their domination was growing. Companies with this kind of market power can artificially restrict production in order to boost price. As a larger and larger part of the economy is found in these industries, a larger and larger part of the economy will not demonstrate a full employment level of production. Furthermore, some employers will not be in competitive labour markets and can hold wages artificially low withholding income from consumers so that they are unable to buy full employment output.
- *Wages and prices are not flexible – they are "sticky" – particularly downward*: Wages and prices do not rapidly

adjust to reflect supply and demand for a variety of reasons.

- *Contracts*: Companies often sign contracts with employees and suppliers – these contracts mean that the company cannot lower the prices it pays for inputs and is, therefore, unwilling to cut the price of their output. It is harder to lower wages and prices since the seller is more motivated to fight a downward move than an upward one.
- *Menu Costs*: It costs a company money to change its prices – someone has to change the information in the computer, someone has to change the prices on the shelf or the individual tags, any "hard copy" that contains prices has to be reprinted, etc. These are called menu costs (when a restaurant changes prices it must reprint the menu). These make a company reluctant to change prices unless they feel the change is not temporary. Obviously, companies are less reluctant to raise price than lower it.
- *Implicit Agreements*: Whether in the labour market or a goods market, both buyers and sellers have an interest in stability over volatility. Workers want a dependable level of income not one that fluctuates with every shift in supply and demand. Firms want a predictable level of cost not one that fluctuates with every shift in supply and demand. Firms don't want to constantly fluctuate price because consumers will learn to wait for the price drops. Consumers want predictable prices both so they can anticipate expenses and to save time – they don't want to constantly be looking at where prices are best this week. Consequently, we tend to accept that wages and prices stay up somewhat when business is weak, but don't rise that much when business is strong.

If wages and prices are somewhat "sticky" and rise more easily than they fall, then we will have at least a temporary problem in the economy, especially in the downward direction. Firms change production and employment rather than wages and prices. When there is a drop in aggregate demand, far from self-correcting, the trend intensifies – falling demand for goods and services leads to layoffs and production cuts. As workers lose jobs they cut their spending – even the workers who are still employed will spend less out of concern for future job cuts. As consumer spending drops, more companies layoff even more workers. The economy will come to an equilibrium far below full employment and remain there for an extended period of time. Since wages and prices are most sticky in the downward direction, the economy is more prone to entering recessions than booms.

There are no forces to make supply equal intended investment at full employment levels: While savings must equal investment, Keynes pointed out that there is no reason that savings will equal intended investment at levels necessary to support full employment. Intended investment refers to what businesses planned to invest in their business – desired changes in asset levels. Let's see why the difference is important. When we looked at Classical economics, we had a situation where full employment was $100 billion, made up of $90 in consumer spending (savings is $10 billion) and $10 billion in business investment. When consumer spending fell to $80 billion (saving rose to $20 billion), business investment rose to $20 billion and we remained at full employment. Now let's break investment down into intended and unintended levels and see the effect it has on economic events. Suppose businesses at full employment intend to invest $10 billion in the following way: $3 billion on replacing old equipment and facilities, $6 billion in expansion and $1 billion in new inventory (this desired inventory is part of their expansion plans). Now consumer spending falls, catching businesses by surprise. Keynes assumed that their investment plans would proceed because of contractual commitments (actually we know today intended investment is more volatile than this) so that businesses continue to allocate this $10 billion in the same way.

If consumers are spending $80 billion and businesses are spending $10 billion, then there are $10 billion worth of unsold goods. Since unsold goods are in inventory and the value of inventory is an asset to the company, these unsold goods constitute investment. Actual investment does equal $20 billion ($10 billion in intended investment plus the $10 billion in unintended investment as undesired inventory changes occur) but there is obviously a problem.

Companies will not continue to produce full employment output when they cannot sell it and we have already seen that they will not cut price in order to sell it – they will cut production instead. Even though actual investment was equal to savings, the economy will not remain at full employment. When savings are greater than intended investment, the remaining amount of national income spent is less than the remaining amount of national output available - unsold goods will pile up in inventory. This situation cannot continue.

Consumption and investment no longer correct for each other, even if intended investment doesn't fall. When C originally fell, businesses saw no reason to increase intended investment since they can't sell current output. We will see layoffs and drops in production, but as households lose income, they cut consumption more and the economy moves further away from full employment.

If anything, firms will cut intended investment as the economy worsens which would increase the drop off seen in the graph to the left. For full employment to exist saving and intended investment must be equal when GDP is at full employment levels and the Keynesians said there is no reason to expect that to happen.

In the Classical model interest rates brought savings and investment together, but the Keynesians believe that interest rates largely lose their power as the economy moves off full employment.

If the economy has dropped significantly below full employment so that companies cannot sell all their output and workers are losing jobs, low interest rates will be relatively powerless to encourage either group to increase their borrowing and spending. If the economy has sped up significantly above full employment so that companies are seeing continually rising revenue and profits while workers are able to get good jobs and overtime, high interest rates may not be sufficient to discourage either to slow their borrowing and spending.

The Velocity of Money Fluctuates

The Keynesians believe that the velocity of money moves with the economy and against the money supply all other things equal. When the economy is strong, people, businesses and financial institutions move money more rapidly and aggressively – they are less inclined to hold it for long periods of time. When the economy is weak, people, businesses and financial institutions move money more slowly and cautiously – they are more inclined to hold it for long periods of time.

$$\text{Money Supply} \times V = P \times Y$$

Since V fluctuates with Y, if the Fed pumps additional money into the financial system, it will have little affect on real GDP (Y) unless people, businesses and financial institutions have the confidence and opportunities to lend, borrow and spend. If the money supply rises, but banks are reluctant to lend it while people and businesses have little incentive to borrow and spend, then the velocity of money will just slow down, negating the effect of the policy.

Fiscal policy on the other hand will now work – since V fluctuates a change in fiscal policy can cause both sides of the equation to rise. Fiscal stimulus can raise real GDP (Y) on the right hand side of the equation because as the fiscal policy works the velocity of money on the left hand side is rising as well.

Crowding out will no longer be a problem since when government takes a larger piece of the economic pie, it causes total output to rise as well and there is more pie to go around. Private sector spending may drop by a very small amount (by $1 billion below) but for the most part, the additional government consumption of goods and services is filled by the expanded production.

The nature of the velocity of money is one of the main differences between Keynesian policy and those that hold opposing theories – it drives the controversies over the nature of monetary and fiscal policy. If velocity is constant or almost constant, then fiscal policy is very weak while monetary policy has a lot of power, at least over nominal measures. If velocity is variable, then fiscal policy is very powerful while monetary policy is fairly weak.

We are not able to answer this by examining the historical data – the velocity of money is not completely constant but its variability is limited. The analysis is further complicated by the fact that the stability of V varies depending on the time period looked at and the money aggregate used. V is less stable for M1 and more stable for M2.

How much variation is needed for the Keynesian view to still work? Keynesians argue that even small variations in V are sufficient since the money supply is so enormous (even a small change multiplied against a large base can have a significant effect). Some other economists say that variations in V are too small and that crowding out will be a significant problem.

Implications of Assumptions

If many markets are not competitive while wages and prices are not flexible for an extended time, then the economy can remain off the natural rate of output for prolonged periods of time. When there are unsold goods, production rather than output prices will fall, employment rather than wages will fall.

This gives us the aggregate supply curve we saw in chapter four – the shape is driven by the fact that some wages and prices are less sticky than others and, in general, are less sticky upward than downward. This aggregate supply curve is a more sophisticated and realistic version of the original Keynesian AS curve and contains three distinct areas. In the horizontal range we see that as the economy contracts, the price level drops very little and the main impact is on production (and, therefore, employment). Since wages and prices are more prone to downward stickyness, the economy has room to fall far below full employment. In the vertical range we see that as the economy booms, the price level starts changing much faster – this is because wages and prices are less sticky in the upward direction. There is still a little stickyness so that the economy can rise above full employment production.

Since the economy lacks rapid and reliable self-correcting mechanisms, it is possible for the economy to become "stuck" far off full employment (especially *below* full employment) for very long periods of time. It is clear why this model gained acceptability during the Great Depression since it reflected the economy of the time – one far below full employment for years. If the private sector does not have the ability to turn the economy around, then it is the necessary role of the government to do so.

Government not only has the ability to stabilise the economy, it has the responsibility to do so. It is unacceptable to allow people, households, businesses to suffer long period of falling income, sales, profits – a financial blow from which many will never recover – when the government can shift aggregate demand in order to restore the natural rate of output more quickly and reliably than the economy could on its own.

THE TERMINOLOGY OF BUSINESS CYCLES

Economy Resources Of Trough

When the economy is at a trough, there are lots of unemployed resources, the level of output is low in relation to the economy's capacity to produce. There is thus a substantial amount of unused productive capacity. Business profits are low; for some individual companies, they are negative. Confidence about the economy in the immediate future is lacking and, as a result, many firms are unwilling to risk making new investments.

Characteristics Of Recovery

The characteristics of a recovery, or expansion, are many: old equipment is replaced; employment, income, and consumer spending all begin to rise; and expectations become more favourable, as a result of increases in production, sales, and profits. Investments that once seemed risky may be undertaken as the climate of business starts to change from one of pessimism to one of optimism. Production can be increased with relative ease merely by reemploying the existing unused capacity and unemployed labour.

PEAK Cycle

A peak is the top of a cycle. At the peak, existing capacity is used to a high degree; labour shortages may develop, particularly in categories of key skills; and shortages of essential raw materials are likely. As shortages develop in more and more markets, a situation of general excess demand develops. Costs rise, but because prices rise also, business remains profitable.

Contraction And Recession

A recession, or contraction, is a downturn in economic activity. Common usage defines a recession as a fall in the *real* GDP for two successive quarters. Demand falls off, and, as a result, production and employment also fall.

As employment falls, so do households' incomes. Profits drop, and some firms encounter financial difficulties. Investments that looked profitable with the expectation of continually rising demand now appear unprofitable. It may not even be worth replacing capital goods as they wear out because unused capacity is increasing steadily. In historical discussions, a recession that is deep and long-lasting is often called a depression. The most famous depression in modern history was the one that took place during 1929-1933.

6

Consumption Management

SIGNIFICANCE

People bought that consumption is the value of goods and services. Individual buying acts are aggregated over time and space. Consumption is normally the largest GDP component. Many persons judge the economic performance of their country mainly in terms of consumption level and dynamics.

Composition

According to the durability of the purchased objects first, consumption may be divided. In this vein, a broad classification separates durable goods (as cars and television sets) from non-durable goods (as food) and from services (as restaurant expenditure). These three categories often show different paths of growth. Second, consumption is divided according to the needs it satisfies.

A commonly used classification identifies ten chapters of expenditure:

- Food
- Clothing and foot wear
- Housing
- Heating and energy
- Health
- Transport
- House furniture and appliances

- Communication
- Culture and schooling
- Entertainment

In respect to income people in different position have systematically different structures of consumption. The rich spend more for each chapter in absolute terms, but they spend a lower percentage in income for food and other basic needs. The percentage values of an aggregation over all the households in a country can thus be used for judging income distribution and the development level of the society.

Both higher levels of consumption and savings are have by rich. In differentiated product markets, the rich can usually buy better goods than the poor. This happens also because they tend to use different decision making rules. In other words, consumption depends on social groups and their behaviours, as well as their proneness to advertising.

Third, for exactness' sake, one should distinguish "*consumption*" as use of goods and services from "*consumption expenditure*" as buying acts. For durable goods this difference may be relevant, since they are used for long time periods. Fourth, only newly produced goods enter into the definition of consumption, whereas the purchase of, say, an old house is not considered consumption, since it was already counted in the GDP of the year in which it was built.

Determinants

The most relevant determinant of consumption is current income. Income comes from labour (employment and wages), capital (*e.g.* profits leading to dividends, rents, etc.), remittances from abroad. In consumption cumulated savings in the past can be squeezed in case of necessity and give rise to a jump, similarly with what happens with wealth increase, due for instance to stock exchange boom or house prices boom.

On future incomes, if expectations especially concerning short-term credible events, it may also play an important role. At household level, there are many possible rules set to control monthly, weekly or even daily consumption expenditure. They relate not only to income but also to the following factors among others:

- General lifestyles, in particular attitudes towards savings or consumption as *"values"* in itself;
- A standard level of consumption the family tries to maintain over time;

decisions regarding active saving strategies, like an investment scheme for pension aims;

- The relative success of past investment in shares or other financial instruments; in fact, a stock-exchange boom is likely to promote an euphoria tide with growing consumption;
- Opportunities of consumer credit, depending in turn by interest rates and marketing strategies by banks and special consumer credit institutions;
- Past decisions on durables. For instance, a family having bought a car will reduce expenditure on public transport in favour *e.g.* Of fuel;
- Status symbols diffusion - "*social musts*";
- New employment perspectives, also as far as the corresponding investments in human and physical capital are concerned;
- Innovative sale proposals in terms of both new products and new services, effectively advertised;
- Temporary money (cash) excess.

In accordance to the age of the decision-maker, individual and household consumption, there exist variation between each of them.

Thus, aggregate consumption may be influenced by demographic factors, such as an older and older population, even though one should not rely too much on these relationships since demographic variables are extremely slow in changes, whereas consumption clearly reacts to economic climate. Other things equal, a higher price level (inflation) reduces the real current income, thus real consumption.

Impact on other Variables

Actually a GDP component consumption has an immediate impact on it. An increase of consumption rises GDP by the same amount, other things equal. Moreover, since current income (GDP) is an important determinant of consumption, the increase of income will be followed by a further rise in consumption: a positive feedback loop has been triggered between consumption and income.

An autonomous increase of consumption, if at the same level of income, would reduce savings, but the positive loop just described (known as the "*Keynesian multiplier*") will imply an increase of income level with a positive impact on future savings.

If directed to goods and services produced abroad, an increase of consumption will immediately push up imports, while a similar indirect effect will result from consuming domestic products requiring foreign raw materials, energy, semi-manufactured goods.

Since usually the States separately tax consumption (say with a VAT tax), an increase of consumption will also boost this type of State revenue, as well as import duties revenue in the case of imported goods. The growth mechanism of consumption-income will also provide State revenue through income taxes. To the extent firms decide to invest forecasting future demand and comparing it with present production capacity, an increase of consumption may induce new investment. particularly:

Soaring consumption rises the production capacity utilization, with positive effects on profits:

- It improves expectations on future demand;
- It improves the financial conditions for funding investment both through profits and loans.

An increase of domestic consumption may decrease export, if an export are a second-best solution for domestic firm since at the same level of production firms would prefer to sell inside the country.

An increased demand may also induce firms to increase prices, the more so when they operate at full production capacity or they operate on monopolized markets. Thus increased price level and accelerated inflation can be an effect of booming consumption.

Long-Term Trends

In the last 50 years in Western countries, consumption has always grown except in few deep recessions. Its growth is smoother than investment's rise or net exports' growth. In particular, services have always systematically grown at a fairly steady pace, non-durables have often mirrored the business cycle and durables have often over-shot the fluctuations in GDP.

Business Cycle Behaviour

As the main component of GDP, it is pro-cyclical almost by definition: *any large fall in consumption would reduce GDP.* Consumption has a smoother dynamics than GDP. During a recovery, it sustains and stabilises the trend. Durable goods are particularly cyclical and they may peak shortly before GDP.

CHANGING PATTERN OF HOUSEHOLD CONSUMPTION EXPENDITURE

National Sample Survey (NSS) carried out the household consumption surveys is now in the public domain. In particular, the large consumer expenditure samples are available over 4 time points covering almost 2 decades, 1983 to 1999-00. Prior to the availability of this data, much of the research was confined to aggregate variables and it was difficult to study the consumption patterns (and hence, the well-being) of micro households. For social welfare policies, the study of household behaviour is essential and this data should therefore serve a useful purpose.

In this report a few calculation are undertake that are feasible with these data sets. The objective of this study is to identify some important estimates of how households behave. It is a purely statistical exercise, suggesting what can be done, rather than what should be done. In particular, it is not an econometric exercise. It is more of an exploratory trip, trying to identify issues that are worth examining in a more rigorous fashion.

Particularly, three types of exercises are done by us. First, we derive the empirical distributions of consumption over the four time points, 1983, 1987-88, 1993-94 and 1999-00. Second, we construct the proportions of expenditure on various commodity groups, by sector and state for the different years. And finally, we calculate the NSS estimates of total expenditure for each of the commodity groups and compare them to what is reported in the National Account Statistics (NAS).

Empirical Distributions

It was calculated by us the empirical distribution of per capita total consumption expenditure (PCTE) for each of the four years 1983, 1987-88, 1993-94 and 1999-2000. Since we are comparing across different years, we had to express the PCTE in real terms. So, the first correction made to the nominal PCTEs was that of transforming them to a common year. We chose 1983 as this base. A second correction was necessary because we had to order the PCTEs when we derived the distributions. For instance, a PCTE of ₹ 100 in the state of Bihar will buy more goods and services than a PCTE of ₹ 101 in Delhi in the same year, simply due to the fact that Delhi prices are higher than Bihar prices. Therefore, in Bihar the ₹ 100 PCTE will have to be greater in real terms than a ₹ 101 Delhi PCTE.

In Maharashtra it has been decided by us to take the 1983 price index as the base for all the years and all the states. The final correction was to take account of the price differences in urban and rural sectors, for the same state in the same year. This we did by keeping the calculations of the two sectors separate. Thus, for the rural sector empirical distributions, all rural PCTEs were expressed in 1983 rural Maharashtra prices. Similarly, all urban PCTEs were expressed in 1983 urban Maharashtra prices.

Consider two distributions *F,G* of PCTE. We say *F* first order stochastically dominates *G* if *F(x)* £ *G(x)* “*x* Î *X*

Where *x* is a given level of PCTE and *X* is the set of admissible PCTEs, which in this case, is the range of PCTEs for all the years. Let *F* be the distribution for a particular year and *G* be that of a previous year. Recall that *F(x)* ° Pr *ob*{*X* £ *x*}, *i.e.*, the proportion of people with a PCTE less than or equal to ₹ *x*. If *F* dominates *G* then, in the later year, for any given PCTE (*x*), the proportion of people consuming below that level is less than or equal to that of the previous year, regardless of the value of *x*. The distribution for a later year first order stochastically dominates (FSOD) the distribution of a previous year is the interesting thing to note. For instance, let us consider the cut-off ₹ 75.15, which in 1999-00 was the rural cut-off for the 15th percentile. In 1993-94, ₹.75.15 is slightly below the 24th percentile, in 1987-88 below the 26th percentile and, in 1983 below the 34th percentile. Thus, the proportion of people whose PCTE was no more than ₹ 75.15 was the highest in 1983, and then consistently fell as one moved to 1999-00.

Over the years, this has an obvious implication for the movement of poverty incidence. Recall that in India, poverty is officially calculated as the proportion of people below the poverty line (PL).

Since we are expressing all PCTEs in 1983 (sectoral) Maharashtra prices, the PL is the 1983 Maharashtra sectoral PL. This, therefore, remains unchanged for all the 4 distributions and is a specific value of *x*. The PL, on the other hand, is the minimum per capita expenditure considered necessary for a decent existence. Given the definition of stochastic dominance, a distribution that dominates another, will have a lower proportion of people below this given minimum and hence, a lower poverty.

Without interruption poverty has been continually declining over these four time points is the simple pictures that emerges from this exercise. There has been a considerable debate in India on what is the correct poverty line. In our scheme of things, if *x*ˆ is the PL, then different approaches will have different values for this cut-off. If the PL is different under different approaches, the incidence of poverty in any given year will be different. However, given that later year empirical distributions exhibit first order stochastic dominance over the previous years, the different PLs will not affect the conclusion regarding the movement of the head count ratio (HCR) over the four time points. A similar exercise can be carried out at the state level. That is to say, for each state, and sector, we can calculate the (comparable) empirical distributions over the different time points.

Weighting Diagrams

A concept about the weighting diagram or the proportion of per capita expenditure on major items of expenditure is constructed by us in this section by sector and state for each of the three years 1987-88, 1993-94 and 1999-00. We carry out this exercise for two types of representative individuals. The first type of individual is the one who has the average PCTE in the sector among all individuals in that sector of the state.

The second type of individual represents all those who are close to the poverty line in that sector of the state. Suppose the PL in a particular sector of a particular state is ₹ x. This divides up the population in to those above (PCTE ^{3} x) and those below (PCTE < x) the poverty line. We took the PCTEs of the top 10 per cent of the total population below the poverty line, and the bottom 10 per cent of the population above the poverty line.

In other words, we took all PCTEs above $x A$ and below xB, with $x A < x < xB$, such that 10 per cent of the total population had a PCTE in the interval (xA, x] and another 10 per cent in the interval (x, xB], where x is the poverty line. While the people in the upper interval were above the poverty line, they were close to the poor population in that sector of the state. People in the lower interval were definitely poor, but not the poorest. In other words, we constructed the expenditure patterns of the people around the poverty line, rather than those at the poverty line. This is because, there could be some movement over time of people around the poverty line — those below, but close to, the PL in a particular year may move, temporarily above it and vice versa for those above the PL but close to it.

In the literature, these people have been referred to as the transient poor. One correction to this procedure had to be made, especially for the later years, for states whose head count ratio was less than 10 per cent. Here we took the PCTEs of the bottom 20 per cent of the population. We broke up the PCTE into its major components, or commodity (and services) groups.

For the urban sector, these groups were Food, Intoxicants, Fuel, Clothing, Rent and Miscellaneous Services. For the rural sector, Rent was clubbed together with Miscellaneous Services, since that is the way the NSS gives the data. Our reason for considering these groups is that there is a time series of available price data (outside of the NSS) for these groups. Recall that the Planning Commission's Expert Group (1987) report on poverty calculations had suggested that price indices of item groups be weighted by their consumption weights of people around the poverty line to arrive at the overall poverty line. Clearly then, the weighting diagram should correspond to the type of price data that are available.

In addition to the practical need for calculating the right price index faced by particular groups of people, the weighting diagram also serves a theoretical purpose. Economic theory tells us that as individuals earn more, the proportion of expenditure on necessities decline and those on other items of consumption increase. In particular, food is a necessity, while many of the items in miscellaneous services are those that increase the quality of life (entertainment, health, etc.).

Thus, if incomes are increasing over time, the proportion spent on food should be falling and those on miscellaneous should be increasing. In both the rural and urban sectors, this is true for the average individual in each sector. In urban areas, the proportion spent on food fell from 63 per cent in 1987-88 to 54 per cent in 1999-00 but in rural areas the drop was from 69 to 62 per cent.

In a corresponding manner, the expenditure on miscellaneous rose from 18 to 25 per cent in the urban sector, while in the rural sector, it went up from 14 to 19 per cent. What is interesting is that this is true also for the average individual around the poverty line. Since the PL is the nominal 1983 value of a given bundle of commodities, it is surprising that the trend here is similar to the overall distribution. If the distribution around the poverty line (as defined by the mass of 20 per cent of the PCTE around the poverty line) is unchanged, and the price increases of each commodity group is similar, then the expenditure proportions should not show any perceptible change. However, there has been a perceptible decline in food expenditure and an improvement in the expenditure proportion on miscellaneous services both in the urban as well as rural poor. This implies that the real income position of people around the poverty line has also improved. Alternately put, if the theory is right, then the average PCTE in the interval $(xA, xB]$ has gone up. This could be either because the interval itself is moving rightwards (with, of course, $xA < x < xB$) or, the distribution within this range is changing. Another possibility is that the commodity bundle that defines basic subsistence is changing over time. After all, the PL has a subjective component associated with it and this cannot be held constant over the years.

If one does the following exercise then the relationship between the theory and what the data say can be seen in a more stark fashion. We consider the major states, whose codes are given. Consider the first 4 states that spend a larger proportion of their total PCTE on food, when compared to the all India rural weight on food. These 4 states also spend on miscellaneous services, a proportion less than the national average.

Moreover, the ratios of their poverty are higher than the national average. To test this theory more rigorously, we estimated the relationship between the proportion spent on food and that on miscellaneous services. The left-hand-side variable FR99ALL is the average food weight in the rural sector for the year 1999-00. FU99ALL is the average urban food weight. FR99 (FU99) is the average rural (urban) food weight in 1999-00 for the 20 per cent people around the poverty line. The right-hand-side variable is miscellaneous services, denoted the same way as the food weights, but with an M in place of the F. In keeping with the theory, one expects a negative relationship. A high R2 implies that the data fits the theory well.

However, for the year 1987-88 we observed that a part of the high R2 could be due to the fact that urban Delhi and Assam, the lowest and highest food weights, respectively, were outliers from the rest of the states, which were clustered closer together. In the rural sector, Delhi alone was the outlier. We repeated the regressions for 1987-88, with and without these outliers. Without the outliers, the negative relationship was weaker. What is of importance is the fact that the R2 is higher for the overall sector rather than for those around the poverty line, which is to be expected from theory.

A BEHAVIOURAL MODEL OF CYCLICAL DIETING

In the US, the problem of increasing obesity in the late years has sparked research interest across a variety of disciplines. Fully 35 per cent of Americans are overweight, and an additional 20 per cent are obese. Excess body weight has been characterized as the second-leading cause of preventable death and disease in the US; 300,000 Americans die annually from obesity-related diseases. It is now refer an excess weight and obesity as an "*epidemic*"by the Centers for Disease Control (CDC) now refer to.

On this topic one branch of the late economics attempts to empirically identify the causes of the observed rise in obesity over time. Another branch has developed behavioural models to explain food consumption choices leading to excess weight and dieting.

This paper contributes to this second branch by developing a behavioural model of food consumption choices that illuminates observed patterns of dieting. Both practical and analytical reasons are there for paying particular attention to dieting behaviour. Dieting efforts appear to be extensive and involve significant expenditures of effort and money on the practical side and on the analytical side, dieting behaviour presents a number of conceptual challenges for rational choice models of human behaviour.

Particularly, "*cyclical*" or "*yo-yo*" dieting —diet, lose weight, stop dieting, gain weight, diet again, etc seems to some observers to be arguably inconsistent with rational behaviour. Also, to the extent that the problems of obesity inspire public policy changes, a model that can capture the behavioural dynamics of overeating and weight gain will be very useful. In behavioural economics, our model departs slightly from the standard.

Much of the previous behavioural economics literature dealing with consumption of potentially harmful products is based on the traditional model of rational intertemporal choice over time. It views individuals as choosing a lifetime consumption path for a product at an initial decision date. If an individual's consumption decision about how much to smoke or eat today affects his future utility, it seems to follow that the "*rational*" way to make choices is to plan over one's lifetime.

In the view of us, this rational choice approach makes for a reasonable prescription about how to make individual choices. However, that approach does not mimic the way a typical individual actually makes consumption decisions. As a consequence this approach has found it difficult to convincingly explain certain features of individual choice including time inconsistency, and regret, among others. A viable alternative is to consider a "*boundedly rational*" choice model, following Suranovic, Goldfarb, and Leonards' model of cigarette consumption.

In that analysis, excessive computational costs constrain decisions to be made only for the current consumption period. It was consider by the individual for the future health of today's smoking but it was inconsiderate of how today's smoking will affect tomorrow's smoking decisions or how tomorrow's decisions will affect today's choice. Several reasons are there to take up this approach. First, individuals are not super-human calculators, projecting all the implications of each decision far into the future. The mental and computational cost of solving an intertemporal decision process is very large for the economic modeler, let alone the typical person.

Second, recent psychological research by Nobel Laureate Daniel Kahneman and others suggests that individuals are very poor at projecting the future utility from even seemingly simple choices.

This makes it extremely dubious that individuals would be capable of a much more complex decision process. At last, the boundedly rational decision process has been able to explain some choice phenomena (such as regret and cold-turkey quitting of smoking) that are more difficult and less intuitive to explain with the intertemporal approach.

We extend this boundedly rational choice process to an individual's food consumption and dieting decisions in today's paper. We develop a model that generates results consistent with important stylized facts about dieting behaviour, including the choice of multiple, or yo-yo diets.

An important outcome of the model is a behavioural rationale for the phenomenon that more frequent dieting attempts tend to result in higher overall weight gain.

Moreover, our modeling framework allows us to identify particular conceptual parameters that affect the patterns of weight change and dieting.

The basic structure of the model including the physiology of weight change is started describing by us. We then turn to specifying specific functional forms for a hypothetical individual who we call Sara.

We next solve for Sara's optimal consumption in an initial period. Based on her choice, we update her weight and other parameters in successive periods and thus simulate Sara's optimal consumption path over an extended period of time. Later, key parameters are adjusted by us to show their impact on Sara's food consumption and dieting behaviour.

THE CONCEPTUAL BEHAVIOURAL CHOICE MODEL

Food consumption has three types of effects on an individual's utility as assume by us:

- A standard benefit effect,
- A weight-utility effect, and
- A dieting cost effect.

Each period an individual maximizes utility, choosing both food and a composite good, considering these three effects of food on utility. A decision making period will initially be assumed to be one month, however parameters can be adjusted to consider alternative time frames. The standard benefit effect is the utility gained from the consumption of food, analogous to the utility that arises from consumption of any good. We assume utility rises at a decreasing rate and there is a satiation point (*i.e.*, too much food ingested in any one day makes the individual sick).

Food consumption are connects to weight by the weight-utility effect. We assume that an individual has an exogenous ideal weight. If food consumption maintains that ideal weight, then there is no weight-utility effect. However, if food consumption leads either to overweight or underweight, then there is a weight-associated disutility effect. We'll assume that the weight disutility effect rises with deviations from the ideal weight. Thus, an additional kilo of weight for a person 10 kilos overweight will have greater disutility than if the person were only 5 kilos overweight.

In GLS, these two effects combine to induce an individual to choose a food consumption level that results in a weight that is greater than ideal. The reason is that small increases in food consumption above one's weight maintenance level do not have a large weight disutility effect. Thus, the normal marginal benefit of greater food consumption will exceed the small weight disutility effect and lead to optimal over weighted ness.

Several motivations for diets are also explore by GLS. However, the basic intuition in all cases is that if weight rises, the disutility effect of food consumption on weight rises at an increasing rate. Eventually, the marginal benefit of food consumption will be less than the weight disutility effect and this inspires a reduction in food consumption, *i.e.*, a diet. However, the GLS analysis does not incorporate the costs or disutility associated with dieting.

Cost of dieting is the third effect of food consumption. In particular, we assume sudden reductions in food consumption have strong negative psychological, and perhaps physical, effects. Typically, individuals choose food consumption levels that are relatively constant over time. We'll refer to that constant level as a habitual level. If consumption is chosen below that habitual level, there is a disutility effect, which increases the greater the reduction. It will be think by us that there is no "*cost*" associated with excessive consumption.

The presence of dieting costs signifies that an additional cost, above the rising disutility of overweight, must be overcome before a diet occurs. Whether a diet occurs will depend on the size of the dieting costs. If they are large, a diet may never occur. But if a diet is chosen, it may not occur until the disutility of overweight is quite high. In order to track the effects of food consumption decisions on weight and the subsequent effects of weight on food consumption choices, we must discuss the physiology of weight change. Incorporating the physiology into our utility model of weight change, will enable us to simulate period-by-period consumption choices and track the effects of these choices on an individual's weight path over time.

The Physiology of Weight Change

The purpose of weight changes is analysing the balance of energy intake and energy expenditure by the nutrition literature models. Weight rises (falls) if energy intake exceeds (falls short of) energy expenditure. Physiologists typically disaggregate energy expenditure into three components: resting or basal metabolism, food digestion, and muscular physical activity. Basal metabolic function accounts for 60 to 75 per cent of energy expenditure in most individuals; another ten per cent is burned eating and absorbing food. Muscular activity accounts for the remaining 15 to 30 per cent in a moderately active individual. It is resulted in weight gain by continuing excess of energy intake over energy expenditure.

A continuing view in the physiology literature is that basal metabolic energy requirements or basal metabolic rate (BMR) can be viewed as a function of age, weight, height and sex. Long-standing empirical estimates widely used in the nutrition literature are provided by the venerable Harris-Benedict equations. Energy expenditure on physical activity (and the thermic effect of food) can then be incorporated by applying a multiplier to the basal metabolism estimates. These long-standing empirical estimates suggest what is well documented elsewhere in the physiology/nutrition literature: that basal metabolism slows with age. There is also evidence, if less extensive, that energy expenditure on physical activity declines later in life.

Various important implications about patterns of weight change are generate by these facts of physiology. First, even with constant calorie intake, age insidiously increases weight, and does so at a faster rate if exercise levels also fall as one ages. Second, these facts by themselves suggest a rationale for dieting. An aging person will, *ceteris paribus,* gain excess weight, and must diet (or exercise more) to avoid weight gain.

Simulation Model

A female call Sara are simulate by us in accordance to the decisions of hypothetical to analyses a series of choices over time. We posit plausible functional forms for each of the three utility effects and calculate Sara's optimal consumption choice for the initial period. Once the optimum is calculated, the functions are updated with a new age, weight level, and age-specific activity (exercise) level. Based on this updated data, Sara's optimal choice is recalculated for this second period. By repeating this process period by period we can describe Sara's time path of food consumption choices and resulting weight path over time.

We next specify specific functional forms for our three utility effects:

- The food benefit function
- The weight loss function
- The dieting cost function.

The Food Benefit Function

The utility or benefits it provides is the main effect of food consumption. Treating food as a normal good, the food benefit function has the following characteristics. Benefits rise at a decreasing rate as daily consumption increases up to a satiation level, given by the parameter M. Beyond that satiation level, benefits fall with increasing consumption. Sara's food consumption benefits are described by the benefit function B(C):

$$B(C)=dK[M^2-(C-M)^2]/M^2$$

where C represents the daily calorie consumption level, the parameter "d" represents the number of days over which the consumption decision is made, and "k" is a scale parameter that determines the peak daily utility attained at the satiation consumption level.

Weight Loss Function

Consumption greater than (less than) necessary to maintain one's weight will cause weight gain (loss). We imagine that an individual chooses an ideal weight, W_I, based on health considerations, social appearance norms, or a combination of the two. The choice of W_I is exogenous to the model.

Dieting Costs

Primarily, people regulate their food consumption by using their own body's hunger signals, eating when hungry and stop after full. The actual calorie intake level is rarely known with any accuracy.

Nonetheless, since people must eat to prevent hunger pangs, food consumption occurs at regular intervals, normally breakfast, lunch, dinner and perhaps snacks. The types of food consumed, the quantities consumed and the pattern of eating typically become extremely regular in form and content. In other words, most people's eating patterns are habitual.

On the other hand, dieting reduced calorie consumption and may force a change in types and quantities of food consumed, and perhaps even the pattern of consumption. These changes are very hard to undertake because they require breaking one's long established habits. These difficulties in adjusting one's food consumption habits constitute dieting, or adjustment, costs. They are not necessarily monetary expenditures, although they certainly can be if one joins a diet center or pays to participate in a weight-loss programme. These dieting costs reflect the disutility that arises from attempts to curtail food consumption and to change one's habits.

SIMULATIONS

Base Case

For example, Sara is a 20-year old woman, 170cm tall (5'6") and has an ideal weight of 60kg. Assume Sara is moderately active with an activity factor AF=1.55. If she initially weighs 60kg, we can multiply her initial BMR by her activity factor to obtain her Total Daily Energy Expenditure (TDEE), measured in calories. Thus, given her energy demands, Sara at age 20 requires 2237 daily calories to maintain her weight. We will assume Sara's satiation consumption level (M) is 2800 calories per day. The function UF(C) represents total utility from food consumption after accounting for the weight losses and the adjustment costs of dieting.

Note the food benefit function rises from zero to a peak at 2800 calories. The losses due to weight concerns increase as consumption rises or falls from the level needed to maintain weight, which for Sara is 2237 calories per day. Finally the dieting/adjustment costs of changing calorie intake becomes larger at a decreasing weight as calorie consumption falls below 2237, but do not arise if consumption is greater than 2237. This feature generates two key features of the food utility function, UF. First, since adjustment costs are assumed only to arise in the downward direction, there is a kink in UF at the weight maintaining calorie level. Second, because adjustment costs rise at a decreasing rate as calories fall below 2237, the total food utility function falls at an increasing, then decreasing rate for reductions in calories. These two features will motivate the incentive to diet.

Dynamics

We'll assume Sara makes a decision once per month about how much to optimally consume. At the end of each month, three things can change. First, if she does not consume precisely the number of calories needed to maintain weight, her weight will change. Second, Sara will become one month older. Both weight change and aging will affect her BMR. Finally, we'll assume her activity factor falls at a gradual linear rate. Our assumption will make Sara more sedentary by the time she is 50 years old. All three changes will affect the number of calories needed to maintain Sara's weight, and are updated monthly in Sara's decision process. We also assume that Sara's habits persist for 6 months. This means that she would need to reduce calorie intake for 6 months in a row to reduce her habitual consumption level to that new lower level.

We'll assume that Sara has a constant annual income of $25,000, approximately equal to average per capita disposable income in the US. The price of food is set at.003 dollars per calorie. At these values, Sara's daily expenditures on food will be between 5 and 10% of her disposable income, which approximates average US consumption patterns. Finally, by optimizing each month and updating based on her choice, we can simulate Sara's time path of food consumption and her weight pattern over time.

Notice that Sara chooses to maintain consumption at her habitual level, 2237 calories per day, until approximately the age of 30. At that point she decides optimally to reduce calorie intake to about 1300 calories for one month. In other words, she chooses to diet. Just prior to her decision to diet, Sara's benefit, weight, and adjustment cost functions. The key difference between the functions for Sara at age 30 compared to age 20 is that the utility cost of higher weight has grown. This is reflected in the downward shift in the loss function L(C), which in turn has rotated the total utility schedule downward. To see the comparison, Also drawn are two lines, labeled Pr20 and Pr30, with slopes equal to the food price. The tangency between the Pr lines and the food utility functions satisfy the first-order conditions given in equation.

In the top curve at age 20, Sara would clearly choose her habitual level of consumption on the kinked part of the food utility function at 2237 calories per day. However, by age 30 the food utility curve has shifted and rotated downward until Sara's optimal choice jumps from the habitual level to a level of about 1300 calories per day. This is shown in the lower set of curves where it appears Sara would be indifferent between consuming 2237 or 1300.

Dieting arises in this model because habitual consumption leads to weight gain and as weight rises there is increasing disutility in consumption from each unit of weight. When the disutility of rising weight becomes larger than the cost of dieting, Sara chooses to cut consumption significantly. That is, she begins a diet. Since Sara's diet is maintained for a 30 day period, Sara's weight will fall. With a reduced weight, the marginal losses due to weight in her utility function will also fall and the total utility function will rotate upwards. For this reason, in subsequent periods she will revert back to nearly her original habitual level.

Immediately after the diet, Sara's new calorie intake will remain below the level needed to maintain her new weight. Thus she will continue to lose weight after she stops dieting, albeit at a much slower rate. However, eventually a rising age, a falling activity level and the difficulty of changing one's habitual consumption level, will again, within several years, result in a rising weight trajectory. Sara's weight trajectory over a 30 year period to age 50.

Notice that Sara will again choose to diet two more times before age 50. This shows the model is capable of explaining cyclical dieting.

Sara's modest success in her first diet does not eliminate the insidious pattern of weight gain since she has not sufficiently reduced her consumption to keep up with her falling caloric needs. Note also that the second diet occurs at a higher weight level than it did previously.

Here's why. When weight rises back up to the level attained at age 30, the marginal effect of weight on utility will be the same as before. However, because the previous diet has reduced the habitual consumption level, the marginal benefits of consumption will be higher.

In other words, the allure of food is greater the less one consumes each day. This implies that weight will need to rise even higher before the losses from weight gain exceed the marginal benefits from consumption. This effect implies that despite several attempts at dieting, Sara's long-term weight trend is rising over her lifetime.

CONSUMER CHOICE IN THE NEOCLASSICAL MODEL FOR MICRO ECONOMICS

In economics, the standard textbook model of consumer is an outstanding example of the neoclassical paradigm: a hyper-rational agent maximises something by choosing an *"optimal"* bundle of things. Here, the hyper-rational consumer maximises utility (i. e. an overall generic measure of well-being) by exhausting a given budget.

He has a pre-defined income to spend on - for simplicity's sake - two goods, called X and Y, respectively. He could spend his entire income buying only X, thus purchasing a quantity of X equal to income divided by the price of X. Let's take a numerical example that you find here in the animated graph and that you can replicate with the software: when his income is 50 and the Y price is 10, the consumer can purchase 5 units of Y (higher red point on Y axis).

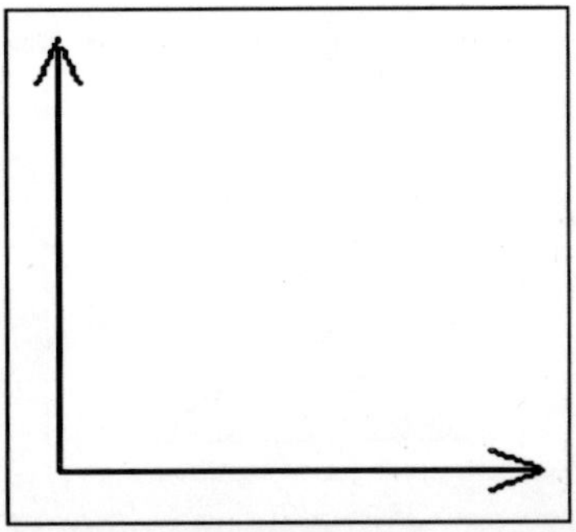

If the graph is not animated, just reload this page.

Or he could spend his entire income buying only X - the other good - thus purchasing a quantity of X equal to his income divided by the price of X. If X price is 6, the consumer can purchase at most 8.33 units of X (lower red point).

Or he can afford (at most) to buy any combination of quantities of X and Y that costs exactly as the income. These combinations give rise to the budget line you see between the two red points. How to choose? Well, by having a consistent set of judgements about how much utility the consumer will enjoy by consuming each possible bundle of goods.

The typical well-behaved structure of utility of bundles is offered by indifference curves, *i.e.* all bundles giving the same level of utility to the consumer. Here below you can see two indifference curves: the higher indifference curve is characterised by a higher level of utility.

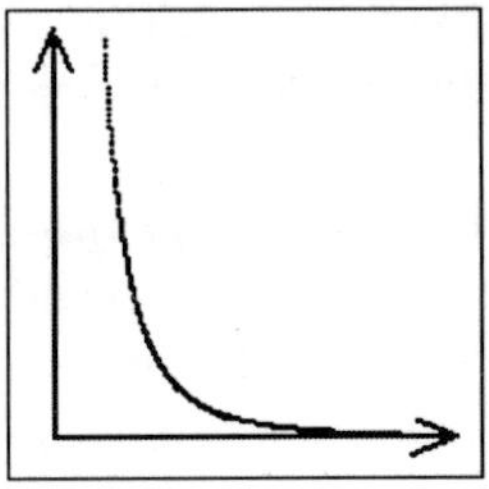

Simultaneously, now we should consider both the budget constraint (the budget line) and the utility structure (the indifference curves). The optimal bundle of goods belongs to the highest possible indifference curve crossing the budget line.

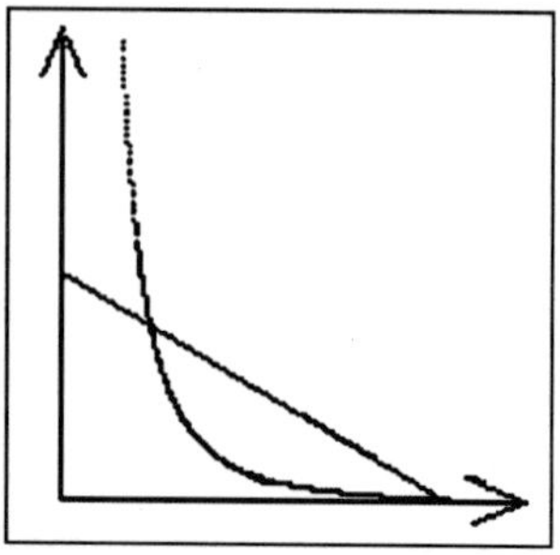

The red point is the rational consumer's choice (the chosen bundle), since it maximises utility, given the budget constraint.

Everything sounds very logical and convincing - within the unrealistic setting offered by this kind of mathematics. The deductive style of this microeconomics in consumer theory takes very little care of empirical analysis and of any reasonably open experimentation.

How to use this Software

Based on Hicksian approach to indifference curves and budget lines, this is free software to draw economic graphs, diagrams, demand curves, singling out individual choices of (hyper) rational consumers choosing the optimal bundle. The programme starts with a consumer having 50 as income and facing the price of some X good of 6 and the price of Y of 10.

The "*Draw*" button produce the graphical representation of the budget line, *i.e.* the quantities of X and Y that the consumer can afford exhausting his income. Push it a first time: you are drawing the budget line and computing the value of its slope, equal - in absolute value - to the relative price of X to Y. Increase income and re-draw the graph. The quantities on the budget line are systematically higher. No surprise. Make more experiments varying income and prices. What happens when you increase the price of X? As we said, the neoclassical approach uses "*indifference curves*" to represent the preferences of the consumer. By choosing an indifference curve type (instead of "*none*" - the default), you'll see - always with the button "Draw" - which combination of X and Y the consumer will optimally choose. For instance, by choosing the well-behaved Cobb-Douglas type you obtain (in the default position of income = 50, px = 6, py = 10) that the consumer buys 5.83 units of X and 1.5 units of Y. In this way he reaches a utility level (a general happiness) of 3.88.

As it can see the effect of changes in income and prices on demanded quantities (so-called "*income elasticity*" and "*price elasticity*") and on utility by changing the input data. In particular, an increase of income will normally boost both quantities of X and Y [1] - as well as the utility enjoyed.

However, the effect of price on demanded quantities shows that the increase of the price of X is a damage: utility falls and the quantity of X decreases as well. Try now some systematic experiment. Keeping income at the same level, gradually increase the price of X, as it would happen maybe due to rising business costs. How does the quantity bought of X change? By collecting your observations, you'll get the demand function, linking the quantity purchased of a good with its price.

Symmetrically, by keeping prices at the same level, changes in income give rise to the Engel curve, as can be seen from the graph in the screen activated by the line "*Engel's curve*" in the "*Issues*" Menu. The (indirect) link from income to utility - mediated by the optimally chosen bundle of goods - can be represented by the so-called "*indirect utility function*". The indirect utility function is the maximum utility attained with given prices and income. It should first experiment in the basic screen by annotating the utility levels obtained at different levels of income, then draw more systematic curves in the new screen opened by the "*Effects of income and prices on utility*" line of the "*Issues*" Menu.

Now reflect: if an increase of income fosters utility whereas an increase of price depresses it - and everything is very precise - there should be the possibility of keeping the consumer exactly at the same level of utility by giving some additional amount of income to compensate for the price increase. This is exactly the idea of the so-called "*Hicksian compensation*": the consumer is given sufficient income to reach his original utility level, the price increase notwithstanding.

7

Price Determination

The interaction of the broad forces of supply and demand which determine the market price level is known as price determination. For fed cattle, supply determinants or factors affecting the quantity of beef produced include input prices (feeder cattle and grain), technology (growth promotants, etc.), and price of outputs produced from those inputs (fed cattle). Broad demand forces or factors affecting the amount of beef consumed include the price of products produced from fed cattle (beef), price of competing products (pork and poultry), consumer income, and consumer tastes and preferences.

Price discrimination, or price differentiation, exists when sales of identical goods or services are transacted at different prices from the same provider. In general, the practice of charging different customers different prices is called price discrimination.

In a theoretical market with perfect information, perfect substitutes, and no transaction costs or prohibition on secondary exchange to prevent arbitrage, price discrimination can only be a feature of monopolistic and oligopolistic markets, where market power can be exercised. Otherwise, the moment the seller tries to sell the same good at different prices, the buyer at the lower price can arbitrage by selling to the consumer buying at the higher price but with a tiny discount. However, product heterogeneity, market frictions or high fixed costs can allow for some degree of differential pricing to different consumers, even in fully competitive retail or industrial markets. Price discrimination also occurs when the same price is charged to customers which have different supply costs.

The effects of price discrimination on social efficiency are unclear; typically such behaviour leads to lower prices for some consumers and higher prices for others. Output can be expanded when price discrimination is very efficient, but output can also decline when discrimination is more effective at extracting surplus from high-valued users than expanding sales to low valued users. Even if output remains constant, price discrimination can reduce efficiency by misallocating output among consumers.

Price discrimination requires market segmentation and some means to discourage discount customers from becoming resellers and, by extension, competitors. This usually entails using one or more means of preventing any resale, keeping the different price groups separate, making price comparisons difficult, or restricting pricing information. The boundary set up by the marketer to keep segments separate are referred to as a rate fence.

Price discrimination is thus very common in services, where resale is not possible; an example is student discounts at museums. Price discrimination in intellectual property is also enforced by law and by technology. In the market for DVDs, DVD players are designed - by law - with chips to prevent use of an inexpensive copy of the DVD from being used in a higher price market. The Digital Millenium Copyright Act has provisions to outlaw circumventing of such devices to protect the enhanced monopoly profits that copyright holders can obtain from price discrimination against higher price market segments.

Price discrimination can also be seen where the requirement that goods be identical is relaxed. For example, so-called"premium products" have a price differential that is not explained by the cost of production. Some economists have argued that this is a form of price discrimination exercised by providing a means for consumers to reveal their willingness to pay.

TYPES OF PRICE DISCRIMINATION

First Degree Price Discrimination

In first degree price discrimination, price varies by customer's willingness or ability to pay. This arises from the fact that the value of goods is subjective. A customer with low price elasticity is less deterred by a higher price than a customer with high price elasticity of demand. As long as the price elasticity for a customer is less than one, it is very advantageous to increase the price: the seller gets more money for fewer goods. With an increase of the price elasticity tends to rise above one. One can show that in the optimum the price, as it varies by customer, is inversely proportional to one minus the reciprocal of the price elasticity of that customer at that price.

This assumes that the consumer passively reacts to the price set by the seller, and that the seller knows the demand curve of the customer. In practice however there is a bargaining situation, which is more complex: the customer may try to influence the price, such as by pretending to like the product less than he or she really does or by threatening not to buy it.

An alternative way to understand First Degree Price Discrimination is as follows: This type of price discrimination is primarily theoretical because it requires the seller of a good or service to know the absolute maximum price that every consumer is willing to pay. It is true that consumers have different price elasticities, but the seller is not concerned with such. The seller is concerned with the maximum willingness to pay of each customer.

By knowing the reservation price, the seller is able to absorb the entire market surplus, thus taking all of the consumer's surplus from the consumer and transforming it into revenues. From a social welfare perspective though, first degree price discrimination is not necessarily undesirable. That is, the market is still entirely efficient and there is no deadweight loss to society.

In a market with first degree price discrimination, the seller(s) simply captures all surplus. Efficiency is unchanged but the wealth is transferred. This type of market does not exist much in reality, hence it is primarily theoretical. Examples of where this might be observed are in markets where consumers bid for tenders, though still, in this case, the practice of collusive tendering undermines efficiency.

Second Degree Price Discrimination

In second degree price discrimination, price varies according to quantity sold. Larger quantities are available at a lower unit price. This is particularly widespread in sales to industrial customers, where bulk buyers enjoy higher discounts.

Additionally to second degree price discrimination, sellers are not able to differentiate between different types of consumers. Thus, the suppliers will provide incentives for the consumers to differentiate themselves according to preference. Quantity"discounts", or non-linear pricing, is a means by which suppliers use consumer preference to distinguish classes of consumers. This allows the supplier to set different prices to the different groups and capture a larger portion of the total market surplus.

In reality, different pricing may apply to differences in product quality as well as quantity. For example, airlines often offer multiple classes of seats on flights, such as first class and economy class. This is a way to differentiate consumers based on preference, and therefore allows the airline to capture more producer's surplus.

Third Degree Price Discrimination

In third degree price discrimination, price varies by attributes such as location or by customer segment, or in the most extreme case, by the individual customer's identity; where the attribute in question is used as a proxy for ability/willingness to pay.

Additionally to third degree price discrimination, the supplier(s) of a market where this type of discrimination is exhibited are capable of differentiating between consumer classes.

Examples of this differentiation are student or senior discounts. For example, a student or a senior consumer will have a different willingness to pay than an average consumer, where the reservation price is presumably lower because of budget constraints.

Thus, the supplier sets a lower price for that consumer because the student or senior has a more elastic price elasticity of demand. The supplier is once again capable of capturing more market surplus than would be possible without price discrimination.

Note that it is not always advantageous to the company to price discriminate even if it is possible, especially for second and third degree discrimination. In some circumstances, the demands of different classes of consumers will encourage suppliers to simply ignore one/some class(es) and target entirely to the other(s). Whether it is profitable to price discriminate is determined by the specifics of a particular market.

Price Skimming

In price skimming, price varies over time. Typically a company starts selling a new product at a relatively high price then gradually reduces the price as the low price elasticity segment gets satiated. Price skimming is closely related to the concept of yield management.

Combination

These types are not mutually exclusive. Thus a company may vary pricing by location, but then offer bulk discounts as well.

Airlines use several different types of price discrimination, including:

- Bulk discounts to wholesalers, consolidators, and tour operators
- Incentive discounts for higher sales volumes to travel agents and corporate buyers
- Seasonal discounts, incentive discounts, and even general prices that vary by location. The price of a flight from

say, Singapore to Beijing can vary widely if one buys the ticket in Singapore compared to Beijing. In online ticket sales this is achieved by using the customer's credit card billing address to determine his location.

- Discounted tickets requiring advance purchase and/or Saturday stays. Both restrictions have the effect of excluding business travellers, who typically travel during the workweek and arrange trips on shorter notice.
- First degree price discrimination based on customer. It is not accidental that hotel or car rental firms may quote higher prices to their loyalty program's top tier members than to the general public.

COMPONENTS AND THEORIES OF DISTRIBUTION

In economics distribution refers to the way total output or income is distributed among individuals or among the factors of production (labour, land, and capital). In general theory and the national income and product accounts, each unit of output corresponds to a unit of income. One use of national accounts is for classifying factor incomes and measuring their respective shares, as in National Income. But, where focus is on income of *persons* or *households*, adjustments to the national accounts or other data sources are frequently used. Here, interest is often on the fraction of income going to the top (or bottom) x per cent of households, the next y per cent, and so forth (say in quintiles), and on the factors that might affect them (globalization, tax policy, technology, etc.).

Descriptive, Theoretical, Scientific, and Welfare Uses

It can be describes by income distribution a prospectively observable element of an economy. It has been used as an input for testing theories explaining the distribution of income, for example human capital theory and the theory of economic discrimination. In welfare economics, a level of *feasible* output possibilities is commonly distinguished from the distribution of income for those output possibilities. But in the formal theory of *social* welfare, rules for selection from feasible distributions of income and output are a way of representing normative economics at a high level of generality.

The species of Exchange by which produce is divided between the parties who have contributed to its production is distribution. Exchange being divided according as both, or one only, or neither of the parties have competitors, Distribution is similarly divided. The case in which both parties have competitors will here be first and principally considered. The simplest type of this distributive exchange would be of a kind which is effected once for all, without reference to a series of future productions and exchanges.

For example, Mr. Henry George used to adapt an illustration, let it be supposed that on a particular occasion each out of a number of white men hires one or more black men to assist in catching seals, on the agreement that each white man shall give his black assistants a certain proportion of the take, the terms having been settled in an open market in which any one white is free to bid against any other white and any one black against any other blacks.

A conception more appropriate to existing industry is that each white agrees to pay in exchange for a certain amount of service a definite quantity of produce, not in general limited to the result of a particular operation. On a particular day less seal may be taken than the employer has agreed to give the employee for the day. In this case, even if payment is not made till the end of the day, the employer must pay for help on a particular day in part with seal caught on a previous day. He must pay altogether out of past accumulations when payment is made before the work is one. When the employer agrees to pay a definite amount, he cannot expect to gain on each day's transaction, but on an average of days.

This example is suited to illustrate some general properties of Exchange which attach to Distribution as a species of Exchange. Such are the laws which connect a change in the supply or demand upon one side of the market with a change in the advantage resulting from the transaction to the parties on either side. Thus, competition on both sides being presupposed, a decrease of supply in a technical sense of the term on the one side is, ceteris paribus, universally attended with detriment to the other side, but is not universally attended with detriment to the side on which the supply is decreased.

A limitation of supply on one side may be advantageous to that side, though not to both sides. The case of Distribution compared with Exchange in general in respect to such limitation of supply has only this peculiarity, — that the danger of this policy defeating itself is in the case of Distribution specially visible and threatening. There is an evident limit to what the black man dealing with the white man can get in exchange for a certain amount of his service; namely, the total product which that service utilized by the white man will on an average produce.

For a true decision, there is here but a case of the general principle that no one will give more for a thing, whether article of consumption or factor of production, than the equivalent of its total utility to him, which total diminishes as the quantity of the commodity is reduced. But this limit is less liable to escape attention when it is fixed by the material conditions of production rather than by the desires of consumers. Conspicuous warning is given to parties in the position of our black men not to attempt to benefit themselves by a considerable reduction in their supply of service; for, though they might possibly obtain a larger proportion, they would probably obtain a smaller portion, of the average product. The laws which have been stated and other general laws of Exchange are equally true in more complicated cases of Distribution.

Till now, only a single factor are supposed to have by us — the service of the black man, or, more generally, the factor beta – offered by the competitors B1, B2, etc., in exchange for some of the produce a offered by the competitors A1, A2, etc. Let us now introduce other kinds of factors, alpha, beta, etc. And let us no longer suppose payment to be made by parties of the type A, in the kind of commodity which is produced, namely, alpha. A more concrete conception is that, besides the group A, B, C, D, there is another and another group, — A',

B', C', D'; A", B", C", D"; — where each capital letter typifies a set of competing individuals. It may be supposed that each A purchases out of the finished product that he turns out — namely, a — portions of the products a', a", etc., which he distributes according to the law of supply and demand among parties of the type B, C, D.

In fine, each A may pay for the factors of production altogether in some one product, a"', — *"numeraire,"* as happily conceived by M. Walras, or, less generally, money — which the purveyors of the factors can exchange for the articles which they want. These articles need not be all commodities ready for consumption: some of the parties may care to purchase factors of production wherewith to play the role which has been assigned to A.

It is now obtained a general idea of the machinery by which distribution in a regime of competition is effected. And, first, of the party that takes factors of production in exchange for products or the means of purchasing the same, the party above represented by the white man and labelled A. The functions of this party may be investigated by an ancient method which Sidgwick has proposed to rehabilitate for the purposes of modern economics, — the search for a definition. What is an entrepreneur? Amid the diversified combinations of attributes which the industrial world presents — innumerable as the varieties in which vegetable nature riots — we ought to fix certain characters agreeably to the rule laid down by Mill under the head of Definition by Type. "*Our conception of the class" should be "the image in our minds which is that of a specimen complete in all the characteristics.*"

Four such type-specimens may be distinguished, ranged in a descending order according to the extent of functions ascribed to the entrepreneur. First, there is the party whom the classical writers designate as the Capitalist, "*who from funds in his possession pays the wages of the labourers, or supports them during the work; who supplies the requisite buildings, materials, and tools, or machinery; and to whom, by the usual terms of the contract, the produce belongs to be disposed of at his pleasure.*"

This party will here be considered as devoting his care and savings to a single business. Second, there is the entrepreneur as portrayed by the late President Walker, "*not an employer because he is a capitalist, or in proportion as he is a capitalist.*"

Third, there is the party to whom Mr Hawley would wish to restrict the term "*entrepreneur,*" the man who undertakes risks, of which class the most prominent, though not the only, species is the investor in joint stock companies. Fourth, at the extreme degree of tenuity, is the entrepreneur who makes no profit. It might seem, indeed, as if this class did not call for special treatment, as differing only in the amount, not in the kind of remuneration. A fig-tree which bears no fruit is not therefore a tree of a distinct species. The horse which the Scotchman its owner had just trained to live upon a minimum, when the animal unfortunately died, was not therefore a new variety of the equine genus, requiring mention in a treatise on Natural History. However, as imposing theories have been connected with this last category, it comes within the scope of the present enquiry.

As our aim in comparing definitions should be, as Sidgwick says, far less to decide which we ought to adopt than to apprehend the grounds on which each has commended itself to reflective minds — the hunt for a definition being followed not so much for the sake of the quarry as of the views which are incidentally presented, — let us go on to consider the principal propositions which the several conceptions are adapted to bring under our notice. In this enquiry much assistance will be obtained from a series of articles on cognate subjects in the Quarterly Journal of Economics, which forms a sort of economic symposium.

The first definition is particularly suited to enquiries in which the parties who are in the habit of saving are contrasted as to their actions and interests with the parties who do not save, — approximately the working classes. It sounds paradoxical to add that the classical conception is not particularly adapted to illustrate the Ricardian theory of rent. But the definition of the capitalist above given is not easily reconciled with the received representation, that the capitalist's remuneration is equal to the number of doses which he lays out, multiplied by the remuneration of the last dose, the ordinary rate of profit. For, as Sidgwick argues, there is no adequate reason for expecting that "*remuneration for management*" as well as interest should tend to be at the same rate for capitals of different sizes.

Probably, the proposition is accurate enough to support the practical consequences which have been deduced from it. But, while fully admitting this, one may still agree with Sidgwick that "*even Mill's exposition*" is "*highly puzzling*." For the idea of an economic person laying out doses up to the margin and obtaining the remuneration equal to the number of doses multiplied by the marginal productivity of each dose is only proper to the case in which the doses are for sale. But it is only in the conditions proper to our third definition that doses of capital are put on a market in exchange for profit. Perhaps the classical writers, having an eye to practice and not restricted by a sharp definition, often tacitly introduce the supposition that it is open to the "*capitalist*" to take part in some other business besides his own.

Our second definition along may employed the classical formula for surplus if we use the phrase "*amount of outlay multiplied by average rate of return*" to designate the amount which the entrepreneur of the Walker type pays in the way of interest from year to year to those who have lent him the means of carrying on his business. The surplus will include not only the landlord's rent, but also the entrepreneur's net income. Any simple formula does not give the portion of this surplus which accrues to the entrepreneur.

Under the two heads, the conditions by which is determined may be considered, corresponding to Cairnes's categories, — commercial and industrial competition. This distinction becomes clearest when, in conformity with the division of employments, we conceive different occupations to be separated by great gulfs, so that they who would pass from one to the other must make a complete, or at least a considerable, change in their business arrangements. In virtue of the first kind of competition the entrepreneur endeavors to make the best possible arrangements within the occupation which he has chosen. In virtue of the second kind of competition he endeavors to choose the occupation which will afford to him the greatest net advantage.

Cairnes's motives under the first head may be understood by likening him to a monopolist who does not control the prices of the factors of production, nor yet the price of the product, the latter being fixed by a maximum law, or, rather, the case being that in which the monopoly is just becoming extinct, as Cournot would say, by the introduction of competitors, so that this entrepreneur can no longer sensibly alter at will the price of the product. Under such circumstances each entrepreneur will vary all the variables under his control up to the margin at which his own advantage becomes greatest. If he or we be content with a rough estimate of this advantage, it may be measured by the difference between his incoming and outgoings.

It may be regarded his incoming as the product multiplied by the price thereof, the amount of the product depending in some definite manner on the amounts of the factors of production which are employed. The outgoings may be regarded as a sum of terms, each of which is the amount of a factor of production multiplied by its price. It follows that in a state of equilibrium the increment of value produced by the last increment of a factor is just equal to its price. "*The marginal shepherd... adds to the total produce a net value just equal to his own wages.*"

So far supposing the entrepreneur's work to be a constant quantity. In a more exact estimate the quantity which the entrepreneur seeks to maximize is the utility to be derived from his net income minus the disutility incident to its production. From this consideration it follows that the increment of utility due to the increment of product which is produced by the last increment of entrepreneur's work is just balanced by the increment of disutility due to that work.

Up to this state is superadded the tendency towards equal net advantages in different occupations, resulting, as Professor

Marshall has shown, not so much in the equal advantageousness as in the equal attractiveness of different occupations. The remuneration of the entrepreneur thus corresponding to his services may be classed along with the remuneration of the workman as "*earnings*," from a certain point of view, which is doubtless proper to the publicist and philosopher. As Mangoldt points out, "*the circumstance that certain services do or do not attain a market price*" does not "*essentially alter the measure of their compensation.*"

But there is another point of view which is proper to those who study the mechanism of distribution. As Professor Taussig well observes, "*The cobbler who works alone in his petty shop gets in the main a return for labour as much as the workman in the shoe factory*"; but "*with regard to the machinery by which distribution is accomplished he [the cobbler] belongs in a different class from the hired labourer.*"

The tendency to quality of net advantages of course only exists with respect to positions between which there is industrial competition. If the union in one person of natural abilities and money constitutes him a member of a "*non-competing group,*" there is no presumption that the remuneration of such an entrepreneur will be exactly equal to the interest which he might have obtained by lending his money plus the salary which a person of his ability could command as a hired manager. There exists an excess above that sum, corresponding to what Mangoldt calls Unternehmergewinn. There may be excesses somewhat similarly caused by different degrees of ability and resources; the various "*rents*" enumerated by Mangoldt, which, as he observes, tend to diminish with the progress of society, so far as education becomes more diffused and it becomes easier for persons properly qualified to obtain the use of capital.

It can be obtained some additional light on the functions of the entrepreneur by comparing the profits in businesses of a different size. Some additional Suppose (for the sake of the argument) that the work and worry of the "*boss*" do not increase with the scale of operations, how is the equality of net advances which theory leads us to expect brought about? Ceteris paribus, might we not expect the entrepreneur's residue to be larger in the large industries?

As the answer may be that as equilibrium is approached under the joint influence of Commercial and Industrial Competition, the amounts of the factors are so varied as to fulfill the condition that equal efforts and sacrifices on the part of the entrepreneur are attended with equal remuneration. This equality is irrespective of identity in the relation between factors and product. It may exist whether that identity is supposed to be present between industries of different sizes or, as in general to be supposed, there is no identity in the relation between factors and product for different individuals and industries.

The sort of adjustment thus postulated may be illustrated by a more familiar kind of surplus, that which accrues to the landlord according to the received theory of rent. Let there be a homogeneous tract of land equally adapted to the cultivation of wheat and barley, owned by a set of competing landlords, who accordingly obtain an equal rent per acre whether wheat or barley is to be grown thereon. Now let a tax be imposed on the rent of land used for growing barley. There must result a new equilibrium, in which it remains true that owners of homogeneous land obtain equal rent per acre for whichever purpose used, and that cultivators of wheat and barley obtain, ceteris paribus, equal profits. These conditions can be fulfilled if the extent of the land applied to the cultivation of wheat is increased while the intensity of cultivation is diminished, and contrariwise for barley the extent is diminished and the intensity increased.

This proposition holds good whether or not the relation between outlay and product— corresponding to the shape of the curve in the illustration which Professor Marshall has made familiar — is supposed identical for wheat and barley, and even if the cultivator seeking the greatest possible profits is able to vary that relation in accordance with the "*law of substitution*." It is here assumed that the case of manufacture is not so different from agriculture, but that an analogous adjustment of "*margins*" must be considered to take place between large and small businesses under the conditions specified, and generally between different industries where industrial competition acts.

A similar adjustment must be postulated when we entertain the third definition of entrepreneur, and consider competing investors in the stock of companies which may at first be supposed equal in respect of risk, though not in size. The competitors being free to invest units consisting, say, of £100 or less in any kind of business (of the given riskiness), large or small, it follows that a return to a dose anywhere invested tends, ceteris paribus, to be the same. This result, which is by no means a deduction from the general formula considered under our second head, may be supposed to be brought about by an adjustment of margins of the sort which has been explained.

Now at length the Ricardian theory of rent as ordinarily stated becomes exact, — the payment for land rented by a joint stock company ought to be Just the difference between the returns (after capital has been replaced and labour paid) and the amount of capital laid out, multiplied by an average rate of profit. Though the class of shareholder is the principal, it is not the only species, of the third kind of entrepreneur, if defined so as to include all risk-takers. As Mr. Hawley observes, workmen take some risk, entrepreneurs who have no capital of their own run the risk of not being paid for their trouble. It might be taken enterprises as the essential attribute of a wide class entitled to a share in the national dividend along with the purveyors of land, labour, and capital. It does not seem to be a fatal objection that enterprise is hardy to be found in the concrete, separate from other factors of production. As Mr. Hawley replies, labour and waiting, the attributes of familiar classes, are not to be found in abstract purity.

To some there may seem a more serious scruple: whether the undertaking of risk does even in thought constitute a fourth factor, whether the distinction between interest and the reward for risk is radical. It is all very well for Jevons to distinguish by different coefficients, p and q, the depreciation of future goods due to uncertainty and to remoteness. But, since the distant pleasure is always uncertain, can we really disentangle the two causes of depreciation?

Luckily, these questions of logical definition and psychological analysis do not affect the important lessons respecting the participation of risk which have been taught by Professor J.B. Clark, — "*that a corporation can run risks which the individual could not with prudence,*" that by forming corporations "*we reduce the initial terrors of business enterprises.*" It is an exemplification of the old maxim not to put all one's eggs in one basket. If a hundred persons are carrying each a hundred eggs, each independently running the risk of tripping and by the loss of all or many of his eggs being exposed to great privation, this great danger will be averted, this chance of great disaster will be commuted for a somewhat higher probability of a much more easily borne loss, if each person carries only one of his own eggs and one belonging to each of the rest, the total to be redistributed at the end of the journey to market or after sale.

It is noticeable that in Professor Clark's nomenclature this risk is borne by the capitalist. "*The hazard of business falls on the capitalist.*" "*Business repays men not only for their labours, but their fears.*" But this repayment is "*not a part of mercantile profit*": it is realised by the capitalist "*as such.*" Admitting a real remuneration for risk, while giving a different name to the recipient from that which others have preferred, Professor Clark is perhaps not committed to the paradox which Mr. Hawley would affix upon the conception of the entrepreneur with vanishing profits, — our fourth species.

To eliminate profit, wholly static conditions must be more absolute.... There must be a cessation of all variations due to the changeableness of the environment due to fire, lightning, hail. We must imagine industrial society in the static condition as an automatic machine,... working without friction in an absolutely unchangeable environment.

This idea of perfect tranquillity is certainly inappropriate to the troubled world in which we live. "*Things are always finding their level,*" like a fluctuating and, in nautical phrase, "*confused*" sea. The oscillating character of the waves is quite consistent with a gradual change of level, as when the tide is flowing. It is a legitimate conception, familiar in statistics, to regard a phenomenon as hovering about an average, even though that average is known to be changing. Let the great tidologist calculate the dynamics of the flow, but let him not convey the impression that but for the action of this flow there would be the level of the proverbial mill-pond.

Professor Clark, almost certainly would recognize the continuance of risk not involving secular progress, — due to unpredictable weather or credit cycles, for example, — but would regard the remuneration for undergoing such risk as accruing to the "*capitalist as such*" rather than, with Mangoldt and others, as a part of the entrepreneur's gain. With regard to other elements of remuneration it is more doubtful whether Professor Clark would accept Mangoldt's statements as to the permanence of the entrepreneur's gain, — statements which read with their context, and attention being paid to Mangoldt's terminology, deserve much consideration.

We must suppose the existence of undertaker's gain [Unternehmergewinn], — otherwise what object has the entrepreneur to increase his business?. The undertaker's gain (Unternehmergewinn) is "*not simply something transitory,*" but a "*permanent species of income*". "*The undertaker's remuneration [Unternehmerlohn] preserves its position, though in a limited form*". However, Professor Clark would be satisfied with the "*limited form*" of the remuneration and the disappearance of certain other elements. It is always pleasant to believe that one's differences with high authorities are only verbal. This satisfaction may now be enjoyed with respect to M. Walras's doctrine that the entrepreneur makes neither gain nor loss. Professor Pareto has made it clear that, as the object of the entrepreneur is to procure the greatest amount of satisfaction, so his income is not to be considered as nil, in the ordinary sense of the term. It was interpreted correctly the doctrine that "*the entrepreneur makes neither gain nor loss,*" taken in connection with the "*coefficients of production,*" appears to cover all the conditions of equilibrium, both those which are involved in what Cairnes called "*industrial competition*" and those which would be satisfied even if we made abstraction of the tendency to equal advantages in different occupations. But, while we accept the ideas, we are not bound to swear to the words, of any master; and the expression in question may be objected to on several grounds which will repay examination. It is violently contrary to usage; it lends itself to a dangerous equivoque; and it has led distinguished economists to paradoxical conclusions.

No amount of authority and explanation can make it other than a strange use of language to describe a man who is making a large income and striving to make it larger, as "*making neither gain nor loss.*" There is an oddity about the phrase which recalls the use of "*gratis*" by Sir Murtagh's lady in Castle Rackrent: "*My lady was very charitable in her own way. She had a charity School for poor children where they were taught to read and write gratis, and where they were kept well to spinning gratis for my lady in return.*"

The term "*making neither gain nor loss*" has to be used in two different senses almost in the same breath is a more serious objection. It is a sufficiently difficult lesson for the plain man to learn that the maximum of income which the entrepreneur aims at realizing is zero. But the difficulty is doubled when he comes to learn as he must in dealing with a maximum problem — that the increment to that income due to the last increment of any factor of production is also zero. There is apt to arise a confusion between conditions belonging to the total and to the marginal quantity, — an ambiguity of a kind which has before now proved detrimental in economics.

A hasty reader of Professor Walras might suppose that it was intended to affirm that the entrepreneur made neither gain nor loss at the margin: whereas the meaning is, rather, that nothing remains to be distributed — on an average and apart from oscillations — after that the entrepreneur has paid a normal alary to himself. The implication that the remuneration of entrepreneur labour may be treated like that of any other labour presents some difficulty. It is the one obscure topic in Professor Barone's brilliant studies on Distribution.

Prof. Barone deserve to be quoted at some length. He first announces as true in a particular case, what is here regarded as true in general, that "*there must be left to the entrepreneur's profit (profitto dell' impresa) the differentiating character of 'residual claimant'; and nothing else can be said but that profit is formed by the difference between the entire product and the remunerations of the various factors corresponding to (raggua gliate) their respective marginal productivities.*" But Professor Barone regards this enunciation as only provisional. He promises to show in a later section that "*with the increase in the number of the competing entrepreneurs the profit of the undertaking tends to lose more and more the character of residual claimant; and tends to conform to that of the law of marginal productivity.*"

In the later section he says:– If on the market there is only one entrepreneur Titius, and if he does not monopolize the product, that is if he in the management of his business arranges to obtain not indeed the greatest monopoly profit, but the greatest profit obtainable in a regime of free competition,... his profit will be [a surplus indicated by a figure which is not here reproduced]. But, if there is an entrepreneur Caius capable of entering into competition with the preceding,... the profit of Titius will be reduced below what he had when he was alone on the market. And, if there is a third employer also capable of entering into competition with the first two, the profit of Titius will be reduced still more. The more the number of employers increases, the more there is a necessary tendency to a limiting state in which all the employers who continue to produce have a remuneration which, like that of any other labour, satisfies the condition that the marginal disutility [penosita] of the same labour [medesimo] shall be equal to the marginal utility of the returns which that labour procures, and not more than this. And, since it is this equality which characterizes the return to labour, it follows (ne viene) as a legitimate consequence that in this limiting state the remuneration of the entrepreneur may be treated like the remuneration of any other species of labour.

The fact that Wages are usually paid in advance is not to the point, as Professor Barone very properly observes. He proceeds:

These considerations seem to me to prove to demonstration how profound and correct is Walras's conception of an entrepreneur who under the conditions postulated makes neither gain nor loss after having paid himself (or others, it is indifferent which) the remuneration of the labour of direction and conduct of production. And, if it is no wonder that this conception should not be comprehended by economists who have really very vague ideas of quantity, it is absolutely astounding that the conception should have been also made the subject of criticism by other economists to whom the notions of quantity are quite familiar.... I frankly must confess myself absolutely incapable of understanding how any difficulty whatever can arise as to the validity [literally, the affirmation] of this conception, which is indeed most simple.

Having called once more attention to the abstract character of the conditions, Professor Barone reiterates:—

In such conditions the law of marginal productivity extends to the remuneration of the entrepreneur; and, after having remunerated all the factors (the work of the entrepreneur included) in proportion to their productivity [with a discount corresponding to the time elapsing between the service and the product], there remains no undistributed residue. About the meaning of this thesis if found any doubt, it would be removed by the unequivocal language of symbols employed, where, by way of illustration, the labour of the entrepreneur is expressed by the total number of hours of work that he devotes to the business. Upon this it may be remarked that the last state of Titius, after Caius and the rest have entered as competitors, seems identical with the case of "*extinct*" monopoly which was above adduced, in order to exhibit the motives of the entrepreneur. As there appears, both before and after the competitors have entered the remuneration of the entrepreneurs, in Professor Barone's phrase, "*satisfies the condition that the marginal disutility of the labour shall be equal to the marginal utility of the return which that labour procures.*"

But neither before nor after the competitors have entered is there any reason for regarding the remuneration of the entrepreneur as the product of the number of doses (*e.g.*, hours worked) and the marginal productivity of a dose (multiplied by a coefficient depending on the length of the productive process). It is only with respect to factors of production which are articles of exchange that the proposed law of remuneration, the "*law of marginal productivity;*" is fulfilled in a regime of competition. Thus, in our typical example of black men assisting white men to catch seals, what the black man gets in a perfect market is an amount of seal equal to the number of units of service which he supplies, multiplied by the quantity of seal for the sake of which he is just induced to offer an additional unit of service, the unit employed being a small quantity.

Similarly, what the white man gets in exchange is an amount of service equal to the amount of seal which he distributes to the black man, multiplied by the quantity of service for the sake of which he is just induced to offer an additional unit of produce. If the amount of service rendered may be taken as the measure of the black man's labour (or of some other factor of production supplied by him), the proposed law holds good for his share of the distributed produce. But, as the amount of produce given by the white man in exchange for services cannot be taken as the measure of his work, the proposed law does not hold for his share of the distributed produce.

This discussion will appear otiose to the economists who are not conversant with the science of quantity. The proposition that the remuneration of the entrepreneur is equal to the amount of his work multiplied by its marginal productivity will be interpreted by them as signifying simply that he will get more, ceteris paribus, the more work he does and the greater the addition to the produce which he would effect by doing a little more work. For them a product will do duty for a function of two variables which increases with the increase of either variable.

However, this simple interpretation is not open to mathematical economists. They must be aware that the formulae in question affirm something more than the simple truth above stated. If nothing more than that simple truth can be deduced from the theory of Exchange, it ought not to be a matter of surprise that the *"law of marginal productivity"* applied to the entrepreneur should be challenged by those who affect mathematical precision. The law of marginal productivity, then, is not fulfilled in the sense that the portion of the national dividend accruing to entrepreneurs is a sum of terms each of which is the product of an entrepreneur's work reckoned in hours, or similar doses, and the marginal productivity of a dose (multiplied by a certain coefficient).

When we take a larger dose that is the total work of an entrepreneur let us see whether the law is fulfilled. The law will then be fulfilled if the net gains of any entrepreneur tend to be equal to what society would lose if he were removed. Can this be generally affirmed? Let us look at the typical case of distribution between whites and blacks above instanced. It may be granted that the white entrepreneur does not normally obtain more than he adds to the common stock. For otherwise the society would gain through his removal, his black assistants either hunting by themselves or being taken on by other entrepreneurs. And neither of these suppositions is possible in a state of equilibrium; for, if either were possible, it would have been already brought about by the free play of self-interest, in a regime of competition. Then, the gain of a white man cannot be greater, but where is the proof that it cannot be less, than the loss which would be occasioned to the society by his removal?

Such a proof might be forthcoming if the white men were not, as hitherto supposed, genuine entrepreneurs, but managers acting under entrepreneurs of our third species, the stockholder.

The income of the managers will fulfill the marginal law of productivity if the new entrepreneurs are conceived as competing against each other in such wise as to bring about the result that no manager earns more or less than what he adds to the profits of his employers. The income of the new entrepreneurs also fulfils the law; for the remuneration of this species of entrepreneur — unlike that of entrepreneurs in general — is proportional to the amount of the factor which they contribute, — namely, capital invested.

In modern industries, the affinity between entrepreneurs and salaried managers supplies the missing link for the general proof of the new law. For, normally, it may be presumed that an independent entrepreneur (of our second species) does not make less (in Edition to the profits that he makes or might have made by investing in some other business money of his own) than a manager of like abilities. And perhaps he does not make much more. The difference is possibly small, probably diminishing, certainly difficult to verify statistically, perhaps hardly worth fighting about. Interpreted cautiously, the law holds good approximately.

If the manager remuneration similar to that of the "*marginal shepherd*," is just equal to the amount that he produces, then the remuneration of the entrepreneur is not very different from the amount that he produces. But, if the law of marginal productivity is fulfilled for the manager only while we consider doses less than his total work, say hours of work, then the law is fulfilled for the entrepreneur only so far as it is presumed from the similarity in nature and habits between the manager and entrepreneur that, when the total remuneration of each is nearly the same, the amount of work and its marginal productivity are not very different. The interpretation which has been suggested, the new law of distribution would be fulfilled by an adjustment of the quantities involved, the amount of each factor, not simply in virtue of the relation which subsists between the product and the factors of production. The sense in which the law is fulfilled is otherwise conceived by a distinguished mathematical economist, Mr. Wicksteed, who regards the law as following from "*the modern investigations into the theory of value,*" and seems to treat it as a clue whereby to investigate the nature of the relation between the product and the factors of production, including the work of the entrepreneur. In fact, he finds that the product depends upon the factors by a relation which mathematicians designate a "*homogeneous function of the first degree.*"

This is certainly a remarkable discovery; for the relation between product and factors is to be considered to hold good irrespectively of the play of the market: "*an analytical and synthetical law of composition and resolution of industrial factors and products which would hold equally in Robinson Crusoe's island, in an American religious commune, in an Indian village ruled by custom, and in the competitive centres of the typical modern industries.*" There is magnificence in this generalization which recalls the youth of philosophy. Justice is a perfect cube, said the ancient sage; and rational conduct is a homogeneous function, adds the modern savant. A theory which points to conclusions so paradoxical ought surely to be enunciated with caution.

To summaries this criticism, as Distribution is a species of Exchange, it seems undesirable to employ a phrase so foreign to the general theory of Exchange as the dictum that one of the parties to an exchange normally gains nothing. Innocently used at first, such paradoxes are calculated to lead to confusion and misrepresentation. Same remark applied to another form of the gain less entrepreneur, involved in Walker's analogy between profits and agricultural rent. Even on the simpler and provisional view which is confined to short periods and commercial competition, this form of expression has no advantage over the terminology proper to the general theory of Exchange. When we consider long periods and industrial competition, Walker's theory has the graver disadvantage of not distinguishing between rent and quasi-rent.

It seems to be generally admitted that Walker's masterly portrait of the industrial captain was not improved by his representation of profits as rent. Lets considered the party that takes factors of production in return for products or the proceeds thereof, let us look at the other side of the counter — the triangular counter across which we may imagine the three factors of land and labour and capital to be exchanged, if we place in the interior of the triangle an entrepreneur of Walker's type, our second species, dealing with three parties in quick succession, and in some sense simultaneously.

At the height of abstraction from which it is here attempted to survey the economic world, what appears the most salient feature in the transactions respecting land is the circumstance that the quantity of ground, or at least space, is limited, not capable of being increased by human effort. From this property flow most of the general theories relating to the landlord's share in distribution, — that a tax on rent (proper) falls wholly on the land, that the remission of agricultural rent by landlords would not benefit the consumer, and other propositions often connected with the formula that "*rent does not enter into the cost of production.*" Some remarks on that time-honoured formula seem called for here. It would not be consistent to have complained of the expression that "*the entrepreneur makes no gain*" as perplexing and apt to mislead, however innocently used by high authorities, and to pass over in silence this dictum about rent, against which and in favour of which much the same is to be said.

Definitely, it is supported by very high authority, — the authority not only of Ricardo and Professor Marshall, but also of Hume, who in the letter which he wrote to Adam Smith on the publication of The Wealth of Nations (the letter which, written a few month before Hume's death, may be considered his economic testament) says, "*I cannot think that the rent of farms makes any part of the price of the produce, but that the price is determined altogether by the quantity and the demand.*" On the other hand, it can hardly be denied that the dictum in question is calculated to obscure the truth that "*land is but a particular form of capital from the point of view of the individual manufacturer or cultivator;*" that, as he doses land with capital and labour, so he doses capital and labour with land, up to a margin of profitableness. And, in fact, the similarity of the factors of production from the entrepreneur's point of view does not seem to have been apprehended in all its generality by the classical writers.

Thus Fawcett, who may be taken as a type, when explaining rent seems to posit the size of the farm as something fixed and constant. J.S. Mill argues that "*there is always some agricultural capital which pays no rent*," not noticing the counter-argument that there is a portion of land which pays no interest. These imperfections belong now, it may be hoped, to past history. And yet that the description of rent as not entering into price is apt to prove misleading may be inferred from the many protests which eminent critics have raised against Professor Marshall's use of the time-honoured phrase. Their criticisms attest the correctness of their own views rather than their capacity of appreciating the views of others. What should we say of critics who should think fit to read Mill a lecture on the errors of the Mercantile system, because Mill had employed the terms "*favourable and unfavourable*" exchanges! To have attributed to Professor Marshall the very error which he by his doctrine of the "*Margin-of-building*" has done more than any other economist to obviate would be unpardonable if it were not excused by the misleading associations of an unfortunate phrase.

Returning to the real from the seeming, import of the phrase, we see that, as the offer of land is in general attended with no real cost, a tax upon the payment for land does not disturb production. On grounds of distribution, too, a sort of income which increases without any effort on the part of the recipient is prima facie a suitable object for a especially heavy impost. On these grounds Mill's proposal to tax away the future unearned increment of rent is defensible, if accompanied with Mill's proviso, that existing interests should not be disturbed.

For, as argued elsewhere, a special tax on existing incomes from land would violate the two principal conditions of a good tax: it would both tend to diminish the amount of production, and also to impair the equality in the distribution of burdens between the owners of incomes derived from land and from other kinds of property. The practical importance of Mill's proposal is greatly reduced by the proviso with which it is accompanied. For, in order that the State may make a good bargain by giving the market price for a certain class of future goods, the State must be able to look further ahead — must exercise the telescopic faculty of prospectiveness in a higher degree — than the ordinary capitalist. And it may well be doubted whether this condition is fulfilled by the politicians who act on behalf of the State.

However, most of the example are heard by us just like that of Chicago, where the value of sites is said to have multiplied some eighty-fold in half a century; but we hear little of proposals to buy up at their present market value the site of some future Chicago, unless, indeed, as part of a scheme for Land Nationalisation, which does not include compensation to vested interests. Unlike the husbandman, who plants trees the fruit of which he will not himself see, the advocates of a single tax and other socialist agitators grasp at the standing crop which has been sown by others, heedless whether cultivation in the future is thereby discouraged.

But, even if their outlook were as distant as it is bounded, there would remain the possibility that, though looking far ahead, they might not discern distant objects clearly. Mill cannot be accused of the shortsightedness which sacrifices the future to the present. He looked very far ahead. But he did not see what was coming, the fall of English rents. Actuated by the highest motives, he proposed an arrangement which was perfectly just to the landlords, and would have proved perfectly disastrous to the State.

Passing in the traditional order from Land to Labour, we may begin by considering a very abstract labour market, in which the difficulty caused by the "*advance*" of wages is kept out of sight. The following example of such a labour market may be worth reproducing, although it is not a genuine case of Distribution:—

Let us suppose several rich men about to ascend some an easy mountain, some a difficult one, each ascent occupying a day.

And let these rich travellers enter into negotiations with a set of porters who may be supposed many times more numerous than the employers. An arrangement according to which the remuneration for ascending the easy and the difficult mountains was the same could not stand: it would not be renewed from time to time. For some of the porters employed on the difficult mountains, seeking to minimise the disutility of their task, would offer their services to travellers on the easy mountains at a rate somewhat less than the temporarily prevailing one. Nor would equilibrium be reached until each porter employed on a difficult mountain received an excess above the fee for the ascent of an easy one sufficient to compensate him for the extra toil. At the same time — simultaneously, in a mathematical sense — the increment of satisfaction due to the last porter taken on by each traveller would just compensate the purchaser of that labour for his outlay on it.

The great number of the employees as compared with the employers is not an accidental circumstance. Suppose that the arrangement which is common in the Tyrol — that each amateur ascensionist should be accompanied by only one guide — were for technical reasons universal. Then the bargain between travellers, on the one hand, and guides, on the other, would not in general be perfectly determinate. It would still indeed be true that "*an arrangement according to which the remuneration for ascending the easy and the difficult mountains was the same could not stand.*" But it would no longer be true that the remuneration for the easy mountain — or, rather, for the average mountain, from which the fares both of the easier and the more difficult ascents might be measured — would be in general determinate.

Generally, there would exist no force of competition by which any particular arrangement (as to the average mountain) initiated by custom and accident could be disturbed. That is, still supposing the service of a guide or porter to be sold as a whole. For, if the labour of the assistants can be sold by the hour, or other sort of differential dose, the phenomenon of determinate equilibrium will reappear. There seems no reason to think that the case of indeterminate equilibrium which has been illustrated is other than exceptional in the actual labour market, even where the bargain appears to be made for totals as distinguished from doses of labour, — situations rather than tasks.

In fact, for there is such a variety of situations attended with different amounts of work as probably in practice to realise that divisibility of the thing supplied — here labour — which, together with the divisibility of the thing demanded, — here money, — constitutes a condition of a perfect market with determinate equilibrium.

Still, the point of theory is worth notice. Perhaps the friction in the labour market would be less if labour were sold freely by the hour (or other small "*dose*").

It ought to be mentioned that a different view of Exchange has been taken by a high authority on Distribution. Professor Bohm-Bawerk presents as the general type of a market that very case which is here regarded as exceptional. On one side of the markets are put dealers each with a horse or it may be a batch of several horses — which he will not sell under a certain price, on the other side buyers each of which will not go beyond a certain price. The following scheme is given as an example of such data:–

Buyers	
Values a horse at........... (and will buy at any price under) ditto:	
A1	£30
A2	£28
A3	£26
A4	£24
A5	£22
A6	£21
A7	£20
A8	£18
A9	£17
A10	£15

Sellers	
Values a horse at..........	(and will sell at any price over)
ditto	
B1	£10
B2	£11
B3	£15
B4	£17
B5	£20
B6	£21 10s
B7	£25
B8	£26

The given data the price of horse is deduced and it must be within £21 and 21/10s. But, if the data had been different, the price might not have been thus determinate. "*If there are, for instance, ten buyers who each value the commodity at £10, and ten sellers who each value it subjectively at £1, obviously all the ten pair can come to terms, and the zone which lies between the valuation of the last buyer and the last seller represents the wide latitude between £1 and £10.*" Of this character are the circumstances of the labour market.

In such a case some further datum is required to determine price. "*That this latitude should be narrowed down, the further circumstance must be present that the desire of the buyers is directed to an limited number of goods, while at the same time the total amount of means of purchase must be strictly limited, and the buyers must be determined to spend the whole of this sum in purchase of the commodities in question.*" This condition is fulfilled, according to Professor Bohm-Bawerk, by the "*general subsistence market.*"

This example will hardly be accepted as typical of a market by the mathematical economists who walk in the way of Gossen. Agreeing with the Austrian leader that value rests at bottom on subjective estimates, they will accept his scheme, just as they would accept the description of a common auction, as illustrative of that attribute. But they may complain that the illustration does not illustrate another attribute which they regard as essential to the determination of value in a market, — the circumstance that each party on the one side is free, in concert with some party or parties on the other side, to vary the amounts of those quantities on which depends his advantage — the quid and the pro quo — up to a limiting point, or margin at which he estimates his advantage to be a maximum.

The law of marginal utility was hardly exemplifies by the "*marginal pair*" of the Austrian scheme. We require knowing, not so much the least price which each horse dealer will take for his horse or stud, but how much horseflesh each individual or at least all collectively, will offer at each of several prices, with similarly graduated data for the would-be buyers.

Granted data of this sort, the mathematical economist need not trouble himself much about a matter which is vital according to the Austrian scheme, — whether the "*subjective valuation*" of a horse is the same (or very similar) for all the sellers, while the dispositions of the buyers are likewise identical. The case of like dispositions does not constitute a special variety of the problem, one which is insoluble without additional data. Far from being anomalous, that case may be normally assumed as a harmless and convenient simplification, very proper to an introductory statement of the general theory.

"Nec Deus intersit, nisi dignus vindice nodus Inciderit"–

The case of like dispositions does not present any peculiar difficulty calling for so very mechanical a Deus ex machina as the hypothesis that "*the total amount of means of purchase must be strictly limited and the buyers must be determined to spend the whole of this sum in purchase of the commodities in question.*" It is riding a one-horse illustration to death to put the accidents of an exceptional sort of auction as representative of the actual transactions by which the great mass of national income is distributed. This criticism, it must be freely admitted, involves an issue about which legitimate differences of opinion may exist; — what is the most appropriate conception of the process by which value is determined through the higgling of the market?

Any simple conception must involve a considerable element of hypothesis, not admitting of decisive proof. The hypothetical character of the enquiry will appear if we look back to that model labour market in which guides or porters were supposed to be hired by amateur mountaineers. It was tacitly assumed that each party has certain dispositions as to the amount of money that he is willing to give or take in exchange for a certain amount of work, — a scale of subjective estimates which is supposed to be formed before the parties come into communication, and not to be modified by the chaffering of the market. The constancy of these dispositions being assumed, it is presumed that somehow a state of equilibrium will be brought about, such that the party on one side cannot improve his position by entering into new contracts with some party or parties on the other side. The better opinion is that only the position of equilibrium is knowable, not the path by which equilibrium is reached. As Jevons says,

It is a far more easy task to lay down the conditions under which trade is completed and interchange ceases than to attempt to ascertain at what rate trade will go on when equilibrium is not attained.

Particular paths may be indicated by way of illustration, "*to fix the ideas*," as mathematicians say. In this spirit two kinds of higgling may be distinguished as appropriate respectively to short and long periods. First, we may suppose the intending buyers and sellers to remain in communication without actually making exchanges, each trying to get at the dispositions of the others, and estimating his chances of making a better bargain than one that has been provisionally contemplated. By this preliminary tentative process a system of bargains complying with the condition of equilibrium is, as it were, rehearsed before it is actually performed. Or, second, one may suppose a performance to take place before such rehearsal is completed.

In our example, on the first day a set of hirings are made which prove not to be in accordance with the dispositions of the parties. These contracts terminating with the day, the parties encounter each other the following day, with dispositions the same as on the first day, — like combatants armis animisque refecti, — in all respects as they were at the beginning of the first encounter, except that they have obtained by experience the knowledge that the system of bargains entered into on the first occasion does not fit the real dispositions of the parties. The second plan of higgling was supposed in the example, — the plan which is more appropriate to "*normal*" value.

Contemplating the theory of exchange in the abstract, we may exclaim with Burke, "*Nobody, I believe, has observed with any rejection what market is without being astonished at the truth, the correctness, the celerity, the general equity, with which the balance of wants is settled.*" But, when we come to the labour market, or any particular market, we must carefully enquire with what degree of approximateness the above-stated fundamental postulate holds good. When the bargaining extends over a considerable time, changes are apt to occur in the dispositions of the parties, whether independently of each other and sporadically, or in a manner even more fatal to the theory, by way of imitation. Also, where there occurs a series of encounters between buyers and sellers, the results of the earlier encounter may affect the dispositions with which the later ones are entered on. The terms which the labourer is ready to offer and accept are altered by the alteration in his habits and efficiency which is the consequence of previous bad bargains.

Professor Marshall pointed out the peculiarities of the labour market pointed out by go far to modify the general presumption in favour of laisser faire. But less careful writers are less successful in supporting the burden of proof which lies on those who profess to add to or take away from that outlined theory of Exchange which seems to express all that is known in general about the working of a market. A warning example of such modification not warranted by specific experience is the doctrine of the wage-fund, which is now universally discredited, and ought always to have excited suspicion and challenged proof because, as already intimated in another connection, it is a supposition repugnant to the general theory of Exchange that *"the total amount of means of purchase must be strictly limited, and the buyers must be determined to spend the whole of this sum in purchase of the commodities in question."*

However, as Sir Leslie Stephen says with reference to the classical writers, *"the assumption slipped into their reasoning unawares."* Sometimes it may have been intended only to convey that early lesson which is contained in our opening paragraphs, — that no party to production can expect to earn more than the total produce. Sometimes there was contemplated a more definite statement true of short periods, — a truth which has been well stated by Professor Taussig in his article on *"The Employer's Place in Distribution,"* and at greater length in his book on Wages and Capital —

The whole of the real income available for the community is not in any substantial sense at the disposal of the capitalists.... A large part of the commodities now on hand would not serve their turn. The supply of bread and flour and grain at any moment is adjusted to the expected needs of the whole mass of consumers.... The effective choice which the capitalists would have... would be thus confined, for the time being at least, within limits not very elastic.

It might be assumes by us that the working classes live on bread only, while the capitalist classes consume buns also. On a day, after a conference between employers and employed, the partition of the national dividend is altered in favour of the capitalists. Yet they will be unable to benefit immediately by the change. On that day more buns will not be forthcoming, all the bakers' ovens being preoccupied with bread. For the purpose of illustration there has been chosen a especially simple case in which the articles consumed by the two classes are formed out of the same material, and by a process which is identical up to the penultimate stage. The stream of production does not bifurcate till it debouches into the mouths of the two parties to Distribution.

When the longer tracts of that stream are consider by us, there comes into view a circumstance to be discussed under the head of Capital, the influence of time on value. To illustrate the distribution of produce between those who have contributed at different times to its production, let us at first make abstraction of other differences, and imagine economic men uniting the functions of workman and capitalist-entrepreneur, differing only in the amount of capitalisation, the length of time during which their labour is invested. One labours at proximate means, another at remote means, tending to the ultimate product out of which all the producers are remunerated. An idea of a train of production formed by successive operations directed to an ultimate product may be obtained by watching any factory.

Here you have the raw cotton-wool put in, there you see a "*sliver*" of carded cotton flowing from one machine en route to another, until at the last stage there comes out the finished article. To illustrate the process of distribution, we must now conceive a backward flow of the ultimate product to the several producers. We might imagine each one's share to be conveyed to him by some contrivance like those wondrous little vehicles in the Boston Public Library, which, as if gifted with human intelligence, find their way about the building to the particular place where each book belongs.

In time of distribution to illustrate the result of distance, we must further modify the model presented by an ordinary factory. We must suppose the interval of time between the processes to be greatly magnified, months being substituted for minutes. Then there will come into view the circumstance to which attention is particularly directed, — that a larger share will be conveyed to each producer (other things being equal), the greater his distance from the final stage. There will thus be a continual flow of materials in process of manufacture onwards and of products ready for consumption backwards, if the work at each stage is steadily maintained, provided that there is a continual stream of raw material, and that the machines are continually renewed.

Considering the continuous round of production and consumption, we realise the important truth which Mill has thus expressed: — "*The miller, the reaper, the ploughman, the plough-maker, the wagoner and wagon-maker, and the sailor and ship-builder, when employed, derive their remuneration from the ultimate product, — the bread made from the corn on which they have severally operated or supplied the instruments for operating.*"

To represent the continual expansion of value as the present ripens into the future, a series of concentric circles has been happily employed by Professor Bohm-Bawerk. Varying his illustration, let us suppose the circles to be drawn on ground which rises uniformly from the outmost circle towards the centre O in the accompanying diagram at which the apex tapers to a needle-point. The circles are drawn at equal distances as measured on the surface, and therefore, in a bird's-eye view which the diagram is intended to represent, become huddled together in the neighbourhood of the central height.

Across the circles, down the hill, flow streams with uniform velocity, so as to pass from circle to circle in a unit of time. The breadth of a stream increases with its length, — not in direct proportion to the length, but according to the law of accumulated price.The volume of the stream is proportioned to its breadth and to its depth (not shown on the figure). The stream takes its rise at some position on the channel (e. g. at a5a'5), the flow per unit of time at that point being proportioned to the energy put forth in pumping from a certain source. As the volume thus originated rolls down the channel, it continually increases by infiltration from the neighbouring soil without any additional pumping, so that, the depth being preserved constant, the volume is proportioned to the increasing breadth. Besides this increase due to its defluxion, the volume may also in the course of its downward flow be increased by additional pumping from a second source (*e.g.* a2a'2). This second increase corresponds to an increase in depth (not shown in the figure); and this second contribution is augmented, like the first, by the infiltration which attends defluxion.

As there may be many sources as circles are cut by the descending stream. But there need not be a source at each interval. The equidistant circles correspond to successive lines, not always coincident with successive stages of production at each of which additional labour is applied. The train of production thus represented terminates in a product ready for consumption — it may be loaves or ribbons, wine or shoes – on the shore of a circumfluent sea of commodities.

As in the natural world rivers are replenished by the melting of the snow, which is formed on mountains by the congelation of vapour, which is wafted up from the ocean, into which the rivers flow down, so in the mundus economicus, by a compensation carried into more just detail, labour is restored and re-created by a refreshing rain of commodities derived from that sea into which all finished commodities are discharged.

Volatile shoes and wine, and other commodities in due admixture up to a certain value, find their way to each point upon the heights from which a source has been tapped, the volume of this return corresponding to the volume of the original contribution, — not indeed the same, but the same increased by a factor of accumulation, the ratio which the breadth of the stream at the littoral bears to its breadth at the point of origin (*e.g.* a1a'1: a5a'5).

The flight of the commodities from the littoral to the heights need not be supposed to occupy an appreciable time. The idea of a Flow which has been illustrated is primary applicable to the case in which materials and consumable commodities aroused up once for all within a unit of time. But the case of labour invested for longer periods is easily assimilated. Suppose that a plough lasts five years, and that in each year of its existence it makes an equal addition to the consumable crop, the year being taken as the unit of time. Then, although the plough may have been made in a week or month, the labour of its production is to be considered as invested in five unequal portions at unequal distances in time from the epoch at which the invested labour meets with its return. The total labour of making the plough may be considered as applied at several positions (a'1a1, a2a'2,... a5a'5) in several contributions, respectively proportioned to the breadth of the stream at these points.

If labour is invested in the production of a machine, imagined by economists, which lasts for ever or what comes to the same, an improvement, such as the draining of land or opening a mine, or cutting an isthmus, which is calculated to yield a constant income for an indefinitely long series of years, then the series of positions along the stream at which the labour is supposed to be invested must be carried back indefinitely up to that needle-point whose tapering dimensions correspond to the perspective of an indefinitely distant future.

Eternal machines are not very common; but the conception may serve to illustrate a species of tool or implement of which the race remains immortal, though the individual is worn out and perishes. Of this kind are implements which are directed not only to produce goods immediately ready for consumption or implements of a kind different from their own, but also to reproduce their own kind. Hammers and axes are presumably of this kind in a primitive society; in an advanced state of industry, some more complicated engines. Such machines may be compared to horses, if used not only as beasts of burden, but also as stations. The demand for such creatures is presumably influenced by the expected series of future generations, so far as commercial prospectiveness may extend. In the stationary state of steady motion, here provisionally contemplated, reproductive machines would be illustrated by beasts of burden of which the breed does not sensibly improve in successive generations.

Two channels only have been represented in the diagram, one of finite, the other of infinite length, with breadth exaggerated for the sake of clearness. Properly, there should be as many channels as there are categories of articles ready for immediate consumption, — "*goods of the first order*," as the Austrians say; and the breadth should be such as to allow of the corresponding number of sectors being fitted into the circle. Another circumstance which must be left to the imagination is the introduction of one and the same article into several streams of production at different distances from the final stage. Coal, for instance, so far as it is used for warming dwelling-houses, is a good of the first order; so far as it is used to drive machines, — they perhaps used only to produce other machines, — coal is to be placed among the higher orders.

The distinction which has been drawn between work which is applied in the neighbourhood of and at a distance from the final stage of production is not coincident with the distinction between the saving and the non-saving classes. The shower of commodities apportioned to each spot according to its height above the littoral as well as to the volume of value which there took its rise, is not "*like the gentle rain from heaven.*"

It does not drop impartially on all who have been concerned with the work of eliciting the stream. Those who have done the common labour of pumping — the drawers of water-fare no better than if that work had been done at the littoral. In fact, it is proper to conceive that it was done at the littoral. As the energy generated at the Falls of Niagara is transmitted for use to a point higher up on the river, so on the stream of production the work of pumping is mostly done at the littoral, though it is applied at the heights.

For instance, on the first stream an amount of work proportioned to a5a'5 might be done at the littoral, and be paid for in commodities at the rate current on the littoral; that is, without the augmentation of value which is due to defluxion. The remainder of the volume of value which is discharged per unit of time flies off to those who occupy the height represented by a5a'5.

If now it is asked where rent comes into this representation of distribution, the answer is to be found in the theory that from the point of view of the entrepreneur the use of land appears in the same light as the use of labourers, — as a factor of production. The idea of a steady cyclic flow which we are striving to win becomes not much more complicated when we imagine that those who, placed on the heights, preside over the origination of productive streams, obtain the material that is to form the current, the precious fluid which it is their office to start upon its downward flow, not solely from a pumping proletariat, but also from the fortunate owners of springs which gush spontaneously.

However, there is difference between the labourer and the land-owner: that, whereas the former (even in the present age and still more when the classical economists flourished) has to spend a great proportion of his daily wage upon his daily necessaries, and therefore in respect of the bulk of his income must be placed at the littoral line, the latter may save a great part of his income, when it is greatly in excess of his daily necessaries, and in particular, with respect to that great portion, may defer fruition until the stream shall have flowed down from the point at which his contribution is applied to the point at which production becomes merged in consummation.

Another difference between land and labour in their relation to capital and enterprise arises from the circumstance that, unlike the labourer (in a free country), land itself, as well as its use, is sold. Whence arises a well-known correspondence between rent and interest in their relation to the capital value of land. This similarity will not be mistaken for identity by those who find the essential attribute of rent in the limitation of the objects for which rent is paid.

To complete the analysis of the parties to Distribution, it may next be required to distinguish the capitalist from the entrepreneur. They are both easily distinguished from the salaried manager in that he is at the littoral, in that respect like the common workman, while they are both above that line. But to draw a line in the series of shades which intervene between the employer of Walker's type and the mere shareholder, to determine at what point the capitalist ends and the entrepreneur begins, appears to defy analysis.

As Thought and Emotion are inseparably blended, though one may so far preponderate as to give its name to the state of consciousness at any time, such is the inseparable connection, such the intelligible but not exactly definable distinction, between Enterprise and Saving. The indefiniteness of the relation is illustrated by the shifting use in economic literature of the term Profit. That profit other than remuneration for managerial work should be transmitted to those who occupy a position on the heights — often the easy position of a dormant shareholder – is certainly invidious and difficult to justify to those who toil below.

Yet it may be reflected that the condition of those below would have been worse if those above, or those from whom they purchased or inherited their position, had not been content to wait for future goods instead of grasping at immediate pleasure. The Flow so beneficial to all classes would never have been set up without abstinence. It could not continue in its present magnitude but for the continued abstinence of each one who has a right to dispose of wealth which is in course of production, make a bonfire of it, if he can get a momentary pleasure from that extravagance, or by some less simple, though more familiar increase of unproductive consumption "*eat up his capital.*"

The consequences of an increase in unproductive consumption may be contemplated by reversing the consequences of an increase in parsimony. The latter increase forms part of a larger subject, economic progress. The progressive change in the volume of value and channels of production cannot be understood until there has been attained what was the object of the preceding paragraphs, — the clear idea of a steady flow in channels for a time unchanged. The study of this stationary state is perhaps the part of economic science which principally deserves to be described as theory of Distribution. In these pages it is not attempted to go far beyond the comparatively narrow round of steady motion in fixed cycles of production and consumption.

It must suffice to indicate three species of progressive alteration in the economic mechanism. There is, first, a uniform increase in the number of both capitalists and labourers, or, more generally, capital and labour, other things being the same. This change presents no difficulty: it may be represented by an increase in the depth of all the channels. Second, the rate at which the breadth of the channels diminishes as one ascends from the littoral — in other words, the rate of interest — might be diminished. A limiting case of this species is put by Mill when he supposes unproductive expenditure of capitalists to be "*reduced to its lowest limit.*"

Conceivably, this change might have no other effect than to reduce the portions accruing to the capitalists — such as a1a'1a2a'2 — to a minimum. The capitalists with new eagerness bid against each other for the service of the labourers; but, if the latter do not give more work for higher pay, the consequences might be a new equilibrium in which the same volume of value is steadily rolled down the same channels of trade, though the portion which flies back to the heights is a minimum. But, even if the quantity of value continued constant, it is hardly to be supposed that the quality of the commodities which make up the amount would remain unchanged. And, in fact, an increase of wages would probably be followed by an increase in the number and efficiency of the wage-earning classes.

And these results would favour the occurrence of a third kind of progress which may, however, be considered as arising independently of the others; namely, the lengthening of the trains of production. It may be doubted whether any great lengthening of the trains is possible without a concomitant improvement in the arts of production; yet, as Sidgwick observes, invention is not necessarily followed by increase of capitalisation. The third head of progress even more surely than the second will be attended with changes in the channels of production.

As already observed with reference to the portion of truth contained in the wage-fund theory, time will in general be required for the carrying out of such changes. The means of production which are rolling down the channels at the instant when the change begins must all or in great part be suffered to run out: otherwise there will probably be a considerable waste of labour, and interruption to consumption.

One delicate adjustment which would be deranged can only be alluded to here – the monetary circulation, especially that form of it which consists of debts that are continually "*cleared,*" or cancelled.

We might imagine the flow of factors in the channels of production and the flight of finished products backward on the way to consumption to be attended each with a displacement of air in a direction opposite to the main movement, — light counter-currents which have their use in facilitating the movements of solid wealth, and in the fulfilment of their useful function continually meet and neutralise each other. But, evidently, we have reached the degree of complexity at which the illustration becomes more difficult to understand than the thing which is to be illustrated. For a more concrete embodiment of a more complete theory the student is referred to the Principles of Economics, — a reference of which the value is, if possible, enhanced by the solid work which Mr. N.G. Pierson has published under the same title.

The preceding hints and metaphors and warnings may assist the student to obtain a general idea of the process by which distribution of the national income is effected. An outline of theory so abstract is not to be despised as useless. It satisfies a legitimate curiosity. It is part of a liberal education. It is comparable in these respects with an elementary knowledge of astronomy.

Such knowledge will not be of much use in navigation. And yet it has a certain bearing on real life. The diffusion of just notions about astronomy has rendered it impossible for astrologers any longer to practise on the credulity of mankind. Knowledge of first principles affords a test by which the authority of those who offer themselves as guides may be estimated. A little science has a further use: it is of assistance in obtaining more.

As the astronomer will proceed from a first approximation to a second, so economists should soften the hard outline of abstract theory by a regard to particular circumstances. As he in dealing with a new object will make certain of his first approximation, will consider, for example, whether an ellipse or a parabola fits better to the orbit of a new comet, — so it behaves us to consider whether the classical hypothesis presupposed in the preceding pages — two-sided competition — is appropriate to the conditions of modern industry. The hypothesis of two-sided monopoly is strongly suggested by what we see before us, — consolidated capital confronted by consolidated trade unions.

But it is alleged that beneath that appearance the forces of competition are effectively at work; that the settlement which is apt to be, and ought to be, agreed to between a combination of Capital and a combination of Labour is no other than that which would have been determined by competition if the individuals now combined had been free to act competitively.

TWO NECESSARY CONDITIONS FOR PRICE DISCRIMINATION

There are two conditions that must be met if a price discrimination plan is to work. First the firm must be able to identify market segments by their price elasticity of demand and second the firms must be able to enforce the plan. For example, airlines routinely engage in price discrimination by charging high prices for customers with relatively inelastic demand - business travellers - and discount prices for tourist who have relatively elastic demand, The airlines enforce the plan by making the tickets non-transferable thus preventing a tourist from buying a ticket at a discounted price and selling it to a business traveller.

Airlines must also prevent business travellers from directly buying discount tickets. Airlines accomplish this by imposing advance ticketing requirements or minimum stay requirements conditions that it would be difficult for average business traveller to meet.

PRICE DETERMINATION UNDER DIFFERENT MARKET SITUATIONS

Price Defined

Among the many responsibilities of the purchasing agent is that of determining the best price for goods and services. What is"price"? Price is the measure of value for a unit of a commodity or service that expresses its worth relative to other goods or services. Economists define price as the value of any item expressed in monetary terms, money. The function of obtaining the best price for the greatest value is an important element in the purchasing cycle.

The best price or correct price is not necessarily the lowest price, for price is only one of the variables a buyer must consider before making the decision to purchase. In the manufacturing industry, the purchasing agent spends up to 60 per cent of the company's income on incoming goods. The purchasing agent has the duty and responsibility to see that these funds are expended to obtain the full measure of value in what is received.

This responsibility is discharged when all prices are carefully reviewed, be they from the past, present, or potential suppliers. Don't become just a"price buyer" by separating price from the considerations of quality and service.

That"Low" Price

There is a tendency to exaggerate the importance of a low price in the purchasing function. The experienced purchasing agent will always avoid quick decisions to buy simply because the seller is quoting a price below the prevailing price. It must be remembered that the quality of the goods and the service offered are as important as the price.

During any recession or depressed market conditions, many firms would be happy just to maintain continuous operation and offer low prices for that purpose. The short-term goal for these firms is survival, with the long-term goal that improved economic conditions will enable them to again operate at a profit. After all, the primary goal of all enterprises is to operate at a profit, thus ensuring continuing and expanding ventures.

If the profit is reasonable and fair for the seller, then the price would be reasonable and fair for the buyer. Good will and cooperation between the seller and buyer makes for a good relationship, which includes reasonable and fair prices for both.

There are situations where a supplier quotes a low price in order to unload excess inventory that is costing carrying charges and thus tying up capital and reducing cash flow. This can be caused by the cancellation of an order by another customer or can be caused by an overstock resulting from anticipation of increased sales that did not materialize. This may be a genuine good buy.

Then there is the low price quoted by a supplier who is financially insecure and just wants your order to get your money. Such low prices lose their attractiveness when deliveries become uncertain and are often late, quality is questionable and requires extensive inspection, and complaints are never promptly resolved. Such purchases are not in the best interest of the buyer's company. Then there is the new supplier who quotes a low price and is willing to take less of a profit at this time in order to become established with the buyer's company. In this type of situation, the purchase may represent a good buy.

When the buyer receives a low price quote from any supplier, that buyer should be alert to all possibilities for that quote and its effect on the operation within the company. Find out the reason for such low price. Reputable suppliers will not hesitate to give you an honest answer. Beware of high-pressure tactics to get you to place the order.

Who Sets The Price?

The primary aim of the supplier is not only to remain in business but to make a profit that will permit expansion and increase profits. It has been assumed that the seller has the"privilege" of establishing the price at which he is willing to shell his product or service. In the economics of the business world, the price must be attractive to the buyer to result in any transaction. Otherwise, there is no market for the goods or services, no business transaction, and no one makes money.

Neither can the buyer establish the price at which he is willing to buy. There would not be a seller willing to sell at a price that does not include a reasonable profit. Thus, to have a business transaction, there must be a"meeting of the minds" to establish a price that is mutually agreeable to both parties.

Economic Considerations

Two types of economic considerations are involved in arriving at the price the seller offers to the buyer. There is the monopolistic approach, where there is only one supplier of the needed goods. This could happen through ownership of the single source, such as a mine, or the exclusive legal protection of a patent or copyright.

Should the supplier's price be exceedingly high, there will be a tendency for the buyers to seek substitute goods or to ask engineering to make some modification in design or variation of the finished product so as not to require those specific goods. This can result in lessening the hold or even eliminating the need for the monopolistic supplier.

The other consideration is the competitive method whereby two or more suppliers make an effort to secure the purchase order by offering the most favourable terms. There are two forms of competition: the perfect competitive method and the imperfect competitive method.

The pure or perfect competitive method exists where there are a large number of independent suppliers and buyers competing for identical commodities, dealing with each other yet retaining the privilege of entering or exiting from the market at any time. The price is usually determined by the supply and demand forces.

The oligopoly form in the imperfect competitive market exists when each of the limited number of suppliers is strong enough to influence the market, but not strong enough to disregard the reaction from his competitors.

In the oligopolistic auto industry, no one auto maker can influence the market without equal or greater counter influences from competitors. When one of the auto makers offers a cash rebate, the others follow with a similar or greater rebate or some other counter influencing offer. We see that each alone cannot influence the market for its own gain without the counteraction of his competitors, resulting in a healthy economic market.

With the lifting of the voluntary import quotas for foreign automobiles, more foreign cars became available to the American consumer, which tended to force a reduction in the price of American-made automobiles to meet foreign competition and enable American auto manufacturers to retain or increase their share of the market.

During the oil shortage, the oligopolistic oil suppliers of the Middle East acted as a monopoly and maximized their profits to such a level that buyers of oil were forced to look for substitute forms of energy. There was an increase in research efforts and exploration activities for new sites of oil reserves. Energy users also looked at coal, solar, and nuclear sources.

This sudden increase in activity in quest of new oil sites caused the Middle East oil suppliers to lower their prices to a level that would"equalize" the expenditures made for research and development activities.

Some exploration projects were halted, but others continued so that we have now developed new sources of crude oil at lower prices. This sudden glut of oil caused some disintegration of the Middle East unity when several of these nations lowered their price to regain and retain their share in the crude market.

The normal imperfect competition exists when there are a great number of sellers of similar products, but each with its own distinguishing feature. These distinguishing features are used by suppliers as persuasive arguments in their attempts to influence buyer's decision.

Fair And Reasonable Prices

One method of determining what is a fair and reasonable price by securing quotations from several potential suppliers. In all governmental agencies, as required by law, purchase contracts are the result of public bidding.

There are exceptions to formal bidding - when there is an emergency, when time is too short to obtain formal quotes, when a patent is involved, or other conditions prescribed under the charter under which the agency or department operates.

In industry, formal competition bidding is used in very limited situations or for special projects. Industrial buyers use the b ding system to build their lists of potential suppliers, especially suppliers of new goods, to seek a replacement for their present supplier, or to seek a quote to use in negotiations.

No two suppliers have identical costs of operation or the same eagerness for that purchase order, resulting in a wide range price quotes.

The buyer should use quotations as a tool in the determination of what is a fair and reasonable price, keeping in Mind our quality and service of that product.

The supplier must quote a price high enough to recover fixed and variable costs plus a profit, sometimes fair and reasonable, sometimes maximized, in order to grow in his business venture. The supplier's profit portion of the price contains what believes his superior manufacturing capabilities are worth for his product.

Factors Influencing Price

It should be recognized that the quoted price reflects more than just costs plus profit. The price is influenced by many factors. Particularly pertinent is competition among the suppliers of that commodity and the buyers of that commodity.

The supplier who faces a limited number of competitors will react differently in his pricing than the supplier who faces many active competitors. Also, the supplier's price is influenced by the number of prospective buyers.

Psychological factors also influence price. One is the prediction of future supply-demand relationships. If there is confidence in the guture of the relationship, there is a tendency towrds higher pricing. In an atmosphere of pessimism, there may be a decline in the pricing. This attitude about the future is a sort of"sixth sense" that buyers develop through experience. An alert buyer can verify his personal attitude by talking with other buyers individually or collectively at meetings.

Another psychological factor is knowing how far you can press a bargaining advantage. Don't press too hard. You may eliminate a good source by attempting to force prices so low that the supplier may refuse to do any business with you. This will force you to look elsewhere to other suppliers whose prices may be higher than you present good supplier's.

A third psychological factor is the practice of haggling over every price quoted. Price haggling has reappeared, especially in the retail market, due to effects of discount outlets on regular retail dealers.

This type of bargaining diverts attention from the quality of the product and services offered. Look at the food supermarts, especially in the produce part, where a low price will often result in poor quality or lesser size, giving rise to a suspicion about future"bargains" that works against the good will between seller and buyer.

Another psychological factor is non business considerations - gifts, entertainment, bribes, etc,. The buyer should be wary of these overtures, for the seller, in the long run, will always recoup these considerations in future prices.

8

Demand for Money

The demand for money is the desired holding of financial assets in the form of money: that is, cash or bank deposits. It can refer to the demand for money narrowly defined as M1 (non-interest-bearing holdings), or for money in the broader sense of M2 or M3.

Money in the sense of M1 is dominated as a store of value by interest-bearing assets. However, money is necessary to carry out transactions; in other words, it provides liquidity. This creates a trade-off between the liquidity advantage of holding money and the interest advantage of holding other assets. The demand for money is a result of this trade-off regarding the form in which a person's wealth should be held. In macroeconomics motivations for holding one's wealth in the form of money can roughly be divided into the transaction motive and the asset motive. These can be further subdivided into more microeconomically founded motivations for holding money.

Generally, the nominal demand for money increases with the level of nominal output (price level times real output) and decreases with the nominal interest rate. The real demand for money is defined as the nominal amount of money demanded divided by the price level. For a given money supply the locus of income-interest rate pairs at which money demand equals money supply is known as the LM curve.

The magnitude of the volatility of money demand has crucial implications for the optimal way in which a central bank should carry out monetary policy and its choice of a nominal anchor. Conditions under which the LM curve is flat, so that increases in the money supply have no stimulatory effect (a liquidity trap), play an important role in Keynesian theory. This situation occurs when the demand for money is infinitely elastic with respect to the interest rate.

A typical *money-demand function* may be written as,

$$M^d = P * L(Rm\ Y)$$

where M^d is the nominal amount of money demanded, P is the price level, R is the nominal interest rate, Y is real output, and $L(.)$ is real money demand. An alternate name for L(R, Y) is the *liquidity preference function.*

Motives for holding money

Transaction Motive

The transactions motive for money demand results from the need for liquidity for day-to-day transactions in the near future. This need arises when income is received only occasionally (say once per month) in discrete amounts but expenditures occur continuously.

Quantity Theory

The most basic "classical" transaction motive can be illustrated with reference to the Quantity Theory of Money. According to the equation of exchange $MV = PY$, where M is the stock of money, V is its velocity (how many times a unit of money turns over during a period of time), P is the price level and Y is real income. Consequently PY is nominal income or in other words the number of transactions carried out in an economy during a period of time. Rearranging the above identity and giving it a behavioural interpretation as a demand for money we have,

$$M^d = P\frac{Y}{V}$$

or in terms of demand for real balances,

$$\frac{M^d}{P} = \frac{Y}{V}$$

Hence in this simple formulation demand for money is a function of prices and income, as long as its velocity is constant.

Inventory Models

The amount of money demanded for transactions however is also likely to depend on the nominal interest rate. This arises due the lack of synchronization in time between when purchases are desired and when factor payments (such as wages) are made. In other words, while workers may get paid only once a month they generally will wish to make purchases, and hence need money, over the course of the entire month. The most well-known example of an economic model that is based on such considerations is the Baumol-Tobin model. In this model an individual receives her income periodically, for example, only once per month, but wishes to make purchases continuously. The person could carry her entire income with her at all times and use it to make purchases. However, in this case she would be giving up the (nominal) interest rate that she can get by holding her income in the bank. The optimal strategy involves holding a portion of one's income in the bank and portion as liquid money. The money portion is continuously run down as the individual makes purchases and then she makes periodic (costly) trips to the bank to replenish the holdings of money. Under some simplifying assumptions the demand for money resulting from the Baumol-Tobin model is given by,

$$\frac{M^d}{P} = \sqrt{\frac{tY}{2R}}$$

where t is the cost of a trip to the bank, R is the nominal interest rate and P and Y are as before.

The key difference between this formulation and the one based on a simple version of Quantity Theory is that now the demand for real balances depends on both income (positively) or the desired level of transactions, and on the nominal interest rate (negatively).

Microfoundations for Money Demand

While the Baumol-Tobin model provides a micro economic explanation for the form of the money demand function, it is generally too stylized to be included in modern macroeconomic models, particularly dynamic stochastic general equilibrium models. As a result most models of this type resort to simpler indirect methods which capture the spirit of the transactions motive. The two most commonly used methods are the cash-in-advance model (sometimes called the *Clower Constraint* model) and the money in the utility function model (sometimes referred to as the 'MIU' or the Sidrauski model).

In the cash-in-advance model agents are restricted to carrying out a volume of transactions equal to or less than their money holdings. In the MIU model, money directly enters agents' utility functions, capturing the 'liquidity services' provided by money.

Asset Motive

The asset motive treats money, in the broader sense of including interest-bearing bank deposits, as a particular type of a financial asset among many others. While it is still assumed that money is held in order to carry out transactions, this approach focuses on the potential return on various assets (including money) as an additional motivation.

Speculative Motive

John Maynard Keynes, in laying out speculative reasons for holding money, stressed the choice between money and bonds. If agents expect the future nominal interest rate (the return on bonds) to be lower than the current rate they will then reduce their holdings of money and increase their holdings of bonds. If the future interest rate does fall, then the price of bonds will increase and the agents will have realized a capital gain on the bonds they purchased. This means that the demand for money in any period will depend on both the current nominal interest rate and the expected future interest rate (in addition to the standard transaction motives which depend on income).

The fact that the current demand for money can depend on expectations of the future interest rates has implications for volatility of money demand. If these expectations are formed, as in Keynes' view, by "animal spirits" they are likely to change erratically and cause money demand to be quite unstable.

Portfolio Motive

The portfolio motive also focuses on demand for money over and above that required for carrying out transactions. The basic framework is due to James Tobin, who considered a situation where agents can hold their wealth in a form of a low risk/low return asset (here, money) or high risk/high return asset (bonds or equity). Agents will choose a mix of these two types of assets (their portfolio) based on the risk-expected return trade-off. For a given expected rate of return, more risk averse individuals will choose a greater share for money in their portfolio. Similarly, given a person's degree of risk aversion, a higher expected return (nominal interest rate plus expected capital gains on bonds) will cause agents to shift away from safe money and into risky assets. Like in the other motivations above, this creates a negative relationship between the nominal interest rate and the demand for money. However, what matters additionally in the Tobin model is the subjective rate of risk aversion, as well as the objective degree of risk of other assets, as, say, measured by the standard deviation of capital gains and losses resulting from holding bonds and/or equity.

Empirical estimations of money demand functions

Is Money Demand Stable?

Friedman and Schwartz in their 1963 work *A Monetary History of the United States* argued that the demand for real balances was a stable function of income and the interest rate. For the time period they were studying this appeared to be true. However, shortly after the publication of the book, due to changes in financial markets and financial regulation money demand became more unstable. Various researchers showed that money demand became much more unstable after 1975. Ericsson, Hendry and Prestwich (1998) consider a model of money demand based on the various motives outlined above and test it with empirical data. The basic model turns out to work well for the period 1878 to 1975 and there doesn't appear to be much volatility in money demand, in a result analogous to that of Friedman and Schwartz. This is true even despite the fact that the two world wars during this time period could have led to changes in the velocity of money. However, when the same basic model is used on data spanning 1976 to 1993, it performs poorly. In particular, money demand appears not to be sensitive to interest rates and there appears to be much more exogenous volatility. The authors attribute the difference to technological innovations in the financial markets, financial deregulation, and the related issue of the changing menu of assets considered in the definition of money.

Later work by Lawrence Ball suggests that the use of adapted aggregates, such as near monies, can produce a more stable demand function. Through his research, Ball was able to show that using the return on near monies produced smaller deviations than previous models.

Importance of money demand volatility for monetary policy

If the demand for money is stable then a monetary policy which consists of a monetary rule which targets the growth rate of some monetary aggregate (such as M1 or M2) can help to stabilize the economy or at least remove monetary policy as a source of macroeconomic volatility. Additionally, if the demand for money does not change unpredictably then money supply targeting is a reliable way of attaining a constant inflation rate. This can be most easily seen with the quantity theory of money equation given above. When that equation is converted into growth rates we have,

$$g_m + g_v = \pi + g_y$$

which says that the growth rate of money supply plus the growth rate of its velocity equals the inflation rate plus the growth rate of real output. If money demand is stable then velocity is constant and $g_v = 0$. Additionally, in the long run real output grows at a constant rate equal to the sum of the rates of growth of population, technological know-how, and technology in place, and as such is exogenous. In this case the above equation can be solved for the inflation rate:

$$\pi = -g_y + g_m$$

Here, given the long-run output growth rate, the only determinant of the inflation rate is the growth rate of the money supply. In this case inflation in the long run is a purely monetary phenomenon; a monetary policy which targets the money supply can stabilize the economy and ensure a non-variable inflation rate.

This analysis however breaks down if the demand for money is not stable — for example, if velocity in the above equation is not constant. In that case, shocks to money demand under money supply targeting will translate into changes in real and nominal interest rates and result in economic fluctuations.

An alternative policy of targeting interest rates rather than the money supply can improve upon this outcome as the money supply is adjusted to shocks in money demand, keeping interest rates (and hence, economic activity) relatively constant.

The above discussion implies that the volatility of money demand matters for how monetary policy should be conducted. If most of the aggregate demand shocks which affect the economy come from the expenditure side, the IS curve, then a policy of targeting the money supply will be stabilizing, relative to a policy of targeting interest rates.

However, if most of the aggregate demand shocks come from changes in money demand, which influences the LM curve, then a policy of targeting the money supply will be destabilizing.

DEMAND BEHAVIOUR

We investigate several topics in demand behaviour. Most of these have to do with special forms of the budget constraint or preferences that lead to special forms of demand behaviour. There are many circumstances where such special cases are very convenient for analysis, and it is useful to understand how they work.

Endowments in the Budget Constraint

In our study of consumer behaviour we have taken income to be exogenous. But in more elaborate models of consumer behaviour it is necessary to consider how income is generated. The standard way to do this is to think of the consumer as having some endowment $\omega = (\omega_1,...\omega_L)$ of various goods which can be sold at the current market prices p. This gives the consumer income m = pω which can be used to purchase other goods.

The utility maximization problem becomes,

$$\max_x u(x)$$

$$\text{such that px} = \text{p}\omega.$$

This can be solved by the standard techniques to find a demand function x(p, pω). The net demand for good i is x_i–ω_i. The consumer may have positive or negative net demands depending on whether he wants more or less of something than is available in his endowment. In this model prices influence the value of what the consumer has to sell as well as the value of what the consumer wants to sell. This shows up most clearly in Slutsky's equation, which we now derive. First, differentiate demand with respect to price:

$$\frac{dx_i(p,p\omega)}{dp_j} = \left.\frac{\partial x_i(p,p\omega)}{\partial p_j}\right|_{p\omega=constant} + \frac{\partial x_i(p,p\omega)}{dm} w_j.$$

The first term in the right-hand side of this expression is the derivative of demand with respect to price, holding income fixed. The second term is the derivative of demand with respect to income, times the change in income. The first term can be expanded using Slutsky's equation. Collecting terms we have

$$\frac{dx_i(p,p\omega)}{dp_j} = \frac{\partial h_i(p,u)}{\partial p_j} + \frac{\partial x_i(p,p\omega)}{\partial m}(\omega_j - x_j).$$

Now the income effect depends on the net demand for good j rather than the gross demand.

Income-Leisure Choice Model

Suppose that a consumer chooses two goods, consumption and "leisure". Let ℓ be the number of hours and $\overline{L}$ be the maximum number of hours that the consumer can work. We then have $L = \overline{L} - \ell$. She also has some nonlabor income m. Let $u(c,L)$ be the utility of consumption and leisure and write the utility maximization problem as,

$$\max_{c,L} u(c,L)$$

such that,

$$pc + wL = w\overline{L} + m.$$

This is essentially the same form that we have seen before. Here the consumer "sells" her endowment of labour at the price w and then buys some back as leisure. Slutsky's equation allows us to calculate how the demand for leisure changes as the wage rate changes. We have,

$$\frac{dL(p,w,m)}{dw} = \frac{\partial L(p,w,u)}{\partial w} + \frac{\partial L(p,w,m)}{\partial m}[\overline{L} - L].$$

Note that the term in brackets is nonnegative by definition, and almost surely positive in practice.

This means that the derivative of leisure demand is the sum of a negative number and a positive number and is inherently ambiguous in sign. In other words, an increase in the wage rate can lead to either an increase or a decrease in labour supply.

Homothetic Utility Functions

A function f: $R^n \rightarrow R$ is homogeneous of degree 1 if $f(t\mathrm{x}) = tf(\mathrm{x})$ for all $t > 0$. A function $f(\mathrm{x})$ is homothetic if $f(\mathrm{x}) = g(h(\mathrm{x}))$ where g is a strictly increasing function and h is a function which is homogeneous of degree 1.

Economists often find it useful to assume that utility functions are homogeneous or homothetic. In fact, there is little distinction between the two concepts in utility theory. A homothetic function is simply a monotonic transformation of a homogeneous function, but utility functions are only defined up to a monotonic transformation.

Thus assuming that preferences can be represented by a homothetic function is equivalent to assuming that they can be represented by a function that is homogeneous of degree 1. If a consumer has preferences that can be represented by a homothetic utility function, economists say that the consumer has homothetic preferences.

It can easily shown that if the utility function is homogeneous of degree 1, then the expenditure function can be written as $e(\mathrm{p}, u) = e(\mathrm{p})u$.

This in turn implies that the indirect utility function can be written as $v(\mathrm{p},m) = v(\mathrm{p})m$. Roy's identity then implies that the demand functions take the form $x_i(\mathrm{p},m) = x_i(\mathrm{p})m$–*i.e.*, they are linear functions of income. The fact that the "income effects" take this special form is often useful in demand analysis.

Aggregating Across Goods

In many circumstances it is reasonable to model consumer choice by certain "partial" maximization problems. We may want to model the consumer's choice of "meat" without distinguishing how much is beef, pork, lamb, etc. In most empirical work, some kind of aggregation of this sort is necessary.

In order to describe some useful results concerning this kind of separability of consumption decisions, as suggested, have to introduce some new notation. Let us think of partitioning the consumption bundle into two "subbundles" so that the consumption bundle takes the form (x, z). For example, x could be the vector of consumptions of different kinds of meat, and z could be the vector of consumption of all other goods.

We partition the price vector analogously into. Here p is the price vector for the different kinds of meat, and q is the price vector for the other goods. With this notation the standard utility maximization problem can be written as

$$\max_{x,z} u(x.z)$$

$$\textit{such that } \mathrm{px} + \mathrm{qz} = m.$$

The problem of interest is under what conditions we can study the demand problem for the *x*-goods, say, as a group, without worrying about how demand is divided among the various components of the *x*-goods.

One way to formulate this problem mathematically is as follows. We would like to be able to construct some scalar quantity index, *X*, and some scalar price index, *P*, that are functions of the vector of quantities and the vector of prices:

$$P = f(\mathrm{p})$$

$$X = g(\mathrm{x}).$$

In this expression *P* is supposed to be some kind of \price index" which gives the "average price" of the goods, while *X* is supposed to be a quantity index that gives the average "amount" of meat consumed. Our hope is that we can find a way to construct these price and quantity indices so that they behave like ordinary prices and quantities.

That is, we hope to find a new utility function *U*(*X;* z), which depends only on the quantity index of *x*-consumption, that will give us the same answer as if we solved the entire maximization problem in.

More formally, consider the problem,

$$\max_{X,z} U(X.z)$$

$$\textit{such that } \mathrm{PX} + \mathrm{qz} = m.$$

The demand function for the quantity index X will be some function $X(P; q;m)$. We want to know when it will be the case that,

$$X(P; q;m) \,' X(f(p); q;m) = g(x(p; q;m)):$$

This requires that we get to the same value of X via two different routes:

1. First aggregate prices using $P = f(p)$ and then maximize $U(X; z)$ subject to the budget constraint $PX + qz = m$.
2. First maximize $u(x; z)$ subject to $px+qz = m$ and then aggregate quantities to get $X = g(x)$.

There are two situations under which this kind of aggregation is possible. The first situation, which imposes constraints on the price movements, is known as Hicksian separability. The second, which imposes constraints on the structure of preferences, is known as functional separability.

Suppose that the price vector p is always proportional to some fixed base price vector p^0 so that $p = tp^0$ for some scalar t. If the x-goods are various kinds of meat, this condition requires that the relative prices of the various kinds of meat remain constant–they all increase and decrease in the same proportion.

Following the general framework, let us define the price and quantity indices for the x-goods by,

$$P = t$$

$$X = p^0x.$$

We define the indirect utility function associated with these indices as,

$$V(P,q,m) = \max_{x,z} u(x,z)$$

$$\textit{such that } Pp^0x + qz = m.$$

It is straightforward to check that this indirect utility function has all the usual properties: it is quasiconvex, homogeneous in price and income, etc. In particular, a straightforward application of the envelope theorem shows that we can recover the demand function for the x-good by Roy's identity:

$$X(P,q,m) = -\frac{\partial V(P,q,m)/\partial P}{\partial V(P,q,m)/\partial m} = p^0 x(p,q,m).$$

This calculation shows that *X(P;* q;*m*) is an appropriate quantity index for the *x*-goods consumption: we get the same result if we first aggregate prices and then maximize *U(X;* z) as we get if we maximize *u*(x; z) and then aggregate quantities.

We can solve for the direct utility function that is dual to *V* (*P,* q,*m*) by the usual calculation:

$$U(X,z) = \min_{P,q} V(P,q,m)$$

such that PX + qz = *m:*

By construction this direct utility function has the property that,

$$V(P,q,m) = \max_{X,z} U(X,z)$$

such that PX + qz = *m*.

Hence, the price and quantity indices constructed this way behave just like ordinary prices and quantities.

The two-good model

One common application of Hicksian aggregation is when we are studying the demand for a single good. In this case, think of the *z*-goods as being a single good, *z*, and the *x*-goods as "all other goods." The actual maximization problem is then,

$$\max_{x,z} u(x,z)$$

such that px + *qz* = *m*.

Suppose that the relative prices of the *x*-goods remains constant, so that p = *P*p^0. That is, the vector of prices p is some base price vector p0 times some price index *P*. Then Hicksian aggregation says that we can write the demand function for the *z*-good as,

$$z = z(P, q,m).$$

Since this demand function is homogeneous of degree zero, with some abuse of notation, we can also write,

$$z = z(q/P;\ m/P).$$

This says that the demand for the z-good depends on the relative price of the z-good to "all other goods" and income, divided by the price of "all other goods." In practice, the price index for all other goods is usually taken to be some standard consumer price index. The demand for the z-good becomes a function of only two variables: the price of the z-good relative to the CPI and income relative to the CPI.

Functional separability

The second case in which we can decompose the consumer's consumption decision is known as the case of functional separability. Let us suppose that the underlying preference ordering has the property that

$$(x, z) \succ (x', z) \text{ if and only if } (x, z') \succ (x', z')$$

for all consumption bundles x, x', z and z'. This condition says that if x is preferred to x' for some choices of the other goods, then x is preferred to x' for all choices of the other goods. Or, even more succinctly, the preferences over the x-goods are independent of the z-goods.

If this "independence" property is satisfied and the preferences are locally nonsatiated, then it can be shown that the utility function for x and z can be written in the form u(x, z) = $U(v(\text{x}), \text{z})$, where $U(v, \text{z})$ is an increasing function of v. That is, the overall utility from x and z can be written as a function of the subutility of x, v(x), and the level of consumption of the z-goods.

If the utility function can be written in this form, as suggested, say that the utility function is weakly separable. What does separability imply about the structure of the utility maximization problem? As usual, as suggested, write the demand function for the goods as,

$$\text{x}(\text{p}, \text{q}, m) \text{ and } \text{z}(\text{p}, \text{q}, m). \text{ Let } m_x = \text{px}(\text{p}, \text{q}, m)$$

be the optimal expenditure on the x-goods. It turns out that if the overall utility function is weakly separable, the optimal choice of the x-goods can be found by solving the following subutility maximization problem:

$$\max\ v(\mathrm{x})$$

$$\textit{such that}\ \mathrm{px} = m_x.$$

This means that if we know the expenditure on the x-goods, $m_x = \mathrm{px}(\mathrm{p,q},m)$, we can solve the subutility maximization problem to determine the optimal choice of the x-goods. In other words, the demand for the x-goods is only a function of the prices of the x-goods and the expenditure on the x-goods mx. The prices of the *other* goods are only relevant insofar as they determine the expenditure on the x-goods.

The proof of this is straightforward. Assume that $\mathrm{x}(\mathrm{p, q},m)$ does not solve the problem. Instead, let x' be another value of x that satisfies the budget constraint and yields strictly greater subutility. Then the bundle $(\mathrm{x}', \mathrm{z})$ would give higher overall utility than $(\mathrm{x}(\mathrm{p,q},m), z(\mathrm{p,q},m))$, which contradicts the definition of the demand function.

The demand functions $\mathrm{x}(\mathrm{p},m_x)$ are sometimes known as conditional demand functions since they give demand for the x-goods conditional on the level of expenditure on these goods. Thus, for example, we may consider the demand for beef as a function of the prices of beef, pork, and lamb and the total expenditure on meat.

Let $e(\mathrm{p}, v)$ be the expenditure function for the subutility maximization problem. This tells us how much expenditure on the x-goods is necessary at prices p to achieve the subutility v. It is not hard to see that we can write the overall maximization problem of the consumer as

$$\max_{\mathrm{v,z}} \mathrm{U}(v,\mathrm{z})$$

$$\textit{such that}\ e(\mathrm{p},v) + \mathrm{qz} = m$$

This is almost in the form we want: v is a suitable quantity index for the x-goods, but the price index for the x-goods isn't quite right. We want P times X, but we have some nonlinear function of p and $X = v$.

In order to have a budget constraint that is linear in quantity index, we need to assume that subutility function has a special structure. For example. Suppose that the subutility function is homothetic.

Then we can write $e(\mathrm{p}, v)$ as $e(\mathrm{p})v$. Hence, we can choose our quantity index to be $X = v(\mathrm{x})$, our price index to be $P = e(\mathrm{p})$, and our utility function to be $U(X, \mathrm{z})$.

We get the same X if we solve

$$\max_{X,z} U(X,z)$$

$$\textit{such that } PX + \mathrm{qz} = m$$

as if we solve,

$$\max_{x,z} u(v(x),z)$$

$$\textit{such that } \mathrm{px} + \mathrm{qz} = m.$$

and then aggregate using $X = v(\mathrm{x})$.

In this formulation we can think of the consumption decision as taking place in two stages: first the consumer considers how much of the composite commodity to consume as a function of a price index of meat by solving the overall maximization problem; then the consumer considers how much beef to consume given the prices of the various sorts of meat and the total expenditure on meat, which is the solution to the subutility maximization problem. Such a two-stage budgeting process is very convenient in applied demand analysis.

Aggregating Across Consumers

We have studied the properties of a consumer's demand function, $\mathrm{x}(\mathrm{p}, m)$. Now let us consider some collection of $i = 1, \ldots, n$ consumers, each of whom has a demand function for some L commodities, so that consumer i's demand function is a vector

$$x_i(p,m_i) = \left(x_i^1(p,m_i),\ldots,x_i^L(p,m_i)\right)$$

for $i = 1,\ldots,n$. Note that we have changed our notation slightly: goods are now indicated by superscripts while consumers are indicated by sub-scripts. The aggregate demand function is defined by,

$$X(p,m_1,\ldots,m_n) = \sum_{i=1}^{n} x_i(p,m).$$

The aggregate demand for good l is denoted by Xl(p;m) where m denotes the vector of incomes $(m_1,\ldots,m_n)$. The aggregate demand function inherits certain properties of the individual demand functions. For example, if the individual demand functions are continuous, the aggregate demand function will certainly be continuous. Continuity of the individual demand functions is a sufficient but not necessary condition for continuity of the aggregate demand functions.

What other properties does the aggregate demand function inherit from the individual demands? Is there an aggregate version of Slutsky's equation or of the Strong Axiom of Revealed Preference? Unfortunately, the answer to these questions is no. In fact the aggregate demand function will in general possess no interesting properties other than homogeneity and continuity.

Hence, the theory of the consumer places no restrictions on aggregate behaviour in general. However, in certain cases it may happen that the aggregate behaviour may look as though it were generated by a single "representative" consumer. We consider a circumstance where this may happen.Suppose that all individual consumers' indirect utility functions take the Gorman form:

$$v_i(\mathrm{p},m_i) = a_i(\mathrm{p}) + b(\mathrm{p})m_i.$$

Note that the a_i(p) term can differ from consumer to consumer, but the b(p) term is assumed to be identical for all consumers. By Roy's identity the demand function for good j of consumer i will then take the form

$$x_i^j(p,m_i) = a_i^j(p) + \beta^j(p)m_i.$$

where,

$$a_i^j(p) = -\frac{\dfrac{\partial a_i(p)}{\partial p_j}}{b(p)}$$

$$\beta^j(p) = -\frac{\dfrac{\partial b(p)}{\partial p_j}}{b(p)}.$$

Note that the marginal propensity to consume good *j*,

$$\partial x_i^j(p, m_i)/\partial m_i,$$

is independent of the level of income of any consumer and also constant across consumers since *b*(p) is constant across consumers. The aggregate demand for good *j* will then take the form,

$$X^j\left(p, m^1, \ldots, m^n\right) = -\left[\sum_{i=1}^{n} \frac{\dfrac{\partial a_i}{\partial p_j}}{b(p)} + \frac{\dfrac{\partial b(p)}{\partial p_j}}{b(p)} \sum_{i=1}^{n} m_i\right].$$

This demand function can in fact be generated by a representative consumer. His representative indirect utility function is given by,

$$V(p, M) = \sum_{i=1}^{n} a_i(p) + b(p)M = A(p) + B(p)M,$$

Where,

$$M = \sum_{i=1}^{n} m_i.$$

The proof is simply to apply Roy's identity to this indirect utility function and to note that it yields the demand function given in equation. In fact it can be shown that the Gorman form is the most general form of the indirect utility function that will allow for aggregation in the sense of the representative consumer model.

Hence, the Gorman form is not only *sufficient* for the representative consumer model to hold, but it is also *necessary*. Although a complete proof of this fact is rather detailed, the following argument is reasonably convincing. Suppose, for the sake of simplicity, that there are only two consumers. Then by hypothesis the aggregate demand for good j can be written as,

$$X^j(p, m_1 + m_2) \equiv x_1^j(p, m_1) + x_2^j(p, m_2).$$

If we first differentiate with respect to m_1 and then with respect to m_2, we find the following identities,

$$\frac{\partial^2 X^j(p, M)}{\partial M} \equiv \frac{\partial x_1^j(p, m_1)}{\partial m_1} \equiv \frac{\partial x_2^j(p, m_2)}{\partial m_2}.$$

Hence, the marginal propensity to consume good j must be the same for all consumers.

If we differentiate this expression once more with respect to m_1, we find that,

$$\frac{\partial^2 X^j(p, M)}{\partial M^2} \equiv \frac{\partial^2 x_1^j(p, m_1)}{\partial m_1^2} \equiv 0.$$

Thus, consumer 1's demand for good j–and, therefore, consumer 2's demand {is affine in income. Hence, the demand functions for good j take the form,

$$x_i^j(p, m_i) = a_i^j(p) + \beta^j(p) m_i.$$

If this is true for all goods, the indirect utility function for each consumer must have the Gorman form. One special case of a utility function having the Gorman form is a utility function that is homothetic. In this case the indirect utility function has the form $v(\mathrm{p}, m) = v(\mathrm{p})m$, which is clearly of the Gorman form. Another special case is that of a quasi-linear utility function. A utility function U is said to be quasi-linear if it has the following functional form:

$$U(x_0, x_1,...,x_L) = x_0 + u(x_1,....,x_L)$$

In this case $v(\text{p},m) = v(\text{p}) + m$, which obviously has the Gorman form. Many of the properties possessed by homothetic and/or quasi-linear utility functions are also possessed by the Gorman form. The class of quasi-linear utility function is a very important class of utility functions which plays an important role in many economics fields such as those of information economics, mechanism design theory, property rights theory due to its important property of no income effect when income changes.

THE MONEY METRIC UTILITY FUNCTIONS

There is a nice construction involving the expenditure function that comes up in a variety of places in welfare economics. Consider some prices p and some given bundle of goods x. We can ask the following question: how much money would a given consumer need at the prices p to be as well of as he could be by consuming the bundle of goods x? If we know the consumer's preferences, we can simply solve the following problem:

$$m(p,x) \equiv \min_{z} pz$$

$$\text{such that } u(\text{z}) \geqq u(\text{x}).$$

That is,

$$m(\text{p, x}) \equiv e(\text{p}, u(\text{x})).$$

This type of function is called money metric utility function. It is also known as the "minimum income function," the 'direct compensation function," and by a variety of other names. Since, for fixed p,m(p, x) is simply a monotonic transform of the utility function and is itself a utility function. There is a similar construct for indirect utility known as the money metric indirect utility function, which is given by,

$$\mu(\text{p,q},m) \equiv e(p, v(q,m)).$$

That is, $\mu(p,q,m)$ measures how much money one would need at prices p to be as well of as one would be facing prices q and having income m. Just as in the direct case, $\mu(p, q,m)$ is simply a monotonic transformation of an indirect utility function.

Example: The CES utility function is given by

$$u(x_1,x_2)=\left(x_1^{\rho}+x_2^{\rho}\right)^{1/\rho},$$

where $0 \neq \rho < 1$. It can be easily verified this utility func-tion is strictly monotonic increasing and strictly concave. Since preferences are invariant with respect to monotonic transforms of utility, we could just as well choose,

$$u(x_1,x_2)=\frac{1}{\rho}ln\left(x_1^{\rho}+x_2^{\rho}\right).$$

The first-order conditions are,

$$\frac{x_1^{\rho-1}}{x_1^{\rho}+x_2^{\rho}}-\lambda p_1=0$$

$$\frac{x_2^{\rho-1}}{x_1^{\rho}+x_2^{\rho}}-\lambda p_2=0$$

$$p_1x_1+p_2x_2=m$$

Dividing the first equation by the second equation and then solving for x_2, we have

$$x_2=x_1\left(\frac{p_2}{p_1}\right)^{\frac{1}{\rho-1}}.$$

Substituting the equation in the budget line and solving for $x1$, we obtain,

$$x_1(p,m)=\frac{p_1^{\frac{1}{\rho-1}}m}{p_1^{\frac{\rho}{\rho-1}}+p_2^{\frac{\rho}{\rho-1}}}$$

and thus,

$$x_2(p,m) = \frac{p_2^{\frac{1}{\rho-1}} m}{p_1^{\frac{\rho}{\rho-1}} + p_2^{\frac{\rho}{\rho-1}}}$$

Substituting the demand functions into the utility function, we get the indirect CES utility function:

$$\upsilon(p,m) = \left(p_1^{\rho/(\rho-1)} + p_2^{\rho/(\rho-1)}\right)^{1-\rho/\rho} m$$

or

$$\upsilon(p,m) = \left(p_1^r + p_2^r\right)^{-1/r} m$$

where r = ρ=(ρ–1). Inverting the equation, we obtain the expenditure function for the CES utility function which has the form,

$$e(p,u) = \left(p_1^r + p_2^r\right)^{1/r} u.$$

Consequently, the money metric direct and indirect utility functions are given by,

$$m(p,x) = \left(p_1^r + p_2^r\right)^{1/r} \left(x_1^\rho + x_2^\rho\right)^{1/\rho}$$

and,

$$\mu(p;q,m) = \left(p_1^r + p_2^r\right)^{1/r} \left(q_1^r + q_2^r\right)^{-1/r} m.$$

The CES utility function contains several other well-known utility functions as special cases, depending on the value of the parameter ρ.

- The linear utility function (ρ = 1). Simple substitution yields

$$y = x_1 + x_2.$$

- The Cobb-Douglas utility function (ρ = 0). When ρ = 0 the CES utility function is not defined, due to division by zero. However, as suggested, show that as ρ approaches zero, the indifference curves of the CES utility function look very much like the indifference curves of the Cobb-Douglas utility function.

This is easiest to see using the marginal rate of substitution. By direct calculation,

$$MRS = -\left(\frac{x_1}{x_2}\right)^{\rho-1}.$$

As ρ approaches zero, this tends to a limit of

$$MRS = \frac{x_2}{x_1},$$

which is simply the *MRS* for the Cobb-Douglas utility function.

- The Leontief utility function (ρ =–∞). We have just seen that the *MRS* of the CES utility function is given by equation. As ρ approaches–∞, this expression approaches

$$MRS = -\left(\frac{x_1}{x_2}\right)^{-\infty} = -\left(\frac{x_2}{x_1}\right)^{\infty}.$$

If $x2 > x1$ the *MRS* is (negative) infinity; if $x2 < x1$ the *MRS* is zero. This means that as ρ approaches–∞, a CES indifference curves looks like an indi®erence curves associated with the Leontief utility function.

Some Important Identities

There are some important identities that tie together the expenditure function, the indirect utility function, the Marshallian demand function, and the Hicksian demand function.

Let us consider the utility maximization problem

$$v(\text{p}, m^*) = \max u(\text{x})$$

$$\text{such that px} \leqq m^*:$$

Let x* be the solution to this problem and let $u^* = u(\text{x}^*)$.

Consider the expenditure minimization problem,

$$e(\mathrm{p}, u^*) = \min \mathrm{px}$$

$$\text{such that } u(\mathrm{x}) = u^*.$$

An inspection of Figure should convince you that the answers to these two problems should be the same x*. Formally, we have the following proposition.

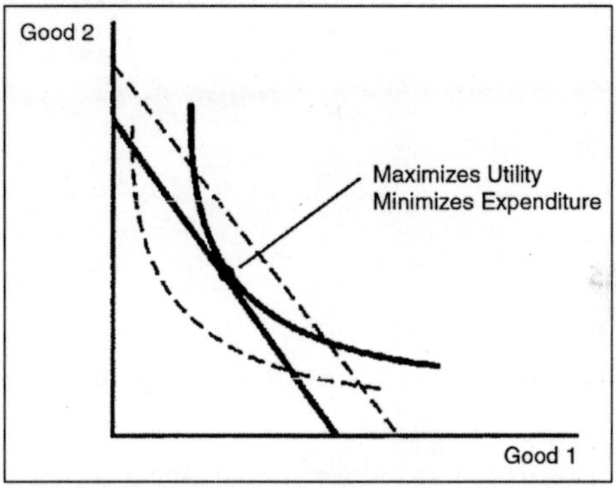

Fig: Maximize Utility and Minimize Expenditure are Normally Equivalent.

Proposition: Suppose the utility function u is continuous and locally non-satiated, and suppose that m > 0. *If the* solutions both problems exist, then the two problems have the same solution x*. That is,

- *Utility maximization implies expenditure minimization*: Let x* *be a solution to, and let* $u = u(\mathrm{x}^*)$. *Then* x* *solves.*
- *Expenditure minimization implies utility maximization*: Suppose that the assumptions are satisfied and that x*solves. Let m = px*. Then x* solves.

Proof:

- Suppose not, and let x′ solve. Hence, px′ < px* and $u(\mathrm{x}') = u(\mathrm{x}^*)$. By local nonsatiation there is a bundle x″ close enough to x′ so that px″ < px* = m and $u(\mathrm{x}'') > u(\mathrm{x}')$. But then x′ cannot be a solution to.
- Suppose not, and let x*0* solve so that $u(\mathrm{x}0) > u(\mathrm{x}^*)$ and px′ = px* = m. Since px* > 0 and utility is continuous,

we can find $0 < t < 1$ such that $ptx' < px^* = m$ and $u(tx')$ $> u(x^*)$. Hence, x cannot solve.

This proposition leads to four important identities that is summarized in the followingn proposition.

Proposition: Suppose the utility function u is continuous and locally non-satiated, and suppose that m > 0. Then we have

- $e(p, v(p,m)) \equiv m$. *The minimum expenditure necessary to reach utility* $v(p,m)$ *is* m.
- $v(p, e(p, u)) \equiv u$. *The maximum utility from income* $e(p, u)$ *is* u.
- $x_i(p,m) \equiv h_i(p, v(p,m))$. *The Marshallian demand at income m is the same as the Hicksian demand at utility* $v(p,m)$.
- $h_i(p, u) \equiv x_i(p, e(p, u))$. *The Hicksian demand at utility u is the same as the Marshallian demand at income* $e(p, u)$.

This last identity is perhaps the most important since it ties together the "observable" Marshallian demand function with the "unobservable" Hicksian demand function. Thus, any demanded bundle can be expressed *either* as the solution to the utility maximization problem or the expenditure minimization problem.

A nice application of one of these identities is given in the next proposition: Roy's identity. *If* x(p,*m*) *is the Marshallian demand function, then,*

$$x_i(p,m) = -\frac{\dfrac{\partial v(p,m)}{\partial p_i}}{\dfrac{\partial v(p,m)}{\partial m}} \; for\, i = 1,...,k$$

provided that the right-hand side is well defined and that pi > 0 and *m* > 0.

Proof: Suppose that x* yields a maximal utility of u^* at (p^*, m^*). We know from our identities that

$$x(p^*, m^*) \equiv h(p^*, u^*).$$

From another one of the fundamental identities, we also know that

$$u^* \equiv v(\mathrm{p},\ e(\mathrm{p},\ u^*)).$$

Since this is an identity we can differentiate it with respect to p_i to get,

$$0 = \frac{\partial \upsilon(p^*, m^*)}{\partial p_i} + \frac{\partial \upsilon(p^*, m^*)}{\partial m}\frac{\partial e(p^*, u^*)}{\partial p_i}.$$

Rearranging, and combining this with identity, we have,

$$x_i(p^*, m^*) \equiv h_i(p^*, u^*) \equiv \frac{\partial e(p^*, u^*)}{\partial p_i} \equiv -\frac{\partial \upsilon(p^*, m^*)/\partial p_i}{\partial \upsilon(p^*, m^*)/\partial m}.$$

Since this identity is satisfied for all (p^*, m^*) and since $\mathrm{x}^* = \mathrm{x}(\mathrm{p}^*, m^*)$, the result is proved.

Example: Consider the indirect Cobb-Douglas utility function:

$$\upsilon(p, m) = \prod_{l=1}^{L}\left(\frac{\alpha_l m}{\alpha p_l}\right)\alpha_l$$

where,

$$\sum_{l=1}^{L}\alpha_l.$$

Then we have

$$\upsilon_{pl} \equiv \frac{\partial \upsilon(p, m)}{\partial_{pl}} = -\frac{\alpha_l}{p_j}\upsilon(p, m)$$

$$\upsilon_m \equiv \frac{\partial \upsilon(p, m)}{\partial m} = -\frac{\alpha}{m}\upsilon(p, m)$$

Thus, Roy's identity gives the demand functions as

$$x_l(p, m) = \frac{\alpha_l m}{\alpha p_l},\ l = 1, 2, \ldots., L.$$

Example: Suppose a preference ordering is represented by the Leontief utility function is given by:

$$u(x) = \min\left\{\frac{x_1}{a_1}, \frac{x_2}{a_2}, \ldots, \frac{x_L}{a_L}\right\}$$

which is not itself differentiable, but the indirect utility function:

$$\upsilon(p,m) = \frac{m}{ap}$$

where $a = (a_1, a_2, \ldots, a_L)$ and ap is the inner product, which is differentiable. Applying Roy's identity, we have

$$x_l(p,m) = -\frac{\upsilon_{p_l}(p,m)}{\upsilon_m(p,m)} = \frac{a_l m}{(ap)^2} / \frac{1}{ap} = \frac{a_l m}{ap}$$

Hence, Roy's identity often works well even if the differentiability properties of the statement do not hold.

Example: The CES utility function is given by,

$$u(x_1, x_2) = \left(x_1^{\rho} + x_2^{\rho}\right)^{1/\rho}.$$

We have derived earlier that the indirect utility function is given by:

$$\upsilon(p,m) = \left(p_1^r + p_2^r\right)^{-1/r} m.$$

The demand functions can be found by Roy's law:

$$x_l(p,m) = \frac{-\partial\upsilon(p,m)/\partial p_l}{\partial\upsilon(p,m)/\partial m} = \frac{\frac{1}{r}\left(p_1^r + p_2^{r\,-\left(1+\frac{1}{r}\right)} mrp_l^{r-1}\right)}{\left(p_1^r + p_2^r\right)^{-1/r}}$$

$$= \frac{p_l^{r-1} m}{\left(p_1^r + p_2^r\right)}, \quad l = 1, 2.$$

9

Demand Forecasting

Today business enterprises are working under the conditions of uncertainties. Uncertainties can be minimized through planning and forecasting. The success of a business firm depends upon its ability to forecast future events.

MEANING OF DEMAND FORECASTING

Future is uncertain. There is great deal of uncertainty with regard to demand. Since the demand is uncertain, production, cost, revenue, profit etc. are also uncertain. Through forecasting it is possible to minimise the uncertainties. Forecasting simply refers to estimating or anticipating future events. It is an attempt to foresee the future by examining the past. Thus demand forecasting means estimating or anticipating future demand on the basis of past data.

Objectives of Demand Forecasting

Short Term Objectives:

- To help in preparing suitable sales and production policies.
- To help in ensuring a regular supply of raw materials.
- To reduce the cost of purchase and avoid unnecessary purchase.
- To ensure best utilization of machines.
- To make arrangements for skilled and unskilled workers so that suitable labour force may be maintained.

- To help in the determination of a suitable price policy.
- To determine financial requirements.
- To determine separate sales targets for all the sales territories.
- To eliminate the problem of under or over production.

Long term Objectives:

- To plan long term production.
- To plan plant capacity.
- To estimate the requirements of workers for long period and make arrangements.
- To determine an appropriate dividend policy.
- To help the proper capital budgeting.
- To plan long term financial requirements.
- To forecast the future problems of material supplies and energy crisis.

Factors Affecting Demand Forecasting

For making a good forecast, it is essential to consider the various factors governing demand forecasting. These factors are summarized as follows.

- *Prevailing business conditions:* While preparing demand forecast it becomes necessary to study the general economic conditions very carefully. These include the price level changes, change in national income, percapita income, consumption pattern, savings and investment habits, employment etc.
- *Conditions within the industry:* Every business enterprise is only a unit of a particular industry. Sales of that business enterprise are only a part of the total sales of that industry. Therefore, while preparing demand forecasts for a particular business enterprise, it becomes necessary to study the changes in the demand of the whole industry, number of units within the industry, design and quality of product, price policy, competition within the industry etc.

- *Conditions within the firm:* Internal factors of the firm also affect the demand forecast. These factors include plant capacity of the firm, quality of the product, price of the product, advertising and distribution policies, production policies, financial policies etc.
- *Factors affecting export trade:* If a firm is engaged in export trade also it should consider the factors affecting the export trade. These factors include import and export control, terms and conditions of export, exim policy, export conditions, export finance etc.
- *Market behaviour:* While preparing demand forecast, it is required to consider the market behaviour which brings about changes in demand. 6. Sociological conditions: Sociological factors have their own impact on demand forecast of the company. These conditions relate to size of population, density, change in age groups, size of family, family life cycle, level of education, family income, social awareness etc.
- *Psychological conditions:* While estimating the demand for the product, it becomes necessary to take into consideration such factors as changes in consumer tastes, habits, fashions, likes and dislikes, attitudes, perception, life styles, cultural and religious bents etc.
- *Competitive conditions:* The competitive conditions within the industry may change. Competitors may enter into market or go out of market. A demand forecast prepared without considering the activities of competitors may not be correct.

Process of Demand Forecasting/ Steps in Demand Forecasting

Demand forecasting involves the following steps:

- Determine the purpose for which forecasts are used.
- Subdivide the demand forecasting programme into small I parts on the basis of product or sales territories or markets.
- Determine the factors affecting the sale of each product and their relative importance.

- Select the forecasting methods.
- Study the activities of competitors.
- Prepare preliminary sales estimates after, collecting necessary data.
- Analyse advertisement policies, sales promotion plans, personal sales arrangements etc. and ascertain how far these programmes have been successful in promoting the sales.
- Evaluate the demand forecasts monthly, quarterly, half yearly or yearly and necessary adjustments should be done.
- Prepare the final demand forecast on the basis of preliminary forecasts and the results of evaluation.

METHODS OF DEMAND FORECASTING (FOR ESTABLISHED PRODUCTS)

There are several methods to predict the future demand. All methods can be broadly classified into two.

Survey Methods

Under this method surveys are conducted to collect information about the future purchase plans of potential consumers. Survey methods help in obtaining information about the desires, likes and dislikes of consumers through collecting the opinion of experts or by interviewing the consumers. Survey methods are used for short term forecasting. Important survey methods are:

- Consumers interview method,
- Collective opinion or sales force opinion method
- Experts opinion method,
- Consumers clinic and
- End use method.

Consumers' Interview Method (Consumers Survey)

Under this method, consumers are interviewed directly and asked the quantity they would like to buy. After collecting the data, the total demand for the product is calculated. This is done by adding up all individual demands. Under the consumer interview method, either all consumers or selected few are interviewed. When all the consumers are interviewed, the method is known as complete enumeration method. When only a selected group of consumers are interviewed, it is known as sample survey method

Advantages:

- It is a simple method because it is not based on past record.
- It suitable for industrial products.
- The results are likely to be more accurate.
- This method can be used for forecasting the demand of a new product.

Disadvantages:

- It is expensive and time consuming.
- Consumers may not give their secrets or buying plans.
- This method is not suitable for long term forecasting.
- It is not suitable when the number of consumer is large.

Collective Opinion Method

Under this method the salesmen estimate the expected sales in their respective territories on the basis of previous experience. Then demand is estimated after combining the individual forecasts (sales estimates) of the salesmen. This method is also known as sales force opinion method.

Advantages: This method is simple.

- It is based on the first hand knowledge of Salesmen.
- This method is particularly useful for estimating demand of new products.
- It utilises the specialised knowledge of salesmen who are in close touch with the prevailing market conditions.

Disadvantages:

- The forecasts may not be reliable if the salespeople are not trained.

- It is not suitable for long period estimation.
- It is not flexible.
- Salesmen may give lower estimates that make possible easy achievement of sales quotas fixed for each salesman.

Experts' Opinion Method

This method was originally developed at Rand Corporation in 1950 by Olaf Helmer, Dalkey and Gordon. Under this method, demand is estimated on the basis of opinions of experts and distributors other than salesmen and ordinary consumers. This method is also known as Delphi method. Delphi is the ancient Greek temple where people come and prey for information about their future.

Advantages:

- Forecast can be made quickly and economically
- This is a reliable method because estimates are made on the basis of knowledge and experience of sales experts.
- The firm need not spare its time on preparing estimates of demand.
- This method is suitable for new products.

Disadvantages:

- This method is expensive.
- This method sometimes lacks reliability

Consumer Clinics

In this method some selected buyers are given certain amounts of money and asked to buy the products. Then the prices are changed and the consumers are asked to make fresh purchases with the given money. In this way the consumers" responses to price changes are observed. Thus the behaviour of the consumers is studied. On this basis demand is estimated. This method is an improvement over consumer's interview method.

Merits:

- It provides an opportunity to study the behaviour of consumers directly.

- It provides reliable and realistic picture about future demand.
- It gives useful information to aid in the decision making process.

Demerits:

- It is a time consuming method.
- Selecting the participants is very difficult.
- It is expensive.
- Consumers may take it as a game. They may not reveal their preferences.

End use Method

This method is based on the fact that a product generally has different uses. In the end use method, first a list of end users (final consumers, individual industries, exporters etc.) is prepared. Then the future demand for the product is found either directly from the end users or indirectly by estimating their future growth. Then the demand of all end users of the product is added to get the total demand for the product.

Statistical Methods

Statistical methods use the past data as a guide for knowing the level of future demand. Statistical methods are generally used for long run forecasting. These methods are used for established products. Statistical methods include:

- Trend projection method,
- Regression and Correlation,
- Extrapolation method,
- Simultaneous equation method, and
- Barometric method.

Trend Projection Method

Future sales are based on the past sales, because future is the grand-child of the past and child of the present. Under the trend projection method demand is estimated on the basis of analysis of past data. This method makes use of time series (data over a period of time). We try to ascertain the trend in the time series. The trend in the time series can be estimated by using any one of the following four methods:

- Least-square method,
- Free-hand method,
- Moving average method and
- semi-average method.

Regression and Correlation

These methods combine economic theory and statistical technique of estimation. Under these methods the relationship between the sales and other variables is ascertained. Such relationship established on the basis of past data may be used to analyse the future trend. The regression and correlation analysis is also called the econometric model building.

Extrapolation

Under this statistical method, the future demand can be extrapolated by applying Binomial expansion method. This method is used on the assumption that the rate of charge in demand in the past has been uniform.

Simultaneous Equation Method

This involves the development of a complete econometric model which can explain the behaviour of all the variables which the company can control. This method is not very popular.

Barometric Technique

This is an improvement over the trend projection method. According to this technique the events of the present can be used to predict the directions of change m the future. Here certain economic and statistical indicators from the selected time series are used to predict variables. Personal income, non-agricultural placements, gross national income, prices of industrial materials, wholesale commodity prices, industrial production, bank deposits etc. are some of the most commonly used indicators.

Advantages of Statistical Methods:

- The method of estimation is scientific
- Estimation is based on the theoretical relationship between sales (dependent variable) and price, advertising, income etc. (independent variables)
- These are less expensive.
- Results are relatively more reliable.

Disadvantages of Statistical Methods:

- These methods involve complicated calculations.
- These do not rely much on personal skill and experience.
- These methods require considerable technical skill and experience in order to be effective.

Methods of Demand Forecasting for New Products

Demand forecasting of new product is more difficult than forecasting for existing product. The reason is that the product is not available. Hence, no historical data are available. In these conditions the forecasting is to be done by taking into consideration the inclination and wishes of the customers to purchase. For this a research is to be conducted. But there is one problem that it is difficult for a customer to say anything without seeing and using the product before. Thus it is very difficult to forecast the demand for new products. Any way Prof. Joel Dean has suggested the following methods for forecasting demand of new products:

- *Evolutionary approach:* This method is based on the assumption that the new product is the improvement and evolution of the old product. The demand is forecasted on the basis of the demand of the old product. For example, the demand for black and white TV should be taken in to consideration while forecasting the demand for colour TV sets because the latter is an improvement of the former.
- *Substitute approach:* Here the new product is treated as a substitute of an existing product, *e.g.* polythene bags for cloth bags. Thus the demand for a new product

is analysed as a substitute for some existing goods or service.

- *Growth curve approach:* Under this method the growth rate of demand of a new product is estimated on the basis of the growth rate of demand of an existing product. Suppose Pears soap is in use and a new cosmetic is to be introduced in the market. In this case the average sale of Pears soap will give an idea as to how the new cosmetic will be accepted by the consumers.
- *Opinion poll approach:* Under this method the demand for a new product is estimated on the basis of information collected from the direct interviews (survey) with consumers.
- *Sales Experience approach:* Under this method, the new product is offered for sale in a sample market, *i.e.* by direct mail or through multiple shop or departmental shop. From this the total demand is estimated for the whole market.
- *Vicarious approach:* This method consists of surveying consumers' reactions through the specialised dealers who are in touch with consumers. The dealers are able to know as to how the customers will accept the new product. On the basis of their reports demand can be estimated.

The above methods are not mutually exclusive. It is de desirable to use a combination of two or more methods in order to get better results.

10

Capital Costs

In business terms the word capital refers to money. Capital costs are the fees associated with the initial setup of a plant or project. Capital costs will usually only occur at the beginning of a project, as the operational costs cover reoccurring business expenses. It may take a wide array of resources to begin a business, so capital costs may finance a number of expenses. The cost of capital will vary depending on the type and size of the business being established.

In order to build an entire plant, capital costs may need to cover the expense of materials and labour to create the new structure. Capital costs tend to mostly cover costs incurred as the result of buying land and building a plant or structure for business use. In order to account for these expenses, they are capitalized and added to the cost of the asset.

If the expenses were deducted in one large sum, it could be potentially devastating to a new business. These costs are instead capitalized and deducted over time from depreciation or depletion. Most capitalized costs are considered to be fixed assets. Since fixed assets are not included in current net income, they tend to affect net income slowly, over several financial periods. Capitalized costs may be considered fixed assets since they include any facility the company constructs for its own use, such as a wind or power plant. Other costs that may be considered fixed assets are real estate developments that may be leased or sold, large office buildings and ships. Being categorized as a fixed asset makes the company's funds both an equity and a debt. Eventually, for a business to remain intact, the return on the capital must reach a higher point than the cost of capital. The company typically needs to make enough money so investors receive at least their original return on the initial investment of capital costs. The Weighted Average Cost of Capital (WACC) is a calculation formula that is used to measure a company's capital costs. This calculation is done prior to financing to estimate if a business venture will be worth the risk. This weighted average includes the cost of debt, the market value of equity equivalents and the total capital amount projected for business start-up. This is a fairly useful tool for determining whether the capital costs are a good investment, but the formula does become more complex if there are multiple funding sources to account for or if there is currency exchange involved in the calculation.

COST STATEMENT OR COST SHEET

You are running a factory which manufactures electronic toys. You incur expenses on raw material, labour and other expenses which can be directly attibuted to cost and which cannot be directly attributed but are incurred upto their sales. You need to know the composition of cost at different stages. This will help you in the analysis of cost of a product so that same can be used for its proper management. In this lesson you will learn about cost sheet and its various components.

Cost Sheet: Meaning And Its Importance

Cost sheet is a statement, which shows various components of total cost of a product. It classifies and analyses the components of cost of a product. Previous periods data is given in the cost sheet for comparative study. It is a statement which shows per unit cost in addition to Total Cost. Selling price is ascertained with the help of cost sheet. The details of total cost presented in the form of a statement is termed as Cost sheet. Cost sheet is prepared on the basis of:

- Historical Cost
- Estimated Cost

Historical Cost

Historical Cost sheet is prepared on the basis of actual cost incurred. A statement of cost prepared after incurring the actual cost is called Historical Cost Sheet.

Estimated Cost

Estimated cost sheet is prepared on the basis of estimated cost. The statement prepared before the commencement of production is called estimated cost sheet. Such cost sheet is useful in quoting the tender price of a job or a contract.

Importance of Cost Sheet

The importance of cost sheet is as follows:

- Cost ascertainment: The main objective of the cost sheet is to ascertain the cost of a product. Cost sheet helps in ascertainment of cost for the purpose of determining cost after they are incurred. It also helps to ascertain the actual cost or estimated cost of a Job.
- Fixation of selling price: To fix the selling price of a product or service, it is essential to prepare the cost sheet. It helps in fixing selling price of a product or service by providing detailed information of the cost.
- Help in cost control: For controlling the cost of a product it is necessary for every manufacturing unit to prepare a cost sheet. Estimated cost sheet helps in the control of material cost, labour cost and overheads cost at every point of production.
- Facilitates managerial decisions: It helps in taking important decisions by the management such as: whether to produce or buy a component, what prices of goods are to be quoted in the tender, whether to retain or replace an existing machine etc.

Components Of Total Cost

The Components of cost are shown in the classified and analytical form in the cost sheet. Components of total cost are as follows:

Prime Cost

It consists of direct material, direct wages and direct expenses. In other words "Prime cost represents the aggregate of cost of material consumed, productive wages, and direct expenses". It is also known as basic, first, flat or direct cost of a product.

Prime Cost = Direct material + Direct Wages + Direct expenses

Direct material means cost of raw material used or consumed in production. It is not necessary that all the material purchased in a particular period is used in production. There is some stock of raw material in balance at opening and closing of the period. Hence, it is necessary that the cost of opening and closing stock of material is adjusted in the material purchased. Opening stock of material is added and closing stock of raw material is deducted in the material purchased and we get material consumed or used in production of a product. It is calculated as:

Material Consumed = Material purchased + Opening stock of material– Closing stock of material.

Factory Cost

In addition to prime cost it includes works or factory overheads. Factory overheads consist of cost of indirect material, indirect wages, and indirect expenses incurred in the factory. Factory cost is also known as works cost, production or manufacturing cost.

Factory Cost = Prime cost + Factory overheads

COST CONTROL

Cost control, also known as cost management or cost containment, is a broad set of cost accounting methods and management techniques with the common goal of improving business cost-efficiency by reducing costs, or at least restricting their rate of growth. Businesses use cost control methods to monitor, evaluate, and ultimately enhance the efficiency of specific areas, such as departments, divisions, or product lines, within their operations.

During the 1990s cost control initiatives received paramount attention from corporate America. Often taking the form of corporate restructuring, divestment of peripheral activities, mass layoffs, or outsourcing, cost control strategies were seen as necessary to preserve—or boost—corporate profits and to maintain—or gain—a competitive advantage. The objective was often to be the low-cost producer in a given industry, which would typically allow the company to take a greater profit per unit of sales than its competitors at a given price level.

Some cost control proponents believe that such strategic cost-cutting must be planned carefully, as not all cost reduction techniques yield the same benefits. In a notable late 1990s example, chief executive Albert J. Dunlap, nicknamed "Chainsaw Al" because of his penchant for deep cost cutting at the companies he headed, failed to restore the ailing small appliance maker Sunbeam Corporation to profitability despite his drastic cost reduction tactics. Dunlap laid off thousands of workers and sold off business units, but made little contribution to Sunbeam's competitive position or share price in his two years as CEO. Consequently, in 1998 Sunbeam's board fired Dunlap, having lost confidence in his "one-trick" approach to management.

Cost Control Applications

A complex business requires frequent information about operations in order to plan for the future, to control present activities, and to evaluate the past performance of managers, employees, and related business segments. To be successful, management guides the activities of its people in the operations of the business according to pre-established goals and objectives. Management's guidance takes two forms of control:

- The management and supervision of behaviour, and
- The evaluation of performance.

Behavioural management deals with the attitudes and actions of employees. While employee behaviour ultimately impacts on success, behavioural management involves certain issues and assumptions not applicable to accounting's control function. On the other hand, performance evaluation measures outcomes of employee's actions by comparing the actual results of business outcomes to predetermined standards of success. In this way management identifies the strengths it needs to maximize, and the weaknesses it seeks to rectify. This process of evaluation and remedy is called cost control.

Cost control is a continuous process that begins with the proposed annual budget. The budget helps:

- To organize and coordinate production, and the selling, distribution, service, and administrative functions; and
- To take maximum advantage of available opportunities.

As the fiscal year progresses, management compares actual results with those projected in the budget and incorporates into the new plan the lessons learned from its evaluation of current operations.

Control refers to management's effort to influence the actions of individuals who are responsible for performing tasks, incurring costs, and generating revenues. Management is a two-phased process: planning refers to the way that management plans and wants people to perform, while control refers to the procedures employed to determine whether actual performance complies with these plans. Through the budget process and accounting control, management establishes overall company objectives, defines the centers of responsibility, determines specific objectives for each responsibility center, and designs procedures and standards for reporting and evaluation.

A budget segments the business into its components or centers where the responsible party initiates and controls action. Responsibility centers represent applicable organizational units, functions, departments, and divisions. Generally a single individual heads the responsibility center exercising substantial, if not complete, control over the activities of people or processes within the center and controlling the results of their activity. Cost centers are accountable only for expenses, that is, they do not generate revenue. Examples include accounting departments, human resources departments, and similar areas of the business that provide internal services. Profit centers accept responsibility for both revenue and expenses. For example, a product line or an autonomous business unit might be considered profit centers. If the profit center has its own assets, it may also be considered an investment center, for which returns on investment can be determined. The use of responsibility centers allows management to design control reports to pinpoint accountability, thus aiding in profit planning.

A budget also sets standards to indicate the level of activity expected from each responsible person or decision unit, and the amount of resources that a responsible party should use in achieving that level of activity. A budget establishes the responsibility center, delegates the concomitant responsibilities, and determines the decision points within an organization.

The planning process provides for two types of control mechanisms:

- Feedforward: providing a basis for control at the point of action; and
- Feedback: providing a basis for measuring the effectiveness of control after implementation.

Management's role is to feedforward a futuristic vision of where the company is going and how it is to get there, and to make clear decisions coordinating and directing employee activities. Management also oversees the development of procedures to collect, record, and evaluate feedback. Therefore, effective management controls results from leading people by force of personality and through persuasion; providing and maintaining proper training, planning, and resources; and improving quality and results through evaluation and feedback.

Control Reports

Control reports are informational reports that tell management about an entity's activities. Management requests control reports only for internal use, and, therefore, directs the accounting department to develop tailor-made reporting formats. Accounting provides management with a format designed to detect variations that need investigating. In addition, management also refers to conventional reports such as the income statement and funds statement, and external reports on the general economy and the specific industry.

Control reports, then, need to provide an adequate amount of information so that management may determine the reasons for any cost variances from the original budget. A good control report highlights significant information by focusing management's attention on those items in which actual performance significantly differs from the standard.

Because key success factors shift in type and number, accounting revises control reports when necessary. Accounting also varies the control period covered by the control report to encompass a period in which management can take useful remedial action. In addition, accounting disseminates control reports in a timely fashion to give management adequate time to act before the issuance of the next report.

Managers perform effectively when they attain the goals and objectives set by the budget. With respect to profits, managers succeed by the degree to which revenues continually exceed expenses. In applying the following simple formula, managers, especially those in operations, realize that they exercise more control over expenses than they do over revenue.

While they cannot predict the timing and volume of actual sales, they can determine the utilization rate of most of their resources, that is, they can influence the cost side. Hence, the evaluation of management's performance and its operations is cost control.

Standards

For cost control purposes, a budget provides standard costs. As management constructs budgets, it lays out a road map to guide its efforts. It states a number of assumptions about the relationships and interaction among the economy, market dynamics, the abilities of its sales force, and its capacity to provide the proper quantity and quality of products demanded.

An examination of the details of the budget calculations and assumptions indicates that management expects the sales force to spend only so much in pursuit of the sales forecast. The details also reveal that management expects operations to produce the required amount of units within a certain cost range. Management bases its expectations and projections on the best historical and current information, as well as its best business judgement.

When calculating budget expenses, management's review of the historic and current data might strongly suggest that the production of 1,000 units of a certain luxury item will cost $100,000, or $100 per unit. In addition, management also determines that the sales force will expend about $80,000 to sell the 1,000 units. This is a sales expenditure of $80. With total expenditures of $180, management sets the selling price of $500 for this luxury item.

At the close of a month, management compares the actual results of that month to the standard costs to determine the degree and direction of any variance. The purpose for analyzing variances is to identify areas where costs need containment.

In the above illustration, accounting indicates to management that the sales force sold 100 units for a gross revenue of $50,000. Accounting data also shows that the sales force spent $7,000 that month, and that production incurred $12,000 in expenses. Table summarizes the data that management reviews to identify variances. While revenue was on target, actual sales expense came in less than projected, with a per unit cost of $70. This is a favourable variance. Production expenses registered an unfavourable variance since actual expenditures exceeded the projected. The company produced units at $120 per item, $20 more than projected. This variance of 20 percent significantly differs from the standard costs of $100 and would call management to action if the variance exceeded acceptable levels.

COST AND CONTROL OF MATERIALS

Understanding the Material

Material is anything made of matter, constituted of one or more substances. Wood, cement, hydrogen, air and water are all examples of materials. Sometimes the term "material" is used more narrowly to refer to substances or components with certain physical properties that are used as inputs to production or manufacturing. In this sense, materials are the parts required to make something else, from buildings and art to stars and computers.

Dispensation and Raw Materials

A material can be anything: a finished product in its own right or an unprocessed raw material. Raw materials are first extracted or harvested from the earth and divided into a form that can be easily transported and stored, then processed to produce semi-finished materials. These can be input into a new cycle of production and finishing processes to create finished materials, ready for distribution, construction, and consumption.

Costing Materials Established

Payments and Discounts

Discounts and allowances are reductions to a basic price of goods or services. The can occur anywhere in the distribution channel, modifying either the manufacturer's list price, the retail price, or the list price. There are many purposes for discounting, including; to increase short-term sales, to move out-of-date stock, to reward valuable customers, to encourage distribution channel members to perform a function, or to otherwise reward behaviours that benefit the discount issuer. Some discounts and allowances are forms of sales promotion.

Types

Dealing with payment:

- *Prompt payment discount:* Trade Discount:Deduction in price given by the wholesaler/manufacturer to the retailer at the list price or catalogue price. Cash Discount:Reduction in price given by the creditor to the debitor is known as cash discount. This discount is intended to speed payment and thereby provide liquidity to the firm. They are sometimes used as a promotional device.

- *Preferred payment method discount:* Some retailers offer discounts to customers paying with cash, to avoid paying fees on credit card transactions.
- *Partial payment discount:* Similar to the Trade discount, this is used when the seller wishes to improve cash flow or liquidity, but finds that the buyer typically is unable to meet the desired discount deadline. A partial discount for whatever payment the buyer makes helps the seller's cash flow partially.
- *Sliding scale:* A discount offered based on one's ability to pay. More common with non-profit organizations than with for-profit retail.
- *Forward dating:* This is where the purchaser doesn't pay for the goods until well after they arrive. The date on the invoice is moved forward - example: purchase goods in November for sale during the December holiday season, but the payment date on the invoice is January 7.
- *Seasonal discount:* These are price reductions given when an order is placed in a slack period. On a shorter time scale, a happy hour may fall in this category. Generally, this discount is referred to as "X-Dating" or "Ex-Dating".

Discounts and allowances dealing with trade:

- *Bargaining:* Bargaining is where the seller and the buyer negotiate a price, which the buyer hopes is lower than the marked price.
- *Trade discount:* These are payments to distribution channel members for performing some function. Examples of these functions are warehousing and shelf stocking. Trade discounts are often combined to include

a series of functions, for example 20/12/5 could indicate a 20% discount for warehousing the product, an additional 12% discount for shipping the product, and an additional 5% discount for keeping the shelves stocked. Trade discounts are most frequent in industries where retailers hold the majority of the power in the distribution channel.

- *Trade-in discount:* This can be a way of reducing the price. By offering more for a trade-in than it is actually worth, the net effect is to reduce the effective price earned by the seller. The advantage of this is it encourages replacement sales without altering the list price or the perceived value.
- *Trade rate discount:* A discount offered by a seller to a buyer in a related industry. For example, a pharmacist might offer a discount for over-the-counter drugs to physicians who are purchasing them for dispensing to the physicians' own patients.

Discounts and Allowances Dealing with Quantity

These are price reductions given for large purchases. The rationale behind them is to obtain economies of scale and pass some of these savings on to the customer. In some industries, buyer groups and co-ops have formed to take advantage of these discounts. Generally there are two types:

- *Cumulative quantity discount:* These are price reductions based on the quantity purchased over a set period of time. The expectation is that they will impose an implied switching cost and thereby bond the purchaser to the seller.
- *Non-cumulative quantity discount:* These are price reductions based on the quantity of a single order. The expectation is that they will encourage larger orders, thus reducing billing, order filling, shipping, and sales personal expenses.
- *Dependence of price on quantity:* An extreme form of quantity discount is when, within a quantity range, the

price does not depend on quantity: if one wants less than the minimum amount one has to be pay for the minimum amount anyway. if one wants an amount between two of the fixed amounts on offer, one has to pay for the higher amount. These also apply in the case of a service with "quantity" referring to time. For example, an entrance ticket for a zoo is usually for a day; if one stays shorter, the price is the same. It is a kind of pass for unlimited use of a service during a day, where one can distinguish whether or not, when leaving and returning, one has to pay again. Similarly a pass can be for another period. In the case of long periods, it is obvious that one can leave and return without paying again. If one has to buy more than one wants, we can distinguish between the surplus just not being used, or the surplus being a nuisance, *e.g.* because of having to carry a large container.

First in first out

FIFO, which stands for "first-in-first-out," is an inventory costing method which assumes that the first items placed in inventory are the first sold. Thus, the inventory at the end of a year consists of the goods most recently placed in inventory. FIFO is one method used to determine Cost of Goods Sold for a business. Here is how inventory cost is calculated using the FIFO method. Assume a product is made in three batches during the year. The costs and quantity of each batch are:

- *Batch 1:* Quantity 2,000 pieces, Cost to produce $8000
- *Batch 2:* Quantity 1500 pieces, Cost to produce $7000
- *Batch 3:* Quantity 1700 pieces, Cost to produce $7700

Let's say you sold 4000 units during the year, out of the 5200 produced. Then calculate the unit costs for each batch:

- *Batch 1:* 8000/2000 = 4
- *Batch 2:* 7000/1500 = 4.667
- *Batch 3:* 7700/1700 = 4.529

So, of the 4000 units sold, using FIFO:

- The first 2000 units sold from the first batch cost $4 per unit.
- The next 1500 units sold from the second batch cost $4.667 per unit.
- And the last 500 units sold from the third batch cost $4.529.

The cost of the remaining 1200 units from the third batch is $4.529. These units will start off the second year.

LIFO

IFO, which stands for "last-in-first-out," is an inventory costing method which assumes that the last items placed in inventory are the first sold during an accounting year. Thus, the inventory at the end of a year consists of the goods placed in inventory at the beginning of the year, rather than at the end. LIFO is one method used to determine Cost of Goods Sold for a business. Here is how inventory cost is calculated using the LIFO method. Assume a product is made in three batches during the year. The costs and quantity of each batch are:

- *Batch 1:* Quantity 2,000 pieces, Cost to produce $8000
- *Batch 2:* Quantity 1500 pieces, Cost to produce $7000
- *Batch 3:* Quantity 1700 pieces, Cost to produce $7700

Let's say you sold 4000 units during the year, out of the 5200 produced. Then calculate the unit costs for each batch:

- *Batch 1:* 8000/2000 = 4
- *Batch 2:* 7000/1500 = 4.667
- *Batch 3:* 7700/1700 = 4.529

So, of the 4000 units sold, using LIFO

- The first 1700 units sold from the last batch cost $4.529 per unit
- The next 1500 units sold from the second batch cost $4.667 per unit
- And the last 800 units sold from the first batch cost $4.

The cost of the remaining 1200 units from the first batch is $4 each. These units will start off the next year.

Highest In, First Out - HIFO

In accounting, an inventory distribution method in which the inventory with the highest cost of purchase is the first to be used or taken out of stock. This will impact the company's books such that for any given period of time, the inventory expense will be the highest possible.

Companies would likely choose to use the HIFO inventory method if they wanted to decrease their taxable income for a period of time. Because the inventory that is recorded as used up is always the most expensive inventory the company has, the company will always be recording maximum cost of goods sold. Contrast this with other inventory recognition methods such as last in, first out, in which the most recently purchased inventory is recorded as used first, or first in, first out, in which the oldest inventory is recorded as used first. Companies may occasionally change their inventory methods in order to smooth their financial performance.

Simple Average

In cost accounting, we can calculate the value of material issue on the basis of simple average price method. Under this method, we can calculate the total of unit cost of each purchase and then it is divided by total no. of units.

Suppose, you have bought the material:

- 1st time 500 units @ Rs. 3
- 2nd time 600 units @ Rs. 4
- 3rd time 200 units @ Rs. 2

Material issue with simple average method = total of unit cost of each purchase/ total no. of units = 3 +4+2/3 = Rs. 3

Now, all material will be issued from store on the price of Rs. 3. This method is more benefited than FIFO and LIFO, if there is very small fluctuation in the buying prices.

Weighted Average

The use of weighted averages is common in many different applications, especially in the fields of accounting and various tasks that involve analysis and mathematical evaluations. Essentially a weighted average involves the assignment of different levels of importance or weights to various components that are used to arrive at a final answer or solution to a question or problem.

This is in contrast to the practice of assigning a common mean value to each component that is relevant to the task at hand. One of the easiest ways to understand the concept of a weighted average is to look at a common grading model used in many schools and colleges.

At the discretion of the instructor, different types of work performed by the student will be assigned a value that will help determine the final grade earned for the course. Successful completion of homework assignments may account for a smaller percentage of the total grade, while one or two major tests may carry additional weight in the final grade earned.

This concept of proportional relevance means that in the greater scheme of things, the tests carry more importance in making a good grade for the course, although the successful completion of both components will ensure earning the highest grade.

This same principle of a weighted average can be applied in other venues as well. Marketing strategists may develop a campaign that is aimed at primary and secondary consumer markets. While the main thrust of the campaign is directly relevant to the primary market, the same techniques are anticipated to be relevant to lesser degree to other markets.

The result is a projection of revenue earned primarily from one sector of the consumer market, but still accounting for smaller percentages of revenue from one or more smaller sectors. A weighted average is somewhat subjective, in that the individual or entity who sets the values for each component involved in the average usually does so with some preconceived ideas about those values. However, it is possible to adjust the criteria used for calculating a weighted average as more facts emerge that could impact the relative value of each component.

Periodic weighted average

This calculation is broadly similar, except that the unit cost is calculated only at the end of a period. Issues during that period are issued at that unit cost. This calculation is simpler, both to calculate and because record keeping is simpler. The disadvantage is obvious: the numbers are not available until the period end. The lower weightings given to the cost of earlier receipts means that both methods are forms of moving average.

Moving Weighted Average

A moving weighted average is an average of multiple figures which has two specific characteristics. First, it gives added emphasis, or weight, to recent figures in preference to older figures. In addition, as a moving average, the set of figures used changes over time to remain up-to-date. The moving weighted average can be used for a wide variety of mathematical purposes, though one of the most common is for making forecasts for either a business or a market. One example of a moving average would be if a store kept track of its average sales over the past thirty days. On the 30th day of the year, this average would cover days 1 to 30.

On the 31st day of the year, the average would cover days 2 to 31. On the 32nd day of the year, the average would cover days 3 to 32, and so on. The main advantage of this method is that it allows the store to get an idea of how sales have varied over time without the trend being heavily distorted by a single event. For example, if the store had spectacular sales one day thanks to a celebrity appearance, it would cause a spike on a traditional graph. With a moving average, these one-off effects would not be so visible and the graph would instead better show long-term trends such as seasonal variations. A weighted average is one where the various numbers involved are not given equal weight. This is common in stock market indices where extra emphasis is given to the largest firms in the market. This avoids sudden movements in the stock of a minor company distorting the overall picture. A moving weighted average brings together these two techniques. It applies its weighting based on how recent each figure is. The idea is to give greater emphasis to the most recent figures, while still taking some account of the past. In finance, it is usually used to get the benefits of the moving average while making sure not to miss strong signals from the most recent events. Producing the moving weighted average is a simple mathematical process. As an example, to produce a five-day moving weighted average, you would multiply the current day's figure by five, the figure from yesterday by four, the figure from two days ago by three, the figure from three days ago by two, and the figure from four days ago by one. You would then add up the five resulting figures and divide the result by five to get the moving weighted average.

Market Price

In finance, the term market price, or market value, refers to the most recent price at which a security transaction took place, if it was completed on an exchange. If the transaction took place over-the-counter, with brokers and dealers negotiating directly with each other, market price refers to the most current bid, the price requested by the broker, and the most current ask, the price demanded by the dealer. As an economic concept, market price is the price at which a good or service is offered at in the marketplace.

This price is reached when market supply and market demand meet. Alfred Marshall, an influential English economist, developed the supply and demand model to explain how human behaviour determined market price. Supply is the service or good that producers are willing to provide at a given price. Demand is the value of a service or good that purchasers are willing to buy at a given price. There is an inverse relationship between price and supply, and a direct relationship between price and demand. On a typical supply and demand graph, the X-axis shows quantity and the Y-axis shows price. The supply curve slopes upward, while the demand curve slopes downwards. The point of intersection between the two curves is the market price, also known as the equilibrium point. Various factors can shift the supply or demand curve significantly, affecting the equilibrium price. For example, change in weather can affect the supply of certain goods while the change in consumer preference can greatly change demand. This supply and demand theory regarding market price, while popular, has been criticized as being too simplistic. It can be argued that a good or service may already have a price before reaching the marketplace. Moreover, buyers are not always considered by producers when creating a commodity. Another contradiction to Marshall's theory comes from Keynesian economics, named after the renowned economist John Keynes. He noted that prices could become "sticky" by not responding to fluctuations in either demand or supply. This is especially likely to occur when prices are decreasing. A noted example of such as situation is the Boston housing market in the 1990s. Buyers and sellers could not agree on a market price as the market dried. Other deterrents to the natural laws of supply and demand are monopoly and oligopoly. The sole or a limited number of providers of a certain commodity has the power to dictate the market price. Similarly, in a monopsony, situations where there are many sellers and one buyer, the buyer is able to dictate the price.

Return of Materials to the Supplier and Storeroom

Where materials are delivered that are either faulty or not in line with the original purchase order then these materials are usually returned to the supplier. Further, suppliers may have overcharged for goods provided, or charged for an incorrect quantity where the invoice quantity and the delivery quantity do not agree. In these situations the purchasing firm will issue a debit note and the supplier will issue a credit note. Where materials have been issued by the storeroom but have not been used up in the production process, then these materials should be returned to the storeroom. The document supporting this transaction may be termed "Materials Returned to Store" form.

Understanding the Materials Control

Material control is a systematic control over the purchasing storing and using of material to minimizing the possible cost.

In every manufacturing concern materials constitute an important factor of production. It is an important element of cost and covering 60-70 percent of the total cost of the production. Material control may be defined as the level of material maintenance so as to ensure uninterrupted production and minimizing the investment of funds.

Thus material control is the proper control of material which reduces the cost of production, minimizing the investment of fund in the purchases of material and increases the profitability of the organisation.

- Essentials of material control: The basic objectives of material control is to obtain requisite quantity of material at right price, right quantity, right quality and from right source. The detailed objectives of material control are as follows:
- Regular supply of material: Material control ensures regular supply of material to the factory so the production may not be held up for want of material.
- No possibility of overstocking and under stocking: By fixing various stock level as minimum level, maximum level ordering level over stocking and under stocking of material can be avoided.
- Minimum Wastage: Proper material management and control reduces wastages of material. Poor stores facilities result deterioration, obsolescence, pilferage, theft, fire, evaporation etc. which directly affect the profitability of the organisation.
- Getting material at reasonable prices: While purchasing materials, it is seen that it is purchased at reasonable low prices but the quality is not to be sacrificed in the plan of low prices.
- Availability of up-to-date information: Up-to-dated and readily material information can be made available to the management, for planning and decision making. The store keeper can supply information because he keeps up-to-dated record of the every item of the store under proper system of material control.

- Adoption of internal check system: Internal check system is the part of material control. Under this system the employees perform their work on rotational basis by which misappropriation of material is minimized.

Purchasing

Purchasing refers to a business or organization attempting for acquiring goods or services to accomplish the goals of the enterprise. Though there are several organizations that attempt to set standards in the purchasing process, processes can vary greatly between organizations. Typically the word "purchasing" is not used interchangeably with the word "procurement", since procurement typically includes Expediting, Supplier Quality, and Traffic and Logistics in addition to Purchasing. Purchasing managers/directors, and procurement managers/directors guide the organization's acquisition procedures and standards.

Most organizations use a three-way check as the foundation of their purchasing programmes. This involves three departments in the organization completing separate parts of the acquisition process. The three departments do not all report to the same senior manager to prevent unethical practices and lend credibility to the process. These departments can be purchasing, receiving; and accounts payable or engineering, purchasing and accounts payable; or a plant manager, purchasing and accounts payable. Combinations can vary significantly, but a purchasing department and accounts payable are usually two of the three departments involved.

When the receiving department is not involved, it's typically called a two-way check or two-way purchase order. In this situation, the purchasing department issues the purchase order receipt not required. When an invoice arrives against the order, the accounts payable department will then go directly to the requestor of the purchase order to verify that the goods or services were received. This is typically what is done for goods and services that will bypass the receiving department. A few examples are software delivered electronically, NRE work, consulting hours, etc... Historically, the purchasing department issued Purchase Orders for supplies, services, equipment, and raw materials. Then, in an effort to decrease the administrative costs associated with the repetitive ordering of basic consumable items, "Blanket" or "Master" Agreements were put into place.

These types of agreements typically have a longer duration and increased scope to maximize the Quantities of Scale concept. When additional supplies are required, a simple release would be issued to the supplier to provide the goods or services. Another method of decreasing administrative costs associated with repetitive contracts for common material, is the use of company credit cards, also known as "Purchasing Cards" or simply "P-Cards". P-card programmes vary, but all of them have internal checks and audits to ensure appropriate use. Purchasing managers realized once contracts for the low dollar value consumables are in place, procurement can take a smaller role in the operation and use of the contracts. There is still oversight in the forms of audits and monthly statement reviews, but most of their time is now available to negotiate major purchases and setting up of other long term contracts.

These contracts are typically renewable annually. This trend away from the daily procurement function resulted in several changes in the industry. The first was the reduction of personnel. Purchasing departments were now smaller. There was no need for the army of clerks processing orders for individual parts as in the past. Another change was the focus on negotiating contracts and procurement of large capital equipment. Both of these functions permitted purchasing departments to make the biggest financial contribution to the organization. A new terms and job title emerged – Strategic sourcing and Sourcing Managers.

These professionals not only focused on the bidding process and negotiating with suppliers, but the entire supply function. In these roles they were able to add value and maximize savings for organizations. This value was manifested in lower inventories, less personnel, and getting the end product to the organization's consumer quicker. Purchasing manager's success in these roles resulted in new assignments outside to the traditional purchasing function – logistics, materials management, distribution, and warehousing. More and more purchasing managers were becoming Supply Chain Managers handling additional functions of their organizations operation. Purchasing managers were not the only ones to become Supply Chain Managers.

Logistic managers, material managers, distribution managers, etc all rose the broader function and some had responsibility for the purchasing functions now. In accounting, purchases is the amount of goods a company bought throughout this year. it is also refers to information as to the kind, quality, quantity and cost of goods bought that should be maintained. They are added to inventory.

Purchases are offset by Purchase Discounts and Purchase Returns and Allowances. When it should be added depends on the Free On Board policy of the trade. For the purchaser, this new inventory is added on shipment if the policy was FOB shipping point, and the seller remove this item from its inventory. On the other hand, the purchaser added this inventory on receipt if the policy was FOB destination, and the seller remove this item from its inventory when it was delivered. Goods bought for the purpose other than direct selling, such as for Research and Development, are added to inventory and allocated to Research and Development expense as they are used. On a side note, equipments bought for Research and Development are not added to inventory, but are capitalized as assets.

Acquisition Process

The process is defined by a series of phases during which technology is defined and matured into viable concepts, which are subsequently developed and readied for production, after which the systems produced are supported in the field. The process allows for a given system to enter the process at any of the development phases. For example, a system using unproven technology would enter at the beginning stages of the process and would proceed through a lengthy period of technology maturation, while a system based on mature and proven technologies might enter directly into engineering development or, conceivably, even production. The process itself includes four phases of development:

- Concept and Technology Development: is intended to explore alternative concepts based on assessments of operational needs, technology readiness, risk, and affordability.
- Concept and Technology Development phase begins with concept exploration. During this stage, concept studies are undertaken to define alternative concepts and to provide information about capability and risk that would permit an objective comparison of competing concepts.
- System Development and Demonstration phase. This phase could be entered directly as a result of a technological opportunity and urgent user need, as well as having come through concept and technology development.
- The last, and longest, phase is the Sustainment and Disposal phase of the programme. During this phase all necessary activities are accomplished to maintain and sustain the system in the field in the most cost-effective manner possible.

Selection of Bidders

This is the process where the organization identifies potential suppliers for specified supplies, services or equipment. These suppliers' credentials and history are analyzed, together with the products or services they offer. The bidder selection process varies from organization to organization, but can include running credit reports, interviewing management, testing products, and touring facilities. This process is not always done in order of importance, but rather in order of expense. Often purchasing managers research potential bidders obtaining information on the organizations and products from media sources and their own industry contacts. Additionally, purchasing might send Request for Information to potential suppliers to help gather information. Engineering would also inspect sample products to determine if the company can produce products they need. If the bidder passes both of these stages engineering may decide to do some testing on the materials to further verify quality standards.

These tests can be expensive and involve significant time of multiple technicians and engineers. Engineering management must make this decision based on the cost of the products they are likely to procure, the importance of the bidders' product to production, and other factors.

Credit checks, interviewing management, touring plants as well as other steps could all be utilized if engineering, manufacturing, and supply chain managers decide they could help their decision and the cost is justifiable. Other organizations might have minority procurement goals to consider in selection of bidders.

Organizations identify goals in the use of companies owned and operated by certain ethnicities or women owned business enterprises. Significant utilizing of minority suppliers may qualify the firm as a potential bidder for a contract with a company or governmental entity looking to increase their minority supplier programmes.

This selection process can include or exclude international suppliers depending on organizational goals and criteria. Companies looking to increase their pacific rim supplier base may exclude suppliers from the Americas, Europe, and Australia. Other organizations may be looking to purchase domestically to ensure a quicker response to orders as well as easier collaboration on design and production. Organizational goals will dictate the criteria for the selection process of bidders. It is also possible that the product or service being procured is so specialized that the number of bidders are limited and the criteria must be very wide to permit competition. If only one firm can meet the specifications for the product then the purchasing managers must consider utilizing a "Sole Source" option or work with engineering to broaden the specifications if the project will permit alteration in the specifications. The sole source option is the part of the selection of bidders that acknowledges there is sometimes only one reasonable supplier for some services or products. This can be because of the limited applications for the product cannot support more than one manufacturer, proximity of the service provided, or the products are newly designed or invented and competition is not yet available.

Bidding Process

This is the process an organization utilizes to procure goods, services or equipment. Processes vary significantly from the stringent to the very informal. Large corporations and governmental entities are most likely to have stringent and formal processes. These processes can utilize specialized bid forms that require specific procedures and detail. The very stringent procedures require bids to be open by several staff from various departments to ensure fairness and impartiality. Responses are usually very detailed. Bidders not responding exactly as specified and following the published procedures can be disqualified.

Smaller private businesses are more likely to have less formal procedures. Bids can be in the form of an e-mail to all of the bidders specifying products or services. Responses by bidders can be detailed or just the proposed dollar amount. Most bid processes are multi-tiered. Acquisitions under a specified dollar amount can be "user discretion" permitting the request or to choose who ever they want. This level can be as low as $100 or as high as $10,000 depending on the organization. The rationale is the savings realized by processing these request the same as expensive items is minimal and does not justify the time and expense. Purchasing departments watch for abuses of the user discretion privilege. Acquisitions in a mid range can be processed with a slightly more formal process. This process may involve the user providing quotes from three separate suppliers. Purchasing may be asked or required to obtain the quotes. The formal bid process starts as low as $10,000 or as high as $100,000 depending on the organization. The bid usually involves a specific form the bidder fills out and must be returned by a specified deadline. Depending of the commodity being purchased and the organization the bid may specify a weighted evaluation criterion. Other bids would be evaluated at the discretion of purchasing or the end users. Some bids could be evaluated by a cross-functional committee. Other bids may be evaluated by the end user or the buyer in Purchasing. Especially in small, private firms the bidders could be evaluated on criteria or factors that have little if anything to do with the actual bid. Examples of these factors are history of the bidder with the company, history of the bidder with the company's senior management at other firms, and bidder's breadth of products.

Technical

Technical evaluations, evaluations of the technical suitability of the quoted goods or services, if required, are normally performed prior to the commercial evaluation. During this phase of the procurement process, a technical representative of the company will review the proposal and designate each bidder as either technically acceptable or technically unacceptable.

Commercial

Cost of Money is calculated by multiplying the applicable currency interest rate multiplied by the amount of money paid prior to the receipt of GOODS. If the money were to have remained in the buyer's account, interest would be drawn. That interest is essentially an additional cost associated with such Progress or Milestone payments. The manufacturing location is taken into consideration during the evaluation stage primarily to calculate freight costs and regional issues which may be considered. For instance, in Europe it is common for factories to close during the month of August for Summer holiday. Labour agreements may also be taken into consideration and may be drawn into the evaluation if the particular region is known to frequent labour unions. The manufacturing lead-time is the time from the placement of the order until the goods are manufactured and prepared for delivery. Lead-times vary by commodity and can range from several days to years.

Transportation time is evaluated while comparing the delivery of goods to the Buyer's required use-date. If Goods are shipped from a remote port, with infrequent vessel transportation, the transportation time could exceed the schedule and adjustments would need to be made. Delivery Charges - the charge for the Goods to be delivered to a stated point. Bid Validity Packing Bid Adjustments Terms and Conditions Seller's Services Standards Organizations Financial Review Payment Currency Risk Analysis - market volatility, financial stress within the bidders Testing

Negotiating

Negotiating is a key skillset in the Purchasing field. One of the goals of Purchasing Agents is to acquire goods per the most advantageous terms of the buying entity. Purchasing Agents typically attempt to decrease costs while meeting the Buyer's other requirements such as an on-time delivery, compliance to the commercial terms and conditions. Good negotiators, those with high levels of documented "cost savings", receive a premium within the industry relative to their compensation. Depending on the employment agreement between the Purchasing Agent and the employer, Buyer's cost savings can result in the creation of value to the business, and may result in a flat-rate bonus, or a percentage payout to the Purchasing Agent of the documented cost savings. Purchasing Departments, while they can be considered as a support function of the key business, are actually revenue generating departments. For example, if the company needs to buy $30 million USD of widgets and the Purchasing Department secures the widgets for $25M USD, the Purchasing Department would have saved the company $5M USD. That savings could exceed the annual budget of the department, which in effect would pay the department's overhead - the employee's salaries, computers, office space, etc.

Post-Award Administration

Post-award administration typically consists of making minor changes, additions or subtractions, that in some way change the terms of the agreement or the Seller's Scope of Supply. Such changes are often minor, but for auditing purposes must be documented into the existing agreement. Examples include increasing the quantity of a Line Item or changing the metallurgy of a particular component.

COSTS FOR DECISION-MAKING AND PLANNING

Opportunity Cost

Scarcity of resources is one of the more basic concepts of economics. Scarcity necessitates trade-offs, and trade-offs result in an opportunity cost. While the cost of a good or service often is thought of in monetary terms, the opportunity cost of a decision is based on what must be given up (the next best alternative) as a result of the decision. Any decision that involves a choice between two or more options has an opportunity cost. Opportunity cost contrasts to accounting cost in that accounting costs do not consider forgone opportunities. Consider the case of an MBA student who pays $30,000 per year in tuition and fees at a private university.

For a two-year MBA programme, the cost of tuition and fees would be $60,000. This is the monetary cost of the education. However, when making the decision to go back to school, one should consider the opportunity cost, which includes the income that the student would have earned if the alternative decision of remaining in his or her job had been made. If the student had been earning $50,000 per year and was expecting a 10% salary increase in one year, $105,000 in salary would be foregone as a result of the decision to return to school. Adding this amount to the educational expenses results in a cost of $165,000 for the degree. Opportunity cost is useful when evaluating the cost and benefit of choices. It often is expressed in non-monetary terms. For example, if one has time for only one elective course, taking a course in micro economics might have the opportunity cost of a course in management. By expressing the cost of one option in terms of the foregone benefits of another, the marginal costs and marginal benefits of the options can be compared. As another example, if a shipwrecked sailor on a desert island is capable of catching 10 fish or harvesting 5 coconuts in one day, then the opportunity cost of producing one coconut is two fish (10 fish/ 5 coconuts). Note that this simple example assumes that the production possibility frontier between fish and coconuts is linear.

Relative Price

Opportunity cost is expressed in relative price, that is, the price of one choice relative to the price of another. For example, if milk costs $4 per gallon and bread costs $2 per loaf, then the relative price of milk is 2 loaves of bread.

If a consumer goes to the grocery store with only $4 and buys a gallon of milk with it, then one can say that the opportunity cost of that gallon of milk was 2 loaves of bread (assuming that bread was the next best alternative). In many cases, the relative price provides better insight into the real cost of a good than does the monetary price.

Applications of Opportunity Cost

The concept of opportunity cost has a wide range of applications including:

- Analysis of comparative advantage
- Career choice
- Consumer choice
- Cost of capital
- Production possibilities
- Time management

Sunk costs

In economics and business decision-making, sunk costs are retrospective (past) costs that have already been incurred and cannot be recovered. Sunk costs are sometimes contrasted with prospective costs, which are future costs that may be incurred or changed if an action is taken.

Both retrospective and prospective costs may be either fixed (that is, they are not dependent on the volume of economic activity, however measured) or variable (dependent on volume). In traditional micro economic theory, only prospective (future) costs are relevant to an investment decision. Traditional economics proposes that an economic actor not let sunk costs influence one's decisions, because doing so would not be rationally assessing a decision exclusively on its own merits. The decision-maker may make rational decisions according to their own incentives; these incentives may dictate different decisions than would be dictated by efficiency or profitability, and this is considered an incentive problem and distinct from a sunk cost problem. Evidence from behavioural economics suggests this theory fails to predict real-world behaviour. Sunk costs greatly affect actors' decisions, because humans are inherently loss-averse and thus normally act irrationally when making economic decisions.

Sunk costs should not affect the rational decision-maker's best choice. However, until a decision-maker irreversibly commits resources, the prospective cost is an avoidable future cost and is properly included in any decision-making processes. For example, if you are considering pre-ordering movie tickets, but have not actually purchased them yet, the cost remains avoidable. If the price of the tickets rises to an amount that requires you to pay more than the value you place on them, the change in prospective cost should be figured into the decision-making, and the decision should be reevaluated.

Description

The sunk cost is distinct from the economic loss. For example, when a car is purchased, it can subsequently be resold; however, it will probably not be resold for the original purchase price. The economic loss is the difference (including transaction costs). The sum originally paid should not affect any rational future decision-making about the car, regardless of the resale value: if the owner can derive more value from selling the car than not selling it, it should be sold, regardless of the price paid. In this sense, the sunk cost is not a precise quantity, but an economic term for a sum paid, in the past, which is no longer relevant to decisions about the future; it may be used inconsistently in quantitative terms as the original cost or the expected economic loss. It may also be used as shorthand for an error in analysis due to the sunk cost fallacy, non-rational decision-making or, most simply, as irrelevant data.

Economists argue that sunk costs are not taken into account when making rational decisions. In the case of the movie ticket, the ticket-buyer can choose between the following two end results:

1. Having paid the price of the ticket and having suffered watching a movie that he does not want to see, or;
2. Having paid the price of the ticket and having used the time to do something more fun.

In either case, the ticket-buyer has "paid the price of the ticket" so "that part" of the decision no longer affects the future. If the ticket-buyer regrets buying the ticket, the current decision should be based on whether he wants to see the movie at all, regardless of the price, just as if he were to go to a free movie. The economist will suggest that, since the second option involves suffering in only one way (spent money), while the first involves suffering in two (spent money plus wasted time), option two is obviously preferable.

Sunk costs may cause cost overrun. In business, an example of sunk costs may be investment into a factory or research that now has a lower value or no value whatsoever. For example, $20 million has been spent on building a powerplant; the value at present is zero because it is incomplete (and no sale or recovery is feasible). The plant can be completed for an additional $10 million, or abandoned and a different but equally valuable facility built for $5 million. It should be obvious that abandonment and construction of the alternative facility is the more rational decision, even though it represents a total loss of the original expenditure—the original sum invested is a sunk cost. If decision-makers are (economically) irrational or have the wrong incentives, the completion of the project may be chosen. For example, politicians or managers may have more incentive to avoid the appearance of a total loss. In practice, there is considerable ambiguity and uncertainty in such cases, and decisions may in retrospect appear irrational that were, at the time, reasonable to the economic actors involved and in the context of their own incentives.

Behavioural economics recognizes that sunk costs often affect economic decisions due to loss aversion: the price paid becomes a benchmark for the value, whereas the price paid should be irrelevant. This is considered non-rational behaviour (as rationality is defined by classical economics). Economic experiments have shown that the sunk cost fallacy and loss aversion are common; hence economic rationality—as assumed by much of economics—is limited. This has enormous implications for finance, economics, and securities markets in particular. Daniel Kahneman won the Nobel Prize in Economics in part for his extensive work in this area with his collaborator, Amos Tversky.

Features Characterizing the Sunk Cost Heuristic

Two specific features characterizing the sunk cost heuristic worth mentioning are:

- An overly optimistic probability bias, whereby after an investment the evaluation of one's investment reaping dividends is increased.
- The requisite of personal responsibility. Sunk cost appears to operate chiefly in those who feel personal responsibility for the investments that are to be viewed as sunk.

Overly Optimistic Probability Bias

In 1968 Knox and Inkster, in what is perhaps the classic sunk cost experiment, approached 141 horse bettors: 72 of the people had just finished placing a \$2.00 bet within the past thirty seconds, and 69 people were about to place a \$2.00 bet in the next thirty seconds. Their hypothesis was that people who had just committed themselves to a course of action (betting \$2.00) would reduce post-decision dissonance by believing more strongly than ever that they had picked a winner. Knox and

Inkster asked the bettors to rate their horse's chances of winning on a 7 point scale. What they found was that people who were about to place a bet rated the chance that their horse would win at an average of 3.48 which corresponded to a "fair chance of winning" whereas people who had just finished betting gave an average rating of 4.81 which corresponded to a "good chance of winning." Their hypothesis was confirmed: after making a $2.00 commitment, people became more confident their bet would pay off. Knox and Inkster performed an ancillary test on the patrons of the horses themselves and managed (after normalization) to repeat their finding almost identically. Additional evidence of inflated probability estimations can be found in Arkes and Blumer and Arkes and Hutzel.

Requisite of Personal Responsibility

In a study of 96 business students in 1976 Staw and Fox gave the subjects a choice between making an R&D investment in either an underperforming company department, or in other sections of the hypothetical company. Staw and Fox divided the participants into two groups; a low responsibility condition and a high responsibility condition. In the high responsibility condition the participants were told that they as manager had made an earlier, disappointing R&D investment. In the low responsibility condition, subjects were told that a former manager had made a previous R&D investment in the underperforming division and were given the same profit data as the other group. In both cases subjects were then asked to make a new $20 million investment. There was a significant interaction between assumed responsibility and average investment, with the high responsibility condition averaging $12.97 million and the low condition averaging $9.43 million. Similar results have been obtained in earlier studies by Staw and by Arkes and Blumer and Whyte.

Loss Aversion and the Sunk Cost Fallacy

Many people have strong misgivings about "wasting" resources. This is called "loss aversion". In the above example involving a non-refundable movie ticket, many people, for example, would feel obliged to go to the movie despite not really wanting to, because doing otherwise would be wasting the ticket price; they feel they passed the point of no return. This is sometimes called the sunk cost fallacy. Economists would label this behaviour "irrational": it is inefficient because it misallocates resources by depending on information that is irrelevant to the decision being made. Colloquially, this is known as "throwing good money after bad".

This line of thinking, in turn, may reflect a nonstandard measure of utility, which is ultimately subjective and unique to the consumer. A ticket-buyer who purchases a ticket to a bad movie in advance, makes a semi-public commitment to watching it. To leave early is to make this lapse of judgement manifest to strangers, an appearance he may rationally choose to avoid. Alternatively, he may take pride in having recognized the opportunity cost of the alternative use of time. The idea of sunk costs is often employed when analyzing business decisions. A common example of a sunk cost for a business is the promotion of a brand name.

This type of marketing incurs costs that cannot normally be recovered. It is not typically possible to later "demote" one's brand names in exchange for cash. A second example is research and development costs. Once spent such costs are sunk and should have no effect on future pricing decisions. So a pharmaceutical company's attempt to justify high prices because of need to recoup research and development expenses is fallacious.

The company will charge the same price whether R & D were one dollar or one million dollars. R&D cost do count when deciding whether to spend the money on research and development but once spent they have no effect on firm decisions. The sunk cost fallacy is in game theory sometimes known as the "Concorde Fallacy", referring to the fact that the British and French governments continued to fund the joint development of Concorde even after it became apparent that there was no longer an economic case for the aircraft. The project was regarded privately by the British government as a "commercial disaster" which should never have been started, and was almost cancelled, but political and legal issues ultimately made it impossible for either government to pull out.

The Sunk Cost Dilemma

The economic approach that sunk costs should not be considered when decisions are being made can lead to a situation where the sum of a number of good decisions can lead to one big disaster. This dilemma situation can be described using a game theory approach for 1-player games. The sunk cost dilemma with its sequence of good decisions should not be confused with the sunk cost fallacy, where a misconception of sunk costs can lead to bad decisions.

Bygones Principle

The bygones principle is an economic theory used in business. Economists stress the "extra" or "marginal" costs and benefits of every decision. The idea is to not look backwards when making decisions and stresses the importance of ignoring past costs in future decision-making. The bygones principle states that when making a decision, one should make a hard-headed calculation of the extra costs one will incur and weigh these against its extra advantages. It emphasizes the importance of only taking into account the future costs and benefits when making decisions.

Bibliography

Aliber, R. Z.: *The International Market for Foreign Exchange,* New York, Praeger, 1969.

Ashok, Vasant: *Indian Economy in the World Setting*, Bombay, Himalaya, 1988.

Bhuleshkar, Vasant: *Indian Economy in the World Setting*, Bombay, Himalaya, 1988.

Connolly, M.: *The International Monetary System: Choices for the Future,* New York, Praeger, 1983.

Deresky, Helen: *International Management: Managing Across Borders and Cultures,* New York, Harper Collins, 1994.

Dornbush, R.: *International Economic Policy,* Baltimore, The Johns Hopkins University Press, 1979.

Fruhan, W. E.: *Financial Strategy, Studies in the Creation, Transfer and Destruction of Shareholder Value.* Homewood, 1979.

Goldsmith, W.: *The Financial Development of India, 1860-1977*, New Haven, Yale University Press, 1983.

Guala, F.: *The Methodology of Experimental Economics,* New York, Cambridge University Press, 2005.

Hart, Oliver: *Firms, Contracts, and Financial Structure,* Clarendon Press, Oxford, 1995.

Hirschey, Mark, and James L. Pappas" *Managerial Economics.* 8th ed. Harcourt Brace Jovanovich College Publishers, 1996.

Hunt, E. K. *History of Economic Thought, A Critical Perspective,* New York, HarperCollins, 1992.

Ishwar, C.: *The Indian Economy: Resources, Planning, Development, and Problems*, Delhi, Sultan Chand, 1983.

Jack Kemp: *A Monetary Agenda for the World Economy,* Boston, Quantum, 1984.

James L. Pappas" *Managerial Economics.* 8th ed. Harcourt Brace Jovanovich College Publishers, 1996.

Jeffrey D. Jones: *Handbook of Business Valuation*, New York: Wiley, 1992.

Johnson, H.: *The Economics of Common Currencies,* London, George Allen & Unwin Ltd., 1973.

Larry J.: *Business Valuations, Advanced Topics,* Westport, CT, Quorum Books, 1997.

Lawrence J.: *Principles of Managerial Finance*, MA: Addison Wesley Longman, 2000.

Le Prestre, Philippe: *The World Bank and the Environmental Challenge,* London, Associated University Presses, 1989.

Magnussen, L., *Evolutionary and Neo-Schumpeterian Approaches to Economics*, Kluwer, Boston, 1994.

Mann, L.: *Decision Making, A Psychological Analysis of Conflict, Choice and Commitment*. New York, Free Press, 1977.

Martin: *Basic Financial Management,* Prentice Hall, 1993.

Meyer, M. W.: *Theory of Organizational Structure*, Indianapolis, 1977.

Michael Connolly, *The International Monetary System: Choices for the Future*, New York, Praeger, 1983.

Ottomar, H.: *Distribution of Stock of Money,* Effingham, London, 1892.

Rappaport, A.: *Creating Shareholder Value, The New Standard for Business Performance,* New York, Free Press, 1986.

Robert H. Litzenberger: *Foundations of Financial Economics,* Prentice-Hall, 1988.

Rothermund, Dietmar: *An Economic History of India from Pre-colonial Times to 1986*, London, Croom Helm, 1988.

Salancik, G. R.: *The External Control of Organizations, A Resource Dependence Perspective*, New York, 1978.

Scott, W. R.: *Organizations: Rational, Natural, and Open Systems,* Englewood Cliffs, 1981.

Subhash, C.: *National Policy Studies*, New Delhi, Tata McGraw-Hill for the Lok Sabha Secretariat, 1990.

Terence, J.: *The State and Development Planning in India*, Delhi, Oxford University Press, 1994.

Vines, David and Christopher Gilbert: *The IMF and its Critics: Reform of the Global Financial Architecture,* Cambridge, Cambridge University Press, 2004.

Index

G

K

L

M

N

P

S

T

U

❑❑❑